America's Suburb

THE SAN FERNANDO VALLEY

America's Suburb

KEVIN RODERICK

Los Angeles Times
BOOKS

For Julie and Rod, who pursued their dreams in

the Valley; and for Judy and Sean, who allow me

to chase mine.

Los Angeles Times
BOOKS

Book Development General Manager: Carla Lazzareschi
Editing: Noel Greenwood, Carla Lazzareschi
Design: G&O Design, Inc.
Copy Editing: Patricia Connell, Steven Hawkins
Maps: Roger Kuo

ISBN 1-883792-55-X
©2001 Kevin Roderick
Published by the Los Angeles Times
202 West 1st Street, Los Angeles, CA 90012

First printing May 2001
Printed in Singapore

Los Angeles Times

Publisher: John P. Puerner
Editor: John S. Carroll

TABLE OF CONTENTS

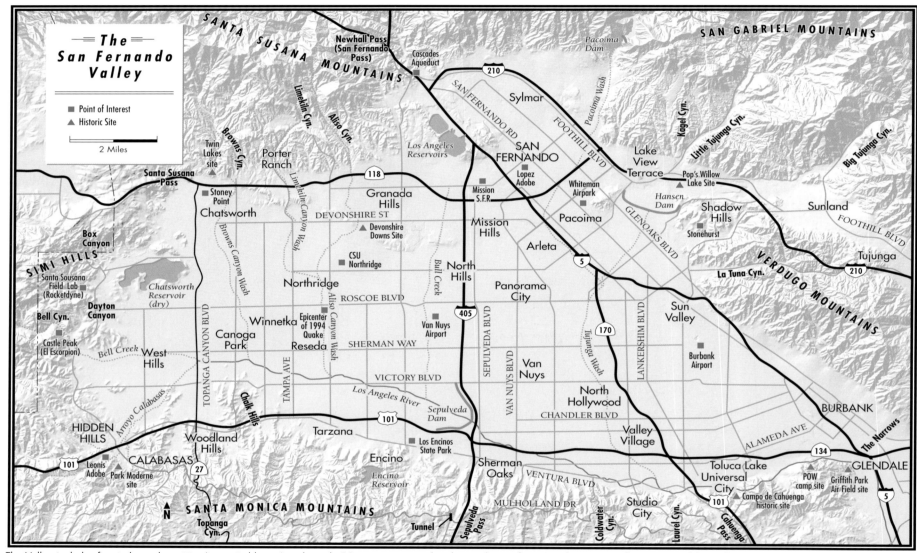

The San Fernando Valley

- ■ Point of Interest
- ▲ Historic Site

2 Miles

The Valley includes five independent cities (in capital letters) and nearly 30 communities within the city limits of Los Angeles. Universal City is an oddity: it fits neither group.

*"I'll forget my sins,
I'll be making new
friends...
It's the San Fernando
Valley for me."*

—From a song made
popular by Bing Crosby
in 1944

My folks arrived in the San Fernando Valley during the great American exodus to the suburbs that began with World War II. It was a fabled place then, a refuge of rustic living where Clark Gable and his studio pals played polo and grew grapefruit on 10-acre ranches. As young families filled the land, a hybrid way of life evolved. The Valley became the swimming pool and sports car capital of the nation, and grew the biggest yards and shopping centers in Los Angeles. We attended the newest and best schools and seldom ventured into the city except to see the Dodgers play or to escape the heat with a day at the beach. Summers were famously torrid, but true Valleyites didn't mind the heat. It made for plumper oranges and longer pool seasons and made us feel somehow superior to the shivering hordes over the hill.

If there were a stigma attached to the Valley then, we never heard of it. We patronized the San Fernando Valley Fair every summer and cheered at local parades like the Northridge Stampede, led by cowboy rider Montie Montana, the honorary sheriff of the Valley. This quirky swirl of country and suburb defined our days. Kids scavenged construction sites for scrap wood to build tree houses, and caught tadpoles in hidden creeks. Even when the ground shook and the night sky glowed from Cold War rocket tests in the western hills, we somehow felt assured that we inhabited a special place. Parents built bomb shelters as protection against Soviet missiles, but nearly everyone left their houses unlocked. Police found it

necessary to run campaigns urging motorists to remove ignition keys and lock their parked cars.

Later I heard about other suburbs, places like Levittown and Lakewood, which were widely reviled as featureless blobs of sameness that rose from nothing. This sounded alien, since the Valley so obviously had a past. Over holiday suppers, families passed along the stories—the years when snow blan-

Mission San Fernando Rey was visible from anywhere in the Valley. The mission *convento* with its 21 arches, shown here in 1895, was the largest adobe in old California.

The Los Angeles River runs the entire length of the Valley, from the Simi Hills on the west to the Narrows near Glendale. This scene at the Narrows, near today's Griffith Park, was photographed in 1898.

keted the Valley floor, the location of a POW camp that operated during the war, the time Dad first cruised Van Nuys Boulevard in his hot rod. They argued over which Ventura Boulevard eatery it was where gangster Mickey Cohen was shot (Rondelli's, now a fondue place, and he wasn't the victim), tested one another's ability to recite the Valley's last alphabet telephone prefixes (DIckens, EMpire, STate, POplar, TRiangle and THornwall) and debated the location of the final orange grove (actually, several are left).

My favorite time to introduce visitors to the Valley is on a sparkling winter morning, with a chilly north wind gusting down from the San Gabriels to sweep the sky clean. The crisp light bouncing off the mountains sharpens the shadows and lets the view spill on forever. I like to drive high into the hills above Studio City, steer around an arresting bend in the road, then wait for my guests to take in the panorama below. Their first words are usually something like: "Wow, it's huge."

But often they already know the landscape, consciously or not, from its role as the backdrop for thousands of television episodes and Hollywood films. Movie classics such as *The Birth of a Nation* and *It's a Wonderful Life* were shot outdoors here. So too were modern blockbusters like *E.T. the Extra-Terrestrial* and forgettables the likes of *Encino Man*, *The Vals* and *San Fernando Valley*, starring cowboy crooner Roy Rogers. On TV the Valley has been home turf for the Lone Ranger, the Real McCoys and the Brady Bunch; it has also been the subject of barbs by funnymen from Bob Hope ("Cleveland with palm trees") to Jay Leno ("Hellholia").

The San Fernando Valley serves, in fact, as the nation's favorite symbol of suburbia run rampant. It is the butt of jokes for its profligate sprawl, kooky architecture, unhip telephone area code and home-grown porno industry, as well as for a mythical tribe of nasal-toned, IQ-challenged teenage girls who like to shop. And yet the Valley only became a suburb fairly late in its history, and whether it qualifies for the label anymore is arguable.

The Cahuenga Pass through the Santa Monica Mountains linked the rural Valley with old Los Angeles, 15 miles away. These bicyclists negotiated the rocky, unpaved pass in 1897.

Teams of horses plowed fields and graded roads across the Valley. These teams are believed to be working around 1900 on the dirt road that became Ventura Boulevard.

Its formal identity is as an oversized appendage of the city of Los Angeles, but that does not tell the real story. The expansive, gently pitched plain has been a destination in at least four centuries now, a landing place for travelers who picked up their lives in search of something better. Where backyard barbecues now reign, two Native American cultures met to celebrate holidays together. The name *El Valle de San Fernando* was bequeathed by colonizers who came from Spain to civilize the Indians and to carve up the land. Later waves of settlers came to escape from shattering winters in cities like Philadelphia and Buffalo, or to try their luck at growing walnuts, or at building airplanes or helping invent the new medium of television. And still they come, from New York and Austin, but more often now from Seoul and Tehran and Guadalajara. All are seeking their piece of the American dream in what has become one of the most richly diverse corners of the country. Once here, they find the miles of walled subdivisions, wide boulevards and corner strip malls that fit with the Valley's popular image as a stucco haven—as well as the million-dollar estates, ethnic enclaves and urban forest of exotic trees and shrubs that suggest a more textured story.

Newcomers are often startled to discover signs of a rural past. Pockets of dirt streets and horse trails remain, along with faded farmhouses, backyard chicken coops, gurgling creeks and overgrown orchards, if you know where to look. This should be no surprise. At the start of the 20th century, the Valley floor contained the world's largest wheat farm, biggest citrus orchard and grandest grove of producing olive trees. The population was scant, just a few thousand, among them Basque sheepherders, Italian orange growers, Japanese strawberry pickers and Midwestern homesteaders. Horse-drawn stages still rattled through a winding mountain pass to Los Angeles.

Some 1.7 million people, more than the populations of 12 states and about a third of that of the entire city of Los Angeles, now reside in the Valley. More than a third of them were born in another country. But some things never change. These denizens of the Valley still live a largely separate existence from their fellow Los Angelenos. They don't share the same climate, flora or fauna, or much of a common history. The two hemispheres of the city have been joined only for a fraction of the Valley's existence—and then only in an audacious arranged marriage recognized in fiction in the film *Chinatown,* but which in real life has yet to be fully consummated. The relationship is like that of step-siblings who have grown closer over time, but who should never be mistaken for blood family. Many residents of the Valley still eschew visits to the city; they treasure the quieter neighborhoods, long summer evenings and ample free parking at the supermarkets found on the inland side of the Santa Monica Mountains.

Locals never refer to the Valley as "L.A." Instead, they claim residence in one of nearly thirty districts recognized as bona-fide addresses by mapmakers and the U.S. Postal Service—but which otherwise don't legally exist. Some of these quasi-communities, such as North Hollywood, Reseda and Canoga Park, sprang into being as dusty farm towns (under different names: Toluca, Marian and Owensmouth, respectively) that were miles from their closest neighbors. Part of the Valley's charm is that sections are named for a fictional ape-man (Tarzana), an English manor (Chatsworth), an Indian settlement (Tujunga) and promotional slogans (Studio City, Sun Valley, Sunland). There is a West Hills, a North Hills, a Shadow Hills, a Woodland Hills, a Granada Hills and a Mission Hills, each distinguishable from another.

The wary relationship with imperial Los Angeles, ingrained since the early 1800s, occasionally erupts into rebellious talk of secession. The notion of breaking off into a new city is absorbing for some and merely amusing to others, including the smaller independent cities that never joined Los Angeles. San Fernando, the Valley's original town, is named for a 13th-century Spanish king, Burbank for a dentist turned land baron, and Calabasas for the wild pumpkins that formerly grew there. The largest of the cities, Glendale, occupies the lone breach in the mountains that surround the Valley. Hidden Hills, a wealthy enclave of horse ranches and estates, bars outsiders from even entering without an invitation.

As a native son, and as a journalist, I set out to discover and clarify the legacy of dreamers and schemers, of milestones and lore, that stamps the Valley as home—to find out what made this place grow up to give the world Valley Girls, mini-malls and the International House of Pancakes, among other institutions. I've lived half of my life elsewhere, but I have always considered the Valley my home-town, and I've yearned to understand why there are no fewer than six historical societies and a half-dozen small museums dedicated to preserving its past—a past that slips further into wispy memory with every new year.

Now that I know at least some of the answers, I see glimpses of history all around. I can imagine *vaqueros* chasing stray mustangs across a grassy plain, and brown grizzly bears snatching steelhead out of the Los Angeles River. Landmarks infused with history are everywhere: the Chatsworth rocks that hid outlaws from *bandito* Joaquín Murrieta to murderer Charles Manson; the quirky church where the Grateful Dead and Ken Kesey's Merry Pranksters staged an "Electric Kool-Aid Acid Test;" the high school that produced Marilyn Monroe, Robert Redford and Don Drysdale.

Some might expect a book on the San Fernando Valley to be a rant against sterile suburban sprawl, or perhaps a celebration of local identity and traditions. I hope this book is neither. Nor is it intended as a work of historical scholarship. I merely found these stories and organized them in a way that made sense to me. If this book helps save any lore from vanishing into the void, and settles a few family arguments, my mission is complete.

Humble thanks are necessary, since many of these accounts and insights and facts were first put on paper elsewhere—in the *Los Angeles Times* and other newspapers, and in the good works of writers who toiled from 1769 to the 21st century. My job was made easier and much more pleasurable by the prodigious talents, diligent efforts and exacting memories of so many. I am hugely indebted to all the reporters, diarists, historians, authors, photographers and storytellers who got there first, and I have taken care to be true to them.

CHAPTER 1

The Land

Looking east from above Encino in 1960, the Ventura Freeway snakes below the Santa Monica Mountains. The Verdugos are the lower range of hills at left in the background.

Viewed from up high in the surrounding hills, the Valley resembles a gargantuan sprawl of asphalt pavement and rooftops peeking through a layer of greenery. The floor of the Valley stretches 20 unbroken miles in length and nearly 12 miles in breadth at the widest point, a flat basin large enough to contain the entire city limits of San Francisco, Washington *and* Boston, with room left over for Beverly Hills.

There is surprising order to the crazed layout, for almost everything one sees occupies a niche on an obsessively perpendicular grid of streets. Long, straight boulevards, most of them too wide for your grandmother to walk across in the span of one green light, are spaced across the plain reliably a half-mile apart. This precision traces from the dictates of early surveyors who mapped the land in sections suited to easy subdivision. Hundreds of feeder streets branch off at right angles from the main arteries to complete the grid.

Other major structures add architectural perspective to the panorama: the Los Angeles River encased in concrete, sidling eastward beneath the eye-catching *art moderne* concrete face of Sepulveda Dam; the San Diego Freeway, a sort of prime meridian splitting the Valley into west and east zones; and landmarks like the retro Warner Bros. studio, the red-and-white-striped quad stacks of the municipal steam plant in Sun Valley, and the faded beige Anheuser-Busch brewery.

The mountain ranges that enclose the basin lend definition to the vista. "Blue, brown and purple contrasting finely with the clear transparent skies, and with the even surface of the valley," a Mrs. E. Williams wrote after visiting the grassy plain of the Valley in 1856, when creaky Spanish *carretas* pulled by oxen were the closest thing to mass transit. Even today, coyotes and rattlesnakes, and the occasional bobcat and black bear, wander out of rocky canyons and down chaparral slopes to excite the human inhabitants.

The Santa Monica Mountains, riddled with fossils of ancient sea creatures and populated by film

The sleek *art moderne* form of Sepulveda Dam has been a roadside landmark in the Valley since 1941. The basin behind is a popular recreation area—weather permitting.

legends and rock stars, form the Valley's south rim. The range reaches 3,111 feet in elevation at its highest point, Calabasas Peak, and influences the climate: By obstructing moist coastal air from reaching inland, the Santa Monicas are a main reason that the Valley's communities bake in summer and that frost forms on lawns and car windows on some winter mornings.

The mountains abruptly vanish from sight in the rugged quasi-wilderness of Griffith Park, at the Valley's southeast corner. There, a low-lying gap about a mile across separates the tip of the Santa Monicas from the toe of the Verdugo Mountains, which rise suddenly and steeply to mark the basin's eastern rim. This gap between the mountain ranges is a crucial point in the geography. The Valley plain tilts imperceptibly toward this corner, pouring all of the rainfall and urban runoff with it. The water eventually gathers in the Los Angeles River, which burbles for nearly the entire length of the Valley floor and then exits through the gap, bound for the Pacific. Without this opening through the Narrows, as the gap has been called historically, the low side of the Valley might be marshland.

The Verdugo range, laced with glens and dells and possessed of marvelous views, marches up the east side of the Valley and stops just short of the soaring exposed granite slabs that define the northeast wall. These higher mountains are the seismically volatile San Gabriels, which reach over 5,000 feet—and rising—above Sunland and Sylmar. They feature deep drainage canyons out of which has tumbled

about a million years of earthen debris to form the foundation of the Valley soil. "Shedding, spalling, self-destructing, they are disintegrating at a rate that is among the fastest in the world," author John McPhee wrote of the turbulent San Gabriels. Over time, this process of erosion filled a gash in the bedrock with a deep layer of rich alluvia—minerals, gravel, sand, kernels of broken-down granite—that enabled fruit trees and row crops to thrive.

Proceeding westward around the rim, the rounded, blond-colored ridges belong to the Santa Susana Mountains. Underlain with rich oil and gas deposits, their highest point, Oat Mountain, tops out at over 3,740 feet—a little higher since the 1994 Northridge earthquake shoved the peak upward. The final segment in the rim, the far western edge of the basin, is defined by the rock crags and sandstone cliffs of the Simi Hills.

Natural passageways through these mountains have played key parts in local lore. The first world travelers to discover the Valley hacked and fought their way over the Santa Monicas through the same canyon where modern commuters struggle against time and traffic in Sepulveda Pass. More history was made where the foothills of the San Gabriels and Santa Susanas blend, in the canyon through which the Golden State Freeway now leaves the Valley, headed north. The ridges there dip to a low saddle, called at various times *Cuesta Vieja* and San Fernando Pass, but most commonly known as Newhall Pass. Through this pass climbed the first horse-drawn

stagecoach from Los Angeles to San Francisco, and beneath it steamed the first northbound locomotive. In a turning point in the nation's history, the American Bear Flag Battalion clambered down the pass to invade the San Fernando Valley and claim victory over Mexico in 1846.

Heat, dust and other forms of torture

The Valley floor in its natural state was a gently sloping grassland of wild oats and foxtail barley. Quail and jack rabbits hid in the tall grass—also antelope and grizzly bears. Red-tailed hawks and turkey vultures, hulking and ugly enough to be mistaken for condors, drifted overhead. In the spring, a sea of wild mustard tinted everything yellow, the stalks swaying chest-high to a man. A river coursed through reeds and marshes. Creeks trickled through willows at the bottom of shallow arroyos.

Early inhabitants found themselves under frequent assault by the elements. Winters brought flash floods that left visible scars across the grassland: wide fans of sand and gravel, decorated with cactus and the yucca plumes called Our Lord's Candle. Summers often meant severe drought and stifling heat. Along the foothills, live oaks with massive limbs offered the only protective shade. Otherwise, the land was treeless for miles and so arid for most of the year that wildfires were not uncommon. Dust kicked up by windstorms tortured animals and people alike.

On November 18, 1871, the *Los Angeles Star*

Trees were scarce on the wide Valley floor until settlers planted windbreaks. This scene looks north from a knoll beside Ventura Boulevard, probably in the early 1900s near present-day Encino.

Tujunga Wash was the most troublesome mountain drainage to spill across the Valley floor. This view, from the Cross aerial photography firm, looks southwest from Big Tujunga Canyon.

Under the sheltering leaves

described a ferocious sandstorm in the Valley that delayed the overland stage from San Francisco by six hours. "The horses refused to face the storm, and the driver had to stop and unhitch, and camp for the night behind the coach. When daylight came, no trace of the road was to be seen; the sand had entirely covered it. At one place on the road near an arroyo, a pile of sand had drifted some 10 feet in height, and stands there now as a landmark."

Farmers drawn to this forlorn grassland planted trees madly, trying to break the north wind and the clouds of dust that it churned up. Well into the 20th century, the battle was still being waged. Dust devils were such a nuisance that early movie crews had to adjust their schedules. Planting wind-breaks "as soon as possible" was urged on land buyers. The *Van Nuys News* of January 12, 1912, published on its front page the advice of C. B. Hewitt, who recommended rows of Monterey cypress and eucalyptus: "Either the red or gray gum is preferable to the blue gum, as they are not so suscepti-ble to cold or drought and are much hardier." Farmers knew the rule: "If the wind started to blow before the fall rains, you had a dust storm," accord-ing to Menton Neggen, whose family raised peaches and apricots after they arrived in 1911 to live in a fledgling Scandinavian pioneer settlement with

The most remarkable physical feature of the modern Valley might be the eclectic forest of trees that covers the terrain like an arboreal blanket. What a magnificent disguise: peppers, gums, sycamores, elms, magnolias, cedars, jacarandas, junipers, at least a dozen species of palms and pines, just about every kind of fruit tree, giant ficus that fracture sidewalks, oaks and walnuts that keep the squirrels stocked for winter—literally millions of trees, native to six continents and a host of islands.

Few of the species grew here naturally. "As we plodded hour after hour along the tedious straight roads, escorted by clouds of pungent

Mature deodar cedars and other species line a Sherman Oaks section of Chandler Boulevard, a favorite route for tree lovers since its creation in 1912 as Sherman Way.

dust...no single tree offered respite of shade, and the two or three ranch houses we passed looked almost hideous in their blistering whitewash," J. Smeaton Chase wrote of a horseback excursion through the Valley in the early 1900s.

The first eucalyptus were put in as windbreaks on the Workman Ranch in the 1870s. Two of the original trees remain in Shadow Ranch Park in West Hills; two others toppled in 1999. Everybody seems to have a favorite tree-lined street: swaying palms along Sherman Way, overgrown deodars planted in 1932 on White Oak Avenue in Granada Hills, century-old olive trees lining Lassen Street in Chatsworth, canopies of live oak limbs south of Ventura Boulevard in Encino.

The demise of Encino's grandest coast live oak—the 75-foot-tall Lang Oak, a state cultural monument since 1963 in the center of Louise Avenue—illustrated the bond. An El Niño storm on February 7, 1998, felled the behemoth *Quercus agrifolia*, believed to be hundreds of years old. Admirers came all weekend to gawk at the limbs, while city crews sought equipment stout enough to penetrate the massive trunk. Some neighbors who had tended the giant through infections, car crash-es and numerous storms carried souvenir branches as they left, wiping away tears. The *Times* headline the next day captured the sentiment: "If a Tree Falls in the Valley, We All Hear It."

Workmen clear debris in 1936 from a section of the Los Angeles River just south of the Narrows. The hills of Griffith Park rise in the background.

the Biblical name of Zelzah.

The newcomers also learned hard lessons about disregarding the canyon washes that plunged out of the San Gabriels and scarred the eastern half of the Valley. Most of the time the sandy washes were dry rattlesnake nests, but in rainy years they could go on rampages. The new town of Van Nuys discovered the truth about the dry channels in February 1914. The heaviest rainfall in 30 years began on a Wednesday. As the water rose higher in Pacoima Canyon wash, crews raced to fill sandbags and keep the town dry.

But on Friday night, February 20, the wash breached the levee and inundated the center of Van Nuys. Bridges tore away and the town was cut off and left without power.

Always the booster, the Van Nuys newspaper tried to assure residents that "the vast benefits gained by the thorough soaking given the lands will offset all damage done." That was of little solace to farmers who found their fields covered with sand and gravel. A visitor, Dr. J. A. Nolen, piled insult on injury and called the Van Nuys denizens a bunch of whiners—"Back in Oklahoma, we have wind and rainstorms that really amount to something worth kicking about!" Flooding returned often to Van Nuys, and the plague wasn't entirely natural. The original town site was planned to be more than a mile farther west, out of harm's way, but the subdividers shifted the locale to add more distance from rivals who owned the historic Encino rancho. In doing so, they moved Van Nuys into the path of Pacoima Wash.

The worst flooding threat was not heavy rain in the Valley itself but the big, wet Pacific storms that smacked into the San Gabriels. If the slopes were already saturated, the rain slid off into the canyons, which gathered the runoff like funnels and pointed the torrents right at the Valley. The highest dam in the country at the time, 330 feet tall, was erected across Pacoima Canyon in 1929 to protect crops and homes in the Valley. A dam was built in Big Tujunga Canyon, the most threatening drainage, in 1931. For a time, everyone felt safe from the washes.

Then, in 1938, the wettest February in half a century ended with a continuous deluge of 4.5 inches. By March 2 the reservoir behind Big Tujunga Dam was nearly full, and there was some minor street flooding, but the morning *Los Angeles Times* still crowed about "the small amount of damage that has resulted." By the time those papers were delivered, the deadliest flood of the century in Southern California was under way. It was classic "torrent and inundation"—heavy rain fell on saturated mountains and rushed toward low ground in the Valley. Rising water washed over farms and ranches and left Van Nuys completely isolated. A fleet of boats was commandeered from the city parks department to move 500 Canoga Park residents to higher ground.

Things got worse when the floodgates on Big Tujunga Dam were opened in order to save the structure. This sent the Valley's most dangerous wash on a rampage, taking out bridges in the foothill area and tossing them down toward the Valley floor. All the creeks and washes were full, and the Los Angeles River was carving big chunks out of its banks. The river swallowed a cafe and 10 houses at Universal City. Five people fell to their deaths when the Lankershim Boulevard bridge collapsed into the river.

The storm finally eased up on the evening of the 3rd, after dropping 12 inches of rain in some areas. But the flood toll mounted as the mountains disgorged their load. At least 96 persons died across Southern California, including five members of the Fujihara family of North Hollywood and 2-year-old

A river runs through it—sometimes

In its natural state, the river, shown here in 1902, meandered through thickets of willows.

Old maps did not agree on the source and the path followed by the Los Angeles River across the Valley. Before the 20th century, mapmakers often believed that the river originated in the San Gabriel Mountains and plunged southward over the Valley floor, since that is where the tormenting winter and spring floods began. Some maps also showed the river rising at Encino and gurgling eastward to the Narrows.

The confusion is due to the river's fickle flow. As understood now, the headwaters of the Los Angeles rise in the Simi Hills, where Bell Creek gathers the runoff from springs and scant rainfall. The creek trickles out of Bell Canyon and across the Valley floor, picks up the runoff from Dayton Canyon and merges with Calabasas Creek to form the river—if the term can be properly applied to a waterway of such dubious existence. Except in rainy season, most of the river's flow across the west Valley is underground. Maps likely showed the river appearing at Encino because, in dry months, the underground flow would first appear on the surface there.

For most of history, the river meandered in a bed lined with willows and reeds. When it periodically escaped its banks, there was little in the way to be destroyed. But after the disastrous flooding of 1938, concrete channeling began. Today the official starting point of the Los Angeles River is where two concrete streams meet behind the bleachers of the Canoga Park High School football field.

Today virtually the entire 51-mile Los Angeles River is entombed in a deep concrete channel designed by flood control engineers. This particularly barren stretch runs behind the Warner Brothers studio in Burbank.

Hansen Dam, a sweeping two miles long, was built to prevent flood waters from tumbling down the Tujunga Wash onto the Valley floor. At its 1940 dedication, VIPs enjoyed lunch atop the dam's spillway.

Construction of Sepulveda Dam, which began in February 1939, was one of several efforts undertaken in the steadily urbanizing Valley after the disastrous flooding of 1938.

The 1938 floods deposited tons of mud and debris on the Valley floor, forcing residents, like the Haley brothers, who operated a grocery store in North Hollywood, to dig out.

of the San Fernando Valley by coalescing the pressure for big public works to prevent future flooding. Almost immediately, work began on Hansen Dam to retain the drainage from Big Tujunga and Little Tujunga canyons. Dedicated on August 17, 1940, at two miles in length it was the largest compacted earth-filled dam in the world. Its construction swallowed up streets, ranches and some of the farming district known as Hansen Heights and also created a new recreation lake. The community and the dam were named for Dr. Homer Hansen, a pioneer subdivider whose home had stood on a knoll known to Valley old-timers as the Mount of Olives.

The 1938 flood also led to the widening, deepening and paving of the Los Angeles River through the Valley and the erection of another signature landmark. Originally called the Van Nuys Retention Basin on the Upper Los Angeles River, the facility now called Sepulveda Dam Basin cost $7 million and consumed 1,000 acres of farmland and ranches. Many residents opposed the dam, calling it a land grab built mainly to protect downstream Los Angeles, but a court order gave the Army Corps of Engineers

Jason Welborn, swept out of his mother's arms in Big Tujunga Wash. As bad as it was, radio reporters described dam failures and catastrophes that never occurred. One announcer reported that Calabasas was wiped off the map. Another shrieked that an auto tunnel in Newhall had collapsed. Neither claim was true. But the Academy Awards, scheduled for the Biltmore Hotel in downtown Los Angeles, were postponed for a week after many stars were stranded in the Valley and elsewhere.

The flood of 1938 was more than a natural disaster—it transformed the landscape and the future

The rampaging Los Angeles River swept away this bridge on Colfax Avenue in Studio City during the March 1938 flooding that claimed 96 lives in Southern California.

emergency possession of the acreage. Work proceeded 24 hours a day. Film actress Jane Wyman, the wife of actor Ronald Reagan, helped cut the ribbon at the dedication in March 1942. If both dams had been in place four years earlier, "there would have been no flood on the Los Angeles River," the local head of the Army Corps of Engineers boldly proclaimed.

Even so, nature's desire to flood the Valley periodically has proven difficult to conquer. In 1958 and 1962, schools had to close briefly because streets were flooded across the Valley—the new suburbs lacked storm drains to move rainwater into flood channels. A crash program was launched to build drains. Torrents washing out of Big Tujunga Canyon in 1969 again knocked down bridges. In 1978, a drought in Southern California ended with such ferocity that mudslides unloosed coffins from a cemetery above Tujunga.

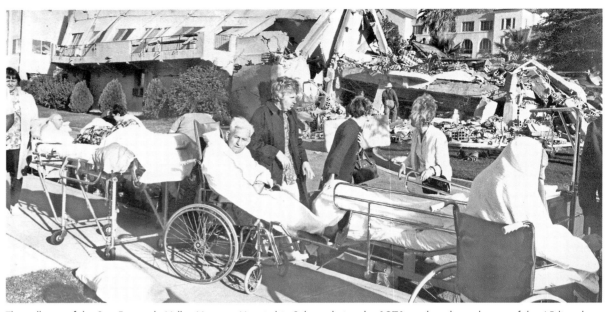

The collapse of the San Fernando Valley Veterans Hospital in Sylmar during the 1971 earthquake took most of the 65 lives lost in the quake. The hospital, which opened in 1926, was not rebuilt.

When the earth moves

Far below the Valley floor, seismic forces of unimaginable strength have bent, twisted and otherwise deformed the bedrock. The Valley, like much of Southern California, is caught in a viselike pinch between rival geologic trends. This squeeze helped create the mountains that encircle the Valley, uplifting and shaping them into their now-familiar contours. The earthen pressure has also riddled the bedrock with small yet potentially dangerous earthquake faults.

Early settlers learned of the geology's ability to inflict damage in 1812, when a three-month swarm of temblors ended with a pair of December earthquakes estimated at magnitude 7.0. The quakes were centered elsewhere, in the Pacific and at the distant end of the San Gabriels, but the adobe church at Mission San Fernando Rey became the Valley's first structural casualty. "As a result of the ruinous events we have to rebuild anew the churches of Missions San Fernando and Santa Barbara," Fray José Senan reported to superiors.

On January 9, 1857, the Great Fort Tejon quake,

estimated as an 8.2-magnitude temblor, was felt across Southern California for two minutes. "Women shrieked, children cried and men ejaculated hastily framed prayers of most ludicrous construction. Horses and cattle fled widely over the plains, screaming and bellowing," historian J. Albert Wilson recorded. This time the mission survived intact. In fact, none of the big quakes in recorded time was located beneath the Valley, although the Chatsworth grammar school was damaged beyond repair in the 1933 Long Beach quake.

A million new inhabitants later, the Valley woke at

The Northridge quake: death, destruction and a land reshaped

The 6.7 quake on January 17, 1994 was the most damaging natural disaster in U.S. history. In addition to 57 deaths, 9,158 people were injured enough to require treatment, 34,000 dwellings were vacated at least temporarily and 12,000 homes and businesses suffered serious structural damage. Economic loss exceeded $20 billion. The fatalities included three cases of Valley fever spread by fungus spores carried in the dust shaken loose by landslides in the Santa Susana Mountains. (The fever gets its name from the San Joaquin Valley, not the San Fernando.)

Cal State University, Northridge was left in shambles, its operations impacted for years afterward. The Valley's biggest shopping mall, Northridge Fashion Center, was nearly destroyed. And almost every remaining adobe building in the Valley was trashed. The Andres Pico adobe needed several years of repairs, displacing the San Fernando Valley Historical Society. Gaping cracks remained six years later in the de Osa adobe and the adjacent limestone Garnier farmhouse at Los Encinos state historic park. The 1870s wood-framed Workman house in Shadow Ranch Park in West Hills—the last building from the Lankershim ranch era—also remained fenced off six years after the quake. At Mission San Fernando Rey, built to modern codes after the 1971 quake, the church opened for funerals the next day.

The thrust fault that broke in the Northridge quake is invisible, and scientists now believe that such "blind" faults pose as great a threat to the Valley and other urban areas as the more visible San Andreas Fault. The worst quakes on these lesser hidden faults won't be as strong, but they can hit right under large populations.

They also can change the actual shape of the land. Scientists calculate that the bedrock lifted on average about three feet in the Northridge quake. Oat Mountain in the Santa Susana range grew by sixteen inches. As a result of the quake, the Valley floor tilted a little more steeply toward the Narrows at Glendale, forcing officials to conduct a new survey of the floodplain.

For all that scientists learned after the quake, a mystery remains. The strongest ground shaking ever measured was detected by a seismic sensor in Tarzana, four miles south of the epicenter, on a knoll above Tarzana Drive. The hill, covered with exotic trees planted before 1917 by former owner Gen. Harrison Gray Otis, was home to the Cedar Hill Nursery at the time of the quake. A sensor fastened into solid rock recorded accelerations so high that experts came from Japan and New Zealand to investigate. Seismologists still aren't sure what caused the extreme shaking.

The Northridge Fashion Center remained closed for 18 months after the 1994 Northridge quake, which leveled this parking structure at the mall. At the nearby state university, quake damage took years to repair.

Clocks at Olive View Hospital in Sylmar stand frozen in time at 6:01 a.m., the exact moment the 1971 quake struck. The hospital was so heavily damaged that it was bulldozed.

6:01 a.m. on February 9, 1971, to a new seismic reality. At that moment, a 6.6-magnitude quake radiated from beneath the mountains northeast of Sylmar, in the San Fernando fault zone—both names have been attached to the quake, which rumbled for 60 seconds. The earthquake caused 65 deaths and more than $500 million in property damage, mostly in the Valley, fracturing the ground for 12 miles and rupturing the state's biggest natural gas preserve beneath Aliso Canyon above Granada Hills. Most deaths occurred in the col-

lapse of the circa-1926 San Fernando Valley Veterans Hospital in Sylmar. A new five-story, quake-resistant tower at Olive View Medical Center in Sylmar also fell apart, and Holy Cross Hospital in Mission Hills incurred heavy damage. The lower dam at Van Norman Reservoir—where the Los Angeles Aqueduct delivers its water—nearly failed, forcing the evacuation of tens of thousands of residents. Aftershocks rattled nerves for months.

A pleasant, shady park now stands on the site of

the fallen Sylmar VA hospital. A plaque mounted at the entrance reads: "Lest We Forget. In loving memory of the many veterans, nurses and aides of the San Fernando Valley Veterans Hospital whose lives were lost during the earthquake of Feb. 9, 1971."

But many people did forget, and even those who remembered were dumbstruck by the terror they woke to on January 17, 1994. At 4:31 a.m., a crack began to rip open in solid rock 11 miles below the intersection of Reseda Boulevard and Arminta Street. The rupture widened into a massive, moving subterranean rift that sped toward the surface at about two miles a second, angling upward and to the northwest, beneath Northridge, Granada Hills and Chatsworth and under the Santa Susana Mountains. Waves of energy radiated outward, in three distinct pulses, as the fracture raced ahead. Eight seconds after the fault snapped, the spreading crack exhausted itself three miles below the surface; it ran into a broken fault from the 1971 quake.

Geologically, the main event of what would be called the Northridge earthquake was over. A huge block of bedrock had been shoved upward by deep and immutable forces. But on the surface, the nightmare had just begun.

Bedrooms contorted and tilted and whipped like a scary thrill ride, or just shook horribly; the sensations varied by location. Doors slammed wildly as if propelled by demonic ghosts. Slumbering families wakened by the gentler first energy wave were tossed from their beds onto floors covered in glass from

Freeway bridges failed in the Newhall Pass during both the Sylmar and Northridge quakes. This was the dramatic scene on Interstate 5 in 1994.

exploding windows. Refrigerators, chests of drawers and china cabinets full of cherished heirlooms toppled. The world had gone berserk, and it all took place in the dark—the power grid had failed. Inky blackness hid what the Valley's inhabitants didn't want to see.

The quake seemed to last so long, and to be so violent, in part because the rock foundations of the surrounding mountains trapped the energy waves, bouncing them back through the basin like ripples of water in a bathtub. Once the sloshing eased, trembling parents felt their way to their children. Tens of thousands fled outdoors onto lawns and sidewalks, where some would remain for days. Many older people lay helpless in their beds, resigned to wait for the sun. Everyone tensed at each sickening quiver as the bedrock slowly settled into its new place.

The first major U.S. earthquake to strike directly beneath an urban area since Long Beach in 1933 generated the most extreme ground motion ever measured in an American city. Freeways and shopping centers toppled and apartment buildings collapsed, crushing the occupants. Remarkably, this was only a medium quake, a 6.7 shaker nowhere near the strongest quake that Southern California urban areas can reasonably expect. On average, about 120 earthquakes of magnitude 6.0 to 6.9 occur annually worldwide. This was the second to emanate from under the Valley in 23 years.

The 57 deaths were fewer than in the 1971 quake. The death toll was that low only because nearly everyone was home asleep, most of them in structures made with relatively forgiving wood frames. Everyone would remember January 17 more somberly if classrooms and department stores had been occupied when the roofs fell in, or if rush-hour commuters had been stalled on the Newhall Pass freeway where CHP motorcycle officer Clarence Wayne Dean plunged to his death in the dark, unable to see that the pavement was gone. A year later to the day, a quake of similar intensity killed 5,000 people in Kobe, Japan.

CHAPTER 2

Early Arrivals

Following decades of neglect and use as a hay barn and hog pen, the historic Mission San Fernando Rey fell into ruin as seen in this 1903 photo of the *convento* and mission outbuildings.

On a summer morning in 1769—Saturday, August 5—a ragged procession of 64 men with almost a hundred mules in tow began ascending the southern slope of the Santa Monica Mountains. Their ranks included a priest who served as diarist for the expedition, and a company of soldiers dressed in leather and armed with muskets. They bushwhacked their way up a canyon thick with sycamores, wild rosebushes and stubby walnut trees until, at midafternoon, they reached the crest of the mountains (near where Mulholland Drive crosses the San Diego Freeway today). There the unsuspecting explorers looked upon "a very pleasant and spacious valley," in the priest's words.

They stumbled down through the brush and, after resting beside a refreshing pool, found their way into "two large villages of very fine, well-behaved and very friendly heathens who must have amounted to about 200 souls, men, women and children. They offered us their seeds in baskets and other things made of rushes.... Each of them brought some food with which to regale us, and we reciprocated with beads and ribbons."

The visitors had come from Spain, in the Old World, and Mexico, her newly established colony in the New World. They had begun walking north from the recently founded settlement of San Diego three weeks earlier, after receiving blessings from Fray Junípero Serra, a learned priest who was intent on creating a string of missions in this land the Spanish called California. Gaspar de Portolá, a captain in the Spanish army, led the expedition. Their goal was to find an overland route to the Spanish outpost at Monterey.

The bearded strangers looked out of place among the Indians, but their manner was more curious than hostile. The Indians, called by later anthropologists the Tongva, responded in kind. They knew of sailing ships passing by the coast beyond the mountains, but these were the first outsiders they had seen. The natives did not act especially concerned; they could not have known that their world

Chumash Indians left rock paintings and other artifacts around the boulder mound known as Stoney Point. The Chatsworth landmark has appeared in many western films.

had in an instant dramatically changed.

At the time, more than a dozen Tongva settlements flourished on the edges of the Valley—among the rocks, under the oaks, away from the open flats that were so foreboding. Their inhabitants ate seeds, berries and acorns and trapped small animals. They fashioned shelters out of river rushes placed over depressions sunk into the ground. Women wore skirts of grass or rabbit skins; the men went naked unless it was cold. The Tongva wore their hair long, crafted flutes from hollow reeds, and played ball-games in large groups. Evidence of their presence in the form of tools and graves has been found throughout the Valley, but nowhere in as much abundance as around the presumed site of the village with its flowing spring, in the modern community of Encino.

Linguistically part of the Shoshone tradition, the Tongva spoke the "nga" sound to indicate a village or special place, as in the now-familiar place names Topanga and Cahuenga. The Tongva also possessed a rich lore of stories and myths. Their village of *Tujunga,* or "old woman place," was where legend said the wife of the chief 'Ra'wiyawi turned herself to stone out of grief for her children who had died. *Siutcanga* was, by some accounts, the name of the village beside the spring, nestled against the mountains among giant live oaks—*siutca* was the native word for the towering shade trees, some of them a thousand years old.

Portolá's weary explorers and the Tongva first met on the Catholic feast day of St. Catherine of Bononia. In tribute to her and the magnificent trees, the Spaniards christened this land *El Valle de Santa Catalina de Bononia de los Encinos*—the Valley of St. Catherine of the Oaks. The next day, Mass was celebrated by the priest, Fray Juan Crespi, and the Spaniards remained in camp and attempted to communicate with the locals. The two groups exchanged gifts while the Indians sketched maps in the dirt showing the Channel Islands off the coast and the course followed by the white men's ships. On Monday afternoon Portolá led his expedition across the broad Valley on the far side of the river. They camped overnight under the San Gabriels, near present-day Sylmar, "in a very green valley grown with large live oaks and alders," Crespi recorded. On Tuesday they climbed through the canyons that later became Newhall Pass and journeyed north.

After the Spaniards returned to San Diego, maps were drawn showing this new place, the valley of *los encinos*. The river was proclaimed to be the *Río Porciúncula,* and a fledgling pueblo, known as *Los Angeles* for short, was founded 15 miles downstream beside another large Indian settlement. In 1774 and 1776, as American colonists in the east were building toward revolt against the king of Great Britain, Juan Bautista de Anza led new expeditions across *el Valle*

In early California, cattle hides and tallow were the unofficial currency. With no fences on the vast Valley plain, *vaqueros* periodically rounded up stray longhorns and checked for branding marks, as depicted here.

de los Encinos in the name of Spain's king. The Valley's destiny as a place to which settlers would flock was sealed—notwithstanding that hundreds, perhaps thousands, of Tongva already considered the grassy plain their world.

Before the century ended, 36,000 acres east of the river narrows were given by Spanish grant to José María Verdugo, an invalid army corporal. His grant was known as *Rancho San Rafael*. His brother, Mariano, received the land straddling the Narrows itself and dubbed it *Rancho Portesuelo*, the gateway. Francisco Reyes, a black-skinned member of the original Portolá expedition also set up a small rancho, across the Valley floor from the spring at *Los Encinos*. By 1795, a quarter-century after the Spaniards' arrival, Reyes had a herd of livestock and an adobe house—and fertile fields of beans, corn and watermelon tended by Tongva Indians wearing shoes and sombreros.

A mission for St. Ferdinand

The native Californians working in Reyes' fields caught the eyes of Franciscan priests scouting a suitable location for a new mission. Reyes' land lay one day's walk between the established missions inland at San Gabriel and on the coast at San Buenaventura. "It has much water, much humid land and also limestone," wrote Father Vicente de Santa María. Reyes agreed to move on, and his adobe became the first building at Mission San

Mission buildings were constructed of mud-and-straw adobe bricks and heavy timbers dragged from the nearby mountains. This 1926 view of a cloister room shows the dirt floor.

Fernando, Rey de España, the seventeenth in the chain of 21 missions in Alta California begun by Fray Serra's order. The name honored Ferdinand III, the Spanish king who had vanquished the Moors in 1248 and been anointed a saint.

On September 8, 1797, Fray Fermín Francisco de Lasuen—president of the missions since Serra's death in 1784—intoned the Litany of All Saints and planted a cross marking the newest outpost in the Spanish empire. He baptized five Indian children of each sex as Catholic neophytes, *neofitos*. The first girl to receive the holy sacrament was christened with her

A mission Indian's life: Field work and prayer

◆ Indians at the mission rose with the sun, answered bells calling them to morning Mass and ate corn mush before reporting to work. A two-hour break at noon was followed by another three hours of toil and a chapel session. A bell at 8 p.m. ordered the Indians to bed. Sundays and feast days were free of work.

◆ In all, 1,586 Indian "neophytes" were baptized at San Fernando Rey. Of the 2,081 Indians who died at the mission, half never reached the age of 20. But 92 San Fernando Indians reportedly lived to the age of 80 or older.

◆ Some historians insist that treatment of the Indians by Spanish soldiers was not excessive. But the soldiers could be brutal, if an account credited to a Russian sea otter hunter captured on the California coast is accurate. Vassili Tarakanoff said he was marched two days to a mission, where he saw Indians tied and flogged with straps—and one chief sewn into the warm skin of a slaughtered calf and tied to a stake until he died. His account, translated into English in 1953, did not name the mission, but the book's editor surmised it was San Fernando. Historical sources confirm the Russian's 1815 arrest but suggest that he was taken not to San Fernando Rey but to Mission Santa Barbara before his release in 1817.

Grizzly bears roamed the Valley grasslands when the Spanish arrived in 1769. ``Roping the Bear'' by artist James Walker, an occasional guest at the San Fernando Mission, depicts a bear being trapped.

new Spanish name, Fernanda María. Other missions donated cattle, sheep, oxen, mules and horses—a thousand head in all. The valley of San Fernando appeared on maps.

The calling of mission priests was to civilize the Indians, baptize them as Christians and put them to work producing goods. Some 147 baptisms and 13 marriages took place the first year. The Indians planted crops and built a small chapel. In concept each mission was a temporary establishment, designed to prepare Indians to run their own self-sustaining Christian pueblo within 10 years. Huge expanses of land were commandeered for the

missions. San Fernando Rey laid claim to its valley and to several others north and west, covering some 130 native settlements.

When the 18th century ended, 541 Indians lived at San Fernando Rey and did the heavy work: making adobe bricks of mud and straw, planting figs, grapes and an olive grove, tending crops and livestock. About half of the *neofitos* came from Tongva-speaking settlements in the San Fernando Valley: from *Ceegenga,* near today's Northridge; from *Momonga,* near Chatsworth; from *Cabuenga* at the mouth of Cahuenga Pass; from *Topanga* and *Tujunga.* The rest came from Chumash lands west of the

Valley, or from tribes further inland. Choosing to accept the mission's lure of food and civilization apparently was voluntary. But once baptized, a neophyte could not leave without permission. Those who fled were hunted down by soldiers, returned to the mission and typically whipped or locked in chains. Floggings of 50 to 100 lashes were not uncommon, though some historians emphasize that the severity of punishment was usual for the times.

Selected Indians became overseers with the authority to mete out punishment, while others were trained as *vaqueros,* the cowboys who tended the free-ranging herds. By 1826 there were 56,000 long-horn cattle and 1,500 horses and ponies foraging on the Valley floor. San Fernando Rey became known for the artistry of its silversmiths, its olives and its vineyard and wine. St. Ferdinand's day, May 30, was the biggest feast of the year. "All attended, from the majordomo to the lowliest Indian," longtime Valley resident T. R. Wilson recounted in the 1920s, recalling his grandmother's stories. "Following the mass was a great feast or banquet. The table was spread between two long rows of pomegranate trees in the orchard at the rear of the old church.... The main event was a bullfight held in the plaza in front of the old church. In the evening, songs and dancing ended the gay fiesta."

The buildings of San Fernando Rey dominated the Valley plain, beckoning travelers on *El Camino Real,* the "king's highway" linking all of the missions, which passed beside the original spring at Los

A landmark rises from the ruins

Restoration of the mission did not progress until the 20th century. In this photo taken about 1888, sunlight filters through the damaged roof as visitors inspect the interior, vandalized by treasure seekers and squatters.

The buildings and gardens of Mission San Fernando Rey were the most visible landmarks on the broad, empty floor of the Valley, an oasis of hospitality and civilization that beckoned travelers across the parched grassland. Stone channels and dams diverted streams from the San Gabriels and kept the mission stocked with cool flowing water.

After the new Mexican landlords of California stripped the missions from church control, the rancho at San Fernando Rey became a semiprivate enterprise under the control of a *mayordomo,* or overseer. The most important of these was Don Pedro López, a rancher whose family remained active in Valley affairs for many decades. His brother, Don Francisco López, became famous as the first discoverer of gold in California in 1842. He found a nugget after pulling up a wild onion while resting under a tree in Placerita Canyon, on the far side of Newhall Pass.

The physical condition of the mission worsened while Andres Pico resided there. On May 31, 1862, President Abraham Lincoln proclaimed that the Mission San Fernando Rey church, clergy residence, cemetery, orchard and vineyard would revert to the control of the Roman Catholic bishop of Monterey. Nonetheless, time and neglect continued to take a toll. Vandals and treasure seekers invaded after Pico's death in 1876, and the elements began to erode the mud-and-straw bricks. Within a few years, the mission was considered to be in ruins.

Around the turn of the century, efforts began to preserve the mission as a historic treasure. Not until 1941 was the mission restored sufficiently that Catholic Mass could be celebrated again in the church.

Encinos. The main church, built between 1804 and 1806, was erected with walls five feet thick at the base tapering to three feet at the top, so that the picturesque structure appeared to lean. The nearby *convento,* at 243 feet in length, was the largest adobe structure ever built in Spanish California. Erected from 1810-22, its 21 Roman arches and long portico became a familiar landmark for travelers (and remain so today). Visitors entered through heavy doors into a *sala,* or grand reception room, the grandest in the province. The *convento* provided quarters for the priests and soldiers, and included the chapel, refectory, winery, kitchen and guest rooms.

Mexico's independence from Spain in 1822 altered the course of the California colony, and set in motion events that would strip the missions of their status. Many citizens of the Los Angeles region wanted the missions' valuable cattle-grazing lands put into private hands; many in the north, including the Mexican governor of the province of Alta California, sided with priests who wished the church institutions to continue operating. The split erupted into an armed rebellion against the governor, Gen. Manuel Victoria.

On December 4, 1831, Victoria led a company of 30 soldiers into the valley of San Fernando Rey, intending to smash the revolt. The troops bivouacked at the mission. The following day, a column of rebels from Los Angeles rode through Cahuenga Pass with lances raised and banners flying. The two forces faced off in the vicinity of today's Studio City and waited for the other side to charge. Finally, Victoria accused his own men of cowardice. In answer to the challenge, Capt. Romualdo Pacheco spurred his horse across the grassland toward the rebels. Responding for the Angelenos was José María Avila, a large man regarded as the region's best horseman. As they met, Pacheco swung his saber, but Avila deflected the blow with his lance and with his other hand fired a pistol shot that found its target. Pacheco crumpled to the ground dead, the first military casualty—and possibly the first gunshot victim of any kind—in the San Fernando Valley.

As the battle raged with swords and muskets, Avila turned to hunt down Victoria. After managing to knock the governor from his horse, Avila himself fell fatally wounded. The undisciplined rebels turned and retreated to Los Angeles, but they had lost the battle and won the war. Victoria had been severely cut over the eye and left soon for Mexico, resigning as governor.

In victory the southerners became more influential and sure of their cause, spelling the end of the missions as all-powerful landholders. San Fernando Rey was still thriving, with 32,000 grapevines, 1,600 fruit trees, 26,000 animals and 792 Indians in residence. "Oranges, lemons, figs and olives hung upon the trees, and the blood-red tuna, or prickly pear, looked very tempting," visitor Edwin Bryant wrote of the mission gardens. But in the new order, the priests became strictly religious functionaries, and the Indians were freed. Some tried to return to their ancestral settlements, but they had become outsiders—if the villages even existed any longer. Some Indians drifted to Los Angeles, but most who did met an unhappy welcome. Many simply vanished into the hills around the Valley or remained near the mission, struggling to eke out a living on the land.

More than a decade later, hostilities flared anew when another unpopular Mexican governor, Jose Manuel Micheltorena, decreed that the missions and their former landholdings should be returned to church control. Ranchers in the south who wanted land for grazing their cattle found this intolerable, and the provincial Assembly voted to unseat Micheltorena as governor and replace him with Pío Pico, a native *Californio.* Another military skirmish followed on the floor of the Valley, pitting dissidents from Los Angeles against forces loyal to the ousted governor.

For this battle, the weaponry had advanced from wooden lances to cannons. Micheltorena marched his ragged army into the Valley in mid-February of 1845 and camped near the spring at *Los Encinos* (the site of his headquarters was pegged in a 1934 history as about where the Balboa Park soccer fields are today, but no supporting evidence was given). Micheltorena's force of 500 men included Americans enticed by his promise to usurp Mexican law and allow them to own land. John Sutter, who played a prominent role in the Gold Rush of 1849, led the American fighters.

In Los Angeles, horses were once again saddled

Castle Peak:
a beacon for the ages

Twelve miles due west of Van Nuys by car, the suburbs bump up against an imposing barrier. Directly behind the backyards on Castle Peak Drive, a scrub-covered slope climbs steeply to a rocky pinnacle with a commanding view over the tract neighborhoods of West Hills.

The promontory looming above Castle Peak Drive looks like just another hill. But through several centuries it served as a sentinel for travelers, guiding visitors to an unusual Indian settlement that flourished beside a creek still flowing out of what is now called Bell Canyon, a crease in the Simi Hills.

Experts think that *Huwam,* the phonetic spelling of the site's name in the Chumash tongue, was a ceremonial meeting place on the border between two Native American lands. The two Indian cultures spoke different languages but evidently interacted peacefully. Chumash celebrants would travel from the western hills and the Malibu coast to mark significant holidays alongside the Shoshone-speaking inland people who lived across the floor of the Valley. These Indians, later designated by anthropologists as the Tongva, apparently knew the ceremonial grounds as *Jucjauynga.*

Some cherished relics of that time remain,

known mainly to native descendants and academics. At a nearby clearing called Burro Flats, a little piece of ancient Chumash culture reveals itself each December on the morning of the winter solstice. When the sun is aligned just right, a little after 7:30 a.m., a dagger of light slips beneath a low rock overhang and illuminates a ring of circles painted on the sandstone. Near the primitive calendar are eight other elaborate pictographs—paintings in red, black and white that depict symbols in Chumash myth like the condor, the centipede and a part-bird, part-man figure. Another half-dozen rock paintings have been studied nearby in Chatsworth, near the rock-climbing landmark known as Stoney Point.

By some accounts, the Chumash had a myth that beneath Castle Peak lived a supernatural being with the body of an iguana. Either because of this myth or by

judging that the ridgeline resembled a scorpion's raised tail, Spanish soldiers labeled the peak and surrounding land *El Escorpión.* The name stuck and appeared on maps well into the 20th century.

Chumash and Tongva Indians congregated in a village beside Bell Creek at the base of Castle Peak, also known as *El Escorpión.* Today, a suburban tract known as Castle Peak Estates covers the lower slope.

up, rusty guns serviced and swords sharpened. The pueblo rebels negotiated the Cahuenga Pass trail into the Valley to head off the invasion. The armies faced off a safe distance apart, drums playing. The exact location is unknown, but it appears to have been near the hills somewhere between Sherman Oaks and Universal City. Micheltorena had three working cannons, the rebels a pair.

All day on February 20, 1845, the two forces lobbed cannonballs across the grasslands at each other, retrieved those that fell and shot them back. The roaring guns could be heard in Los Angeles and implied a ferocious battle. Anxious citizens streamed to the top of Lookout Mountain in the Santa Monicas to catch a view. "The scene upon the hill was a remarkable one," wrote William Heath Davis in his book, *Seventy Five Years in California.* "Women and children with crosses in their hands, kneeling and praying to the Saints for the safety and protection of their fathers, brothers, sons, husbands, lovers, cousins…"

In truth, no one was being killed or even scratched; the only fatality was one animal, either a horse or a mule. Acting to break the standoff, three Americans on the Los Angeles side arranged a secret rendezvous in a ravine with three Yankees fighting for Micheltorena. The negotiators struck a truce and summoned Pío Pico, the rebel governor-in-waiting, to get his assent. Showing good political acumen, Pico assured the Americans that if they stopped fighting and took steps to become Mexican citizens, they could secure title to their land despite laws restricting foreign ownership. To cinch the deal, he winked that they could take their time about the formality of Mexican citizenship. The Americans quit the battle, dooming Micheltorena, who was captured near the Narrows. The victorious *Californios* from Los Angeles put him on board a ship and sent him back to Mexico. Never again would Mexico send a governor to rule California.

The brothers Pico

Pío Pico became the last Mexican governor of Alta California—and the first subdivider of the San Fernando Valley. Born at Mission San Gabriel in 1801, he was neither well liked nor widely respected. "Pío Pico had always been looked upon, by the better element of California, as a clown," J. Gregg Layne of the California Historical Society wrote. In his younger days Pico was called *la breva aplastada,* the squashed fig. When he grew a beard, he became *el oso sentado,* the sitting bear.

Pico did possess a keen sense of the future, and he warned his fellow *Californios*—citizens born in the province—to pay attention to the growing American presence. "We find ourselves suddenly threatened by hordes of yankee emigrants, who have already begun to flock into our country, and whose progress we cannot arrest. Already have the wagons of that perfidious people scaled the almost inaccessible summits of the Sierra Nevada…. What that aston-ishing people will next undertake, I cannot say; but in whatever enterprise they embark they will be sure to prove successful."

The province was land rich but poor in every other way, lacking in cash, gunpowder and support from Mexico. In preparation for war between Mexico and the United States, Pico began dispersing the vast holdings of Mission San Fernando Rey. He gave a large square of land around Los Encinos to three former mission Indians—Tiburcio Cayo, Francisco Papabubaba and, simply, Roman—and entered the grant as *Rancho Encino.* At the west end of the Valley, beneath Castle Peak, Pico's grant to Indians Odon Chihuya, Urbano Chari and Manuel was mapped as *Rancho El Escorpión.* A colony of 40 to 50 Indians—possibly descendants of the original *Huwam* population—settled there.

Pico put the rest of the Valley in the hands of his brother Andres, who leased the grazing rancho and the mission itself—which became his home—for $1,120 a year. But events forced Don Pío to raise even more cash. After the United States declared war on May 13, 1846, Gov. Pico sold the bulk of the Valley, including the mission, for $14,000 to an acquaintance in Los Angeles. Eulogio de Celis, a Spaniard, paid 12 cents an acre for more than 116,858 acres, the largest parcel of privately owned land in Alta California. De Celis agreed to take care of the resident priest at the mission and to let the older remaining Indians keep growing crops, and he also agreed to honor the lease with Andres Pico, his friend and antelope-hunting partner. The generous arrangement raised many suspicions, but Gov. Pico later testified that he had made the sale at the instruction of the Mexican government.

Once it became clear that California would fall to the Americans, Pío Pico fled to Mexico. His departure cleared a place on the historical stage for his youngest brother Andres, a more statesman-like figure. A 36-year-old hero of the *Californio* militia for leading the defeat of an American force at the Battle of San Pasqual, near Escondido, Don Andres accomplished a peaceful surrender of the province to American hands. His small remaining force was camped in a secluded canyon of the Verdugo Mountains on January 11, 1847, when the U.S. Bear Flag Battalion, led by Colonel John C. Frémont, climbed down Newhall Pass and occupied Don Andres' home at the mission. The American soldiers lodged in the grand *convento*, took what horses they could find, and slaughtered Pico livestock for meat. Frémont then sent emissaries to negotiate peace.

Both Frémont and Pico moved their camps the next day across the Valley floor to Rancho Cahuenga at the mouth of Cahuenga Pass. Surrender language was worked out in English and Spanish. On the morning of January 13, Don Andres and Col. Frémont met at a simple adobe on the rancho and signed the Capitulation of Cahuenga. The former

Justice, Pico style

If the stories passed down are true, Andres Pico seldom turned away visitors to his quarters at the former mission. In one legend, the notorious outlaw Tiburcio Vasquez rode in late one night and shared a room with two state senators. The next morning, the senators informed Pico of their chamber mate's identity. Pico confirmed that the much-hunted bandit was welcome at the rancho, and that in return Vasquez had promised not to harm anyone in the Valley.

But Pico was no friend of bandits. He helped hunt for one of the most wanted outlaws of the 1850s, a time of tension between *Californios* and the growing number of Americans in the state. Juan Flores, a 22-year-old horse thief and robber, escaped from San Quentin and assembled a gang of young *Californios* to seek revenge against the Los Angeles sheriff, James Barton, who exacted harsher justice on those with brown skin. In a gunfight in the foothills of Orange County, Flores' gang killed the sheriff and two deputies.

Pico led a posse that nabbed and summarily lynched two suspects, but Flores eluded capture. To make sure he could not escape north through the Valley, soldiers guarded the Newhall and Santa Susana passes, a posse camped at *Rancho El Escorpión* and more than a dozen men watched the trail west from *Rancho Encino*.

Flores made it to Mission San Fernando Rey and stole a horse from Pico's herd, then rode for Santa Susana Pass, where he was captured. At the gallows in Los Angeles, Flores proved stubborn as ever. The drop was too brief to snap his neck, and he struggled for his life. He managed to free his arms and grab hold of the noose, desperate to take a breath, but the lynch mob fought to pry his hands loose, succeeding with some effort.

"After a protracted struggle, very painful to behold, the limbs became quiet and finally stiff in death. Thus ended the brief but stormy life of the bandit captain, Juan Flores," the *Los Angeles Star* reported on February 21, 1857.

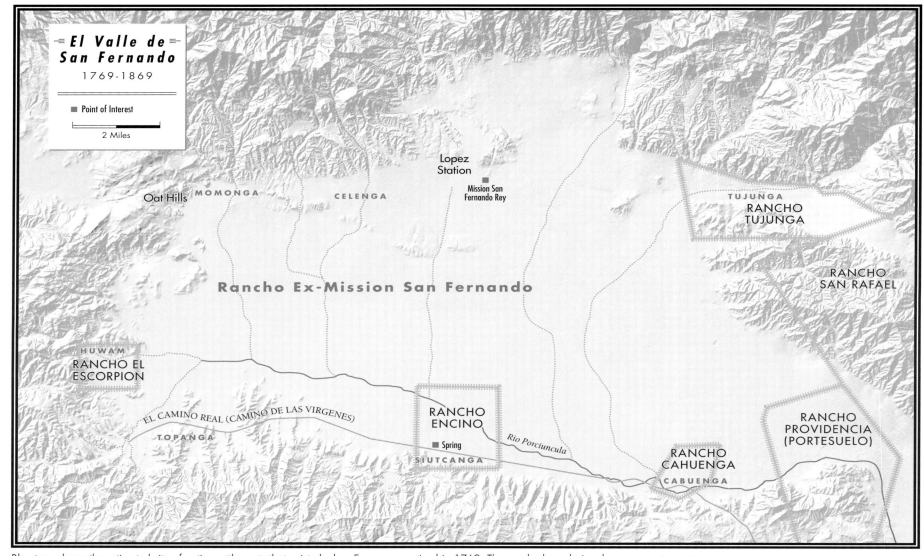

El Valle de San Fernando

1769-1869

■ Point of Interest

2 Miles

Oat Hills

MOMONGA

CELENGA

Lopez
Station

Mission San
Fernando Rey

TUJUNGA

RANCHO
TUJUNGA

RANCHO
SAN RAFAEL

Rancho Ex-Mission San Fernando

HUWAM

RANCHO EL
ESCORPION

EL CAMINO REAL (CAMINO DE LAS VIRGENES)

TOPANGA

RANCHO
ENCINO

■ Spring

SIUTCANGA

Rio Porciuncula

RANCHO
CAHUENGA

CABUENGA

RANCHO
PROVIDENCIA
(PORTESUELO)

Blue type shows the estimated site of native settlements that existed when Europeans arrived in 1769. The rancho boundaries shown are not exact.

An artist's rendering depicts the *Rancho Cahuenga* house where Andres Pico surrendered to Col. John Fremont in 1847. The adobe's foundations were unearthed in the late 1990s during subway construction near Universal City.

Spanish realm of Alta California became the American territory of California. Despite the surrender, Andres Pico had pulled off a diplomatic feat. The terms of surrender were easy on the beaten *Californios*. They handed over their artillery and agreed not to take up arms again, but they were free to leave for Mexico or to stay and enjoy all the protections of American citizens. Most stayed—and Pico became fast friends with Frémont (who later was convicted at court-martial of exceeding his authority, then pardoned).

With the war over, Andres Pico returned to his leased rancho and made the former mission one of the most celebrated homes in the new California. Most historians and writers have little bad to say about Andres, save for his bacchanalian ways. He was "brave, reckless, jovial, kindhearted, popular," historian Hubert Howe Bancroft wrote. After California became a state on September 9, 1850, Don Andres served as an elected state assemblyman and senator, and when California voted for U.S. president for the first time in 1852 he was among the state's presidential electors. He carried the title of brigadier general of the state militia, developed an oil field near today's Newhall and may have been the first Valley secessionist—he authored a bill in the state Legislature in 1859 that would have allowed the five Southern California counties to form their own state, but the outbreak of the Civil War tabled the issue. "He never did an act beneath the dignity of an officer, and was humane and generous," wrote William Heath Davis.

Lopez Station, seen here in 1885, housed the Valley's first stagecoach rest stop, post office and English-speaking school. Located in the hills west of San Fernando, it was torn down in 1912 for a reservoir.

sion treasures, "many of the ancient trinkets of the church, some of which are solid silver." Truman reported that Pico showed off two tallow candles used at the first Mass in 1797, the original mission cattle brands, a stockpile of empty French wine bottles, old spears and flintlock guns and half a dozen cannons called *cámaras*.

Feasts and bullfights at the Pico rancho were legendary affairs. "Don Andres keeps a fine lot of native wine and brandy [and] takes his 'snifters' with marked promptness and exceeding regularity," Truman wrote. Prominent painters and citizens of Los Angeles attended parties at which watermelons were a prized delicacy, picked ripe and cooled in a tank of water until Don Andres gave the word to crack open a sweet melon. A visitor named J. E. Pleasant wrote this account of a week-long stay in 1856:

"His silver and china table-service made a brilliant display. His household furnishings were plain but massive and luxurious.... The dinners consisted of five to six courses, all of the far-famed California-Spanish cookery.... Two young Indian boys served as waiters. They were clad in the simple tunic of the day. Before the meal, one of them stood by the host, Don Andres, at the head of the table and said grace, and at the end of the meal the other took his place and returned thanks.... After the noon dinner, all work was suspended for the customary two-hour siesta. The cool rooms of the thick-walled adobe afforded a refreshing change from the July sunshine

Andres Pico lived in the old *convento* in high style, receiving visitors and hosting parties with his mate Catalina, whom historians say he never formally married. They had Indian servants—one ring of the bell summoned Timetejas; two rings, José. In the verdant gardens were 300 olive trees, 12,000 grapevines, and groves of fig, peach, pear, walnut, almond and pomegranate trees. Their home was "the

most pretentious adobe in the state," wrote Los Angeles merchant and chronicler Harris Newmark.

Another writer of the time, Ben C. Truman, described the Pico home as a vast collection of rooms unlike any house in America, with a library "where have been hoarded hundreds of thousands of Spanish doubloons." Above the wine cellar, Truman claimed, Pico kept a locked chest containing old misof the open plains."

Pico enjoyed the most notoriety, but others began settling in the Valley. The first American land-holders were Alexander Bell and David Alexander, who purchased *Rancho Providencia*—which included part of the original *Rancho Portesuelo*—in 1851. At *Rancho Encino*, the Indian owners had cattle and a stable of 20 horses, but they could not keep up with the taxes and lost the land to Vicente de la Osa, the former holder of *Providencia*. At *Rancho Encino*, de la Osa built an adobe house with nine rooms for himself, his wife and their 14 children. Near their house gurgled the historic Encino spring, said to flow with a thousand gallons a day of water "very palatable, as soft as water possibly can be. Horses and cattle will come for miles to drink from this spring," wrote Ben Truman.

De la Osa's ranch at Encino became a way station for travelers on the dirt *camino* across the Valley. By tradition, voyagers could expect gracious free lodging at ranches they visited. But as more traffic came through the Valley, de la Osa was forced to humble himself and insist on payment. An ad in the *Los Angeles Star* in 1859 delicately announced the new realities. "I have

Perilous new passes

◆ Phineas Banning opened a new route out of the Valley by coaxing the first Concord stagecoach, pulled by six mustangs, to the top of San Fernando Pass in December 1854. "A rather broad trail already existed there, but such was its grade that many a pioneer…will never forget

Horse-drawn stages departing Los Angeles for the coast crossed the Valley, then negotiated Devil's Slide, which was carved into Santa Susana Pass in 1860.

the real perils of the descent," Los Angeles merchant Harris Newmark wrote.

◆ Beale's Cut, completed in 1863, made it even easier to exit the Valley. Edward F. Beale dug a narrow passage in the hills—the site remains a hidden but easily reachable piece of history in Newhall Pass. Beale made another contribution to the lore of the area. As an Army lieutenant in 1857, he led camels over Newhall Pass and across the Valley to ferry supplies between Los Angeles and Fort Tejon. The camel experiment was abandoned after the Civil War.

◆ A precarious passage cut through the rocks of Santa Susana Pass in 1860 became a new coast stage route. "Devil's Slide" challenged horses and men alike, the "nearest thing to an escalator without power that has ever been constructed," according to stage historian Charles F. Outland. An Overland Mail Company stage began using the new pass in September 1861. The summit was crossed about a half mile south of the current Santa Susana Pass Road, almost at the end of Lilac Lane. It cost $1.50 to ride the 18 miles from Los Angeles to *Rancho Encino*, and $4 to go the next 14 miles over the Devil's Slide.

established at my ranch, known by the name of El Encino…on the road to Santa Barbara, a place for affording the accommodation to the people traveling on this road…. I hope those wishing to call at our place will not forget to bring with them what is necessary to defray their expense."

The flow of visitors had surged after the horse path through Cahuenga Pass was opened to wagons in 1851. The old *El Camino Real* trail west past Los Encinos was declared a public highway, *Camino de las Virgenes*. Butterfield Overland Mail began stage service across the Valley from Los Angeles three times a week in 1858. The stages creaked and rattled up Newhall Pass and followed a circuitous route to San Francisco via Elizabeth Lake and Fort Tejon.

At the north end of the Valley, in hills west of the mission, the stages stopped for fresh horses at a new landmark. Lopez Station was run by Gerónimo López and his wife, Catalina, the daughter of the mission's former *mayordomo*. The general store and roadhouse occupied 40 acres that had once belonged to an Indian named José Miguel, a former captain of the guard at the mission. Miguel had planted the Valley's first private orchard, according to a history by the Daughters of the American Revolution. Lopez Station accommodated travelers and also hosted the first public school in the Valley, with classes taught for the first time in English.

A new era begins

The year 1869 was a momentous one for the American West. On May 10 a golden spike was driven at Promontory Point, Utah, joining the first railroad across the continent. Migrants no longer faced long wagon train journeys and dangerous crossings of the Sierra Nevada or the desert to reach the Pacific. It became relatively easy to check out this place called California.

It was a big year too in the San Fernando Valley—exactly a century since the Portolá expedition first arrived in the Tongva homeland. A U.S. post office opened at Lopez Station. Nels Johnson and his wife, Ann, rode into the Valley, enjoyed a meal at Lopez Station, then headed for the hills beneath Santa Susana Pass. They homesteaded 160 acres just outside the boundary of the mission rancho's lands—a boundary marked today by Andorra Avenue in Chatsworth.

Around this time, *Rancho Encino* was sold to a French sheepherder, Eugène Garnier. He and his brother Philippe bred fine Merinos for wool. "These gentlemen have the reputation of producing as fine wool as is sent to market," Ben Truman wrote. The Garniers improved the de la Osa adobe, putting in wooden floors and kerosene lamps. They also erected a two-story farmhouse from limestone rock quarried on the ranch. The house featured sleeping rooms, kitchen and dining room. Finally, the Garniers captured the spring water in a pond formed of bricks laid out in the shape of a Spanish guitar—the buildings and pond exist today within Los Encinos state historic park.

The death in 1869 of Eulogio de Celis brought even more dramatic changes. He had tried to sell the Valley for 50 cents an acre years before, but found no takers. At his death he owned a half share of 181 square miles of land; the other half share belonged to Pío Pico, the former governor who returned from Mexico. Andres Pico at the time retained ownership of only 2,000 acres around the old mission, including his prized vineyard, and he continued to live in the *convento*. A surviving landmark a few minutes walk from the mission is known today as the Andres Pico Adobe, but he apparently never resided there.

On July 2, 1869, desperate for cash to pay off mortgage debts, Pío Pico sold his half share for $115,000. The buyer, Isaac Lankershim, had come to California from West Prussia and gone into farming around Sacramento. Though he called himself a Protestant, he was born and raised Jewish. His investors in the San Fernando Farm Homestead Association included other German Jewish immigrants to California, among them Levi Strauss, the biggest name in blue jeans. Rancho Ex-Mission San Fernando—the awkward name given to the Valley floor by American land recorders—was split lengthwise to complete the sale of Pico's half. Lankershim's group received the southern section, while the heirs of de Celis kept the northern half. Lankershim and friends had paid $2 an acre for a swath of open grass-

This two-story farmhouse was built of limestone quarried on *Rancho Encino* by sheep breeder Eugène Garnier. The house, shown in 1915, still stands in Los Encinos state historic park.

land twice the size of modern San Francisco. They planned to raise sheep.

Soon the de Celis family also wanted to sell. Coincidentally, the former governor of California, railroad baron Leland Stanford, was eager to extend his Southern Pacific line to new towns. When he heard in 1872 that the northern half of the Valley was for sale, Stanford contacted a state senator from the San Francisco Bay area whom he knew was looking to get into the land game. Stanford made Sen. Charles Maclay a pledge: If he would erect a town, Stanford would lay a railroad across the San Fernando Valley.

This was valuable information. Stanford's railroad made and broke fortunes with its decisions to route through—or to shun—a place. A railroad would make land in the Valley much more valuable. Maclay, who already had founded the Bay Area town of Saratoga, vowed to name his new town's widest and longest street after his benefactor; then he traveled south to negotiate a price. He paid $117,500 for 56,000 acres, just over $2 an acre—not counting the cost of a bribe to the de Celis family lawyer that drew Maclay a rebuke from the state Supreme Court.

Maclay picked a flat spot about a mile northeast of the crumbling mission to lay out his town. He considered giving it the name Pico, after the area's most famous family, but he opted for San Fernando. As promised, he named the wide street out to the scenic mission Stanford Avenue. The Valley had the beginnings of its first town. The Spanish rancho era was truly over.

CHAPTER 3

Boom Towns

Reaping the wheat crop was arduous work for men and horses alike in the heat of Valley summers. Harvester teams like this one, in about 1905, could cut 60 acres a day.

By the year 1880, the Western world was modernizing in some haste. Rodin finished sculpting *The Thinker,* and Gilbert and Sullivan wrote *The Pirates of Penzance.* Electric lights illuminated the streets of New York, population 1,206,299. San Francisco teemed with almost 234,000 souls. Wild Los Angeles exhibited few conveniences, but the former Mexican pueblo's population had swelled to nearly 10,000. Upriver from Los Angeles, the San Fernando Valley had no streetlights, electricity or indoor running water. A few hundred homesteaders, Indians and ranch hands were scattered across the plain and up the canyons. If dust devils and flash floods did not pose enough hazards, wildfires periodically raged—a range fire in 1878 scorched 18,000 acres of pasture and grain.

The lone township, San Fernando, counted just 1,305 inhabitants; its chief attraction, other than the nearby ruins of the former mission, was plentiful cheap land. But change was coming. Leland Stanford's Southern Pacific had done its part to lure settlers, beginning service to San Fernando early in 1874 after Chinese track layers scribed a nearly straight line across the virgin grassland at the foot of the Verdugo Mountains. Any male adult could ride

Voracious jackrabbits were the scourge of farmers on the Valley plain. In this 1892 scene, a crowd looked on as hundreds of rabbits were rounded up and trapped in pens.

The January 21, 1874 arrival of the Southern Pacific from Los Angeles allowed San Fernando to become the first town settled in the Valley. The engine barn in San Fernando is shown here about 1900.

sands of head of livestock died of thirst or starvation across the Valley. The disastrous drought that escorted out the 1870s prompted Isaac C. Ijams, a pioneer resident, to observe: "I could have walked across the Valley on the bones of sheep and cattle."

Raising San Fernando

Maclay had no taste for cattle or sheep. He was the first in a long line of San Fernando Valley town builders. His town took on the roughshod character one might expect of a place at the end of the line,

The first office building in the fledgling township of San Fernando rose at Maclay and Celis streets. The corner remains at the city's center today, but the building is gone.

the SP 22 miles from Los Angeles to San Fernando for half price—the railroad figured a man curious enough to visit the remote, upstart town must be a live prospect. Sales agents met every train and offered free barbecue lunches and a pitch. Town lots sold for $50 to $100 each, farmland for $5 to $40 an acre.

Shortly after his town opened for business, Charles Maclay was the center of attention at a feast on the mission grounds. "Music filled up the pauses between libations, and beautiful women lent the charm of their presence to the occasion. The Senator was happy…surrounded by all that makes life beautiful," Benjamin Truman, editor of the *Los Angeles*

Star, wrote in his flowery prose.

Always cheerfully boosterish, Truman painted an exaggerated portrait of San Fernando's charms. "Water bubbles up from springs, flows through pipes, is delivered to people at their doors, and is found in abundance wherever it is wanted…. In a few years San Fernando will be adorned with groves and orchards. It will become the site of a resort for seekers after health…. The sea breeze wanders there, but is tempered by its passage over 20 miles of intervening plains."

About the same time that Truman spun his tale of windblown San Fernando as Eden, tens of thou-

The sad final days of Rogeria Rocha

More has been written about Rogerio Rocha than about any other Indian who lived at Mission San Fernando Rey. Sorting out fact from fiction, though, is a challenge.

Rocha died April 6, 1904. After his death he was labeled the last Mission Indian *neofito,* which probably was so. He had played violin in the mission orchestra and had served as leader of the Indians who remained near the mission after the priests left. Legend said he died at 110 years of age, but a reexamination of mission records casts doubt on this. John R. Johnson, curator of anthropology at the Santa Barbara Museum of Natural History, found reason to believe that Rocha was born in 1824, to a Ventureno-Chumash and a Tongva woman from the village of *Tujunga,* and so was either 79 or 80 years old at death.

Before his death, Rocha figured in an unsavory bit of business that soiled the reputation of Charles Maclay, San Fernando's founder, and led to some public sniping in the letters column of the *Los Angeles Times.* During a cold autumn rain in 1885, Maclay, a Methodist preacher before arriving in California, forcibly evicted Rocha and his frail wife from their adobe house and farm beside Pacoima Wash. They had lived in the adobe for decades, but the land grant—apparently made by a former Mexican governor of California—was not recognized. Maclay wanted the land and its spring for a brickworks to supply his new subdivision outside San Fernando.

The life of Rogerio Rocha, seen here in 1898, inspired the sympathies of writers and others who heard his story.

Even the deputy sheriffs who carried out the eviction called it ``disagreeable duty...a hard cruel thing." In some accounts, the Rochas and nine other Indians were hauled to the nearest road and dumped in the rain with all of their belongings. Rocha walked to Los Angeles and won permission to squat in a shed at the Mission San Fernando Rey ruins. This took him many days, and his wife caught pneumonia during her exposure and died.

In a letter published in the Times on November 22, 1885, Maclay's nephew and attorney, R. M. Widney, insisted the eviction was handled mercifully and that Rocha, on bad advice from a lawyer, had rejected offers of housing elsewhere and $100 in cash. ``The Indians have been a great nuisance and their rancheria has been a rendezvous for horse thieves and other bad characters," Widney wrote.

E. F. de Celis, whose family had sold the land to Maclay, retorted the following day that Maclay had violated an agreement that ``the old Indians were to be protected...as long as they lived." Rocha had been born on the land and had planted fruit trees and vines, de Celis said, and harbored no thieves. As for Rocha being offered compensation, ``the Indian denies it, and I believe the Indian."

In the end, Rocha lived out his years in a canyon above the Valley. ``Rogerio had the great mistake of having a fine spring of water on his place," the former Indian agent for the area wrote later in Out West magazine.

since the Southern Pacific at first went no farther than San Fernando. There were two hotels—Kittridge House and the Fernando—and seven saloons. The town saw its share of drunks. Twice a year, a local yahoo named John Dagon came into town to get plastered. When he got good and loaded, Dagon would grit his teeth, stare at the sun and wave a green flag.

The toughest customers were probably the teamsters who drove heavy ore wagons to and from the mines in the distant Owens Valley, crossing the Mojave Desert en route. Each evening two laden wagons pulled by teams of 16 mules reached San Fernando, announcing their arrival by bumping and sliding down the treacherous dirt grade over Newhall Pass. Two fresh wagons departed for the mines in the morning. Remi Nadeau, who ran the operation, built a hotel in San Fernando for his men, a barn for his mules and a warehouse for feed and equipment. He also cleared and packed a dirt track to Los Angeles (it became San Fernando Road). Nadeau's community spirit was limitless: The town's Christmas Eve dance in 1877 was held in the Nadeau warehouse, the headlight from a locomotive providing illumination.

Stanford's vision for the Southern Pacific was to blow past San Fernando and connect Los Angeles by rail with San Francisco. For that, he needed to bore one of the longest tunnels in the world through the mountain barrier blocking the northern end of the Valley—and he wanted the tunnel in a hurry. Work began in April 1875 with 1,500 men working by can-

dlelight in two deep shafts beneath Newhall Pass. Chinese, Mexican and Indian workers did most of the hazardous labor, using picks and shovels to hack through the rock and connect the shafts. Quicksand, disease and frequent landslides harassed the laborers. The only man who knew how many tunnel moles died was the project's coroner, A. B. Moffitt, "and he never told. He did this so that the work might go forward without delay...," a 1924 history by the local Daughters of the American Revolution chapter reported bluntly.

In September 1876 the tunnel was finished—a triumph of engineering haste that was 6,964 feet long and showed what was possible with virtual slave labor. Hundreds of Chinese workers stood at attention beside the joined tracks, tools on their shoulders, as a spike forged of gold was driven at Lang Station in the Santa Clarita Valley. With the extended railroad carrying more people through the Valley, San Fernando took on the trappings of a real town. A school opened. Maclay, a Methodist minister before his years in the Senate, put up a share of the money

The Maclay College of Theology opened near San Fernando in 1885, reflecting the religious beliefs of the town and its founder. Charles Maclay had been a Methodist preacher before coming to California.

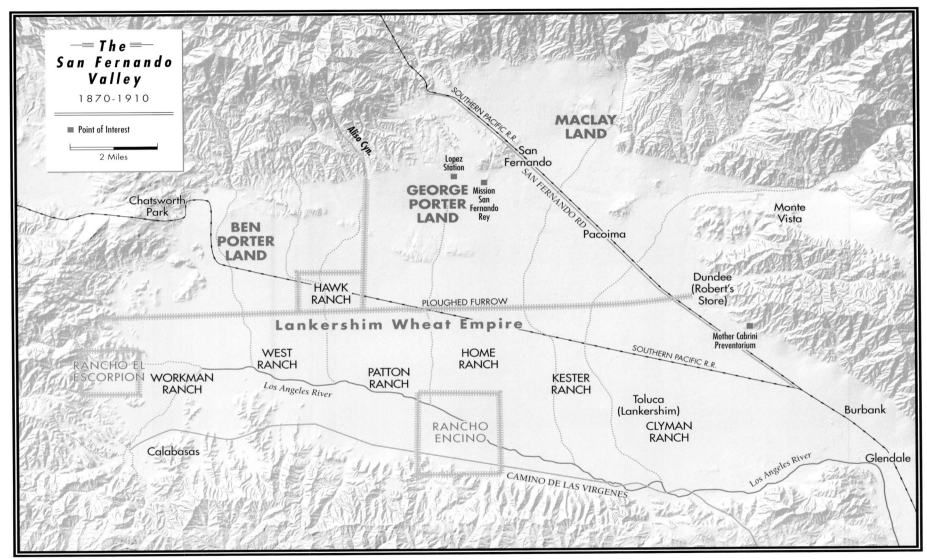

The San Fernando Valley
1870-1910

■ Point of Interest

2 Miles

Aliso Cyn.

SOUTHERN PACIFIC R.R.

MACLAY LAND

San Fernando

Lopez Station ■

GEORGE PORTER LAND

Mission San Fernando Rey ■

SAN FERNANDO RD

Chatsworth Park

BEN PORTER LAND

Pacoima

Monte Vista

Dundee (Robert's Store) ■

HAWK RANCH

PLOUGHED FURROW

Lankershim Wheat Empire

SOUTHERN PACIFIC R.R.

Mother Cabrini Preventorium ■

WEST RANCH

HOME RANCH

RANCHO EL ESCORPION

WORKMAN RANCH

PATTON RANCH

KESTER RANCH

Los Angeles River

Toluca (Lankershim)

Burbank

RANCHO ENCINO

CLYMAN RANCH

Calabasas

CAMINO DE LAS VIRGENES

Los Angeles River

Glendale

The Valley was largely divided between the Lankershim ranches and the Maclay-Porter lands. Towns appeared after 1873, among them San Fernando, Burbank and Toluca.

to erect a Methodist church and invited guest speakers: a rabbi from Los Angeles, a Presbyterian clergyman. One Sunday a noted violinist from San Francisco was enticed to give a concert in this town in the middle of nowhere.

Maclay often hosted chicken dinners after

church in his two-story Colonial house at Celis and Workman streets. "On Sunday afternoons after dinner they played the piano and sang hymns until it was almost dark," his granddaughter, Catherine Hubbard Egbert Dace, told an interviewer in 1960. Chinese servants tended the house and grounds.

Maclay alone was the father of San Fernando, but his land venture had two partners whose names live on in the Valley. George K. Porter was a former colleague in the state Senate, a persuasive voice who urged against California joining the Confederacy during the Civil War. His cousin Benjamin F. Porter ran a tannery in the Santa Cruz area. The partners divided the northern half of the Valley into roughly equal thirds.

Maclay, intent on creating towns, kept all the land east of the Southern Pacific tracks, up to the base of the San Gabriels. George Porter took the center third, everything west of the railroad as far as Aliso Canyon (a line marked approximately today by Zelzah Avenue in Granada Hills and Northridge). His piece surrounded the mission, which he leased as headquarters for his "Middle Ranch." Under his watch, the crumbling mission buildings were used as hay barns and hog pens and fell into even worse repair. Nearby he built a 30-room mansion for his family and the Mission Hotel, a three-story frame structure with steep peaked roof and gables, private bathrooms and verandas with views of the mission ruins. He also planted a navel orange grove that stretched nearly three miles in length. The "long orchard" covered 170 acres and became famous. "What a grand sight to stand at the upper end of this magnificent tract and glance down the rows for such a distance," wrote J. E. Straw, a correspondent for the journal *Rural Californian*. The third partner, Benjamin Porter, had little interest in the Valley. He

A chronic shortage of fresh water threatened the Valley's boom towns. Hoping to capture subterranean runoff, Pacoima's founders in 1888 sunk an innovative dam in the sand of Pacoima Wash.

accepted the least desirable share of land, the farthest from the railroad, west of Aliso Canyon.

As San Fernando grew, the town cleaned up and went dry, pressured by an active chapter of the Woman's Christian Temperance Union. Deeds issued to land buyers by Maclay included the proviso that if any liquor was sold, the property would revert to the former owners. Maclay also opened the Valley's first institution of higher education, the Maclay College of Theology. The college had a grand building that stood alone on the open plain, though it never enrolled more than about a dozen students before the Methodist church moved the college to Los Angeles (where it merged into the University of Southern California).

The 1880s brought a frenzy of subdivision and new town creation to Southern California, forever altering the Valley map. Maclay and George Porter joined in the boom. Porter sold some of his land southwest of the mission, today's Mission Hills, for small ranches under the name of the Porter Land and Water Company. Maclay subdivided 20,000 acres north and east of the original San Fernando settlement, cleared the land with Chinese workers and called the new tract Maclay Colony. This land later became part of San Fernando and Sylmar.

Elsewhere, the first subdivision map for the town of Glendale was filed in March 1887, on the old *Rancho San Rafael* land grant. The hamlet of Dundee opened with a post office and a handful of homes along the SP tracks, in the vicinity of a locomotive

Isaac Lankershim planted wheat fields in the Valley after losing his sheep to drought. In 1888 his son founded the town of Toluca, which became today's North Hollywood.

watering station called Robert's Store, about where Sun Valley is today. On *Rancho Providencia*, dentist David Burbank founded a settlement that took his name. Burbank was "a town of magnificent promise in its early days," historian J. M. Guinn wrote. Monte Vista (sold under the slogan "The Gem of the Mountains") opened on the former *Rancho Tujunga* in the Tujunga Valley, tucked between the San Gabriels and the Verdugos. Until the post office opened in 1887, mail for Monte Vista was collected at the railroad by local pioneer Daisy Bell Rinehart, who drove her pony and buckboard over a rugged wagon

track through the canyon where Sunland Boulevard runs now.

One of the most ambitious of the 1880s subdivisions sprouted along the train line down-rail from San Fernando. Jouett Allen, a lawyer and real estate gambler from Chattanooga, Tenn., called his 1,000 acres Pacoima, said to be an Indian word for "rushing waters." He built a brick train depot, one of the most attractive on the Southern Pacific. Chinese workers carved streets and lots into the hard soil. Pacoima's main street, eight miles long, was named Taylor Avenue for President Zachary Taylor—and today is Van Nuys Boulevard.

In order to compete with San Fernando for the higher classes of settlers, Pacoima had strict rules— an early form of suburban CC&Rs. Each house was required to cost at least $2,000 to build. Anything less grand was labeled a barn. Pacoima streets had the Valley's first curbs and cement sidewalks, which attracted roller skaters. Children played in the nearby hills, gathering relics from Indian burial grounds. Water, always an issue in these new towns, came from a clever structure buried 50 feet deep in the sand of Pacoima Wash. It was believed to be the first subterranean dam in the world, designed in 1888 to catch submerged water flowing from Pacoima Canyon. It had its doubters, however. "Pacoima always was a desert, is a desert today and will be a desert for all future time," Maj. Horace Bell, who gave his name to Bell Canyon, wrote in his memoir *On the Old West Coast*.

When the Southern California town boom went

Isaac Newton Van Nuys, shown here in 1912, ran the Lankershim ranches. He built and lived in the first wood frame house on the Valley floor and wed the boss's daughter.

bust in the 1890s, dreams of a prosperous future were dashed. Dundee vanished. Pacoima slipped into obscurity, its soil too sandy for growing much, and Monte Vista all but disappeared. San Fernando, Glendale and Burbank hung on, as did the even smaller settlements of Calabasas and Chatsworth Park.

The last big ranch

The lower half of the former mission rancho remained in Isaac Lankershim's spread. He had been wrong about grazing sheep—the drought of the 1870s quashed that notion—but he had recovered well by deciding to experiment with wheat. When enough rain fell, the crop thrived. Before long, Lankershim headed the largest wheat-growing empire in the world. His vital partner in the operation was Isaac Newton Van Nuys, the son of Dutch New York farmers, who had arrived in Northern California at the age of 30 and made the acquaintance of the more senior Lankershim.

Van Nuys came south to work with Lankershim and deserves credit for a bold stroke of Valley map-making. Wishing to mark where the Lankershim half of the Valley began, Van Nuys stood near the Verdugo Mountains and sighted on a faint peak in the Simi Hills more than 20 miles off to the west. He instructed a ranch hand to start walking with his plow and to furrow a line in the dirt all the way to the distant hills. It took the man two days to reach the end of the property. Everything to the left—the south side—belonged to Lankershim; everything to the right was Maclay or Porter land. That boundary gouged in the dirt eventually scribed the route of Roscoe Boulevard.

Van Nuys built and lived in the first wood-frame ranch house in the land of the adobe—erected all by itself, nearly in the center of the Lankershim acreage. This house became the Home Ranch, headquarters of the farming enterprise. Lankershim and Van Nuys organized their wheat lands into self-sustaining ranches. After the first fall rain, horses would scrape plows across the ground and drop seeds. Starting in June, giant combines pulled by as many as 36 horses and mules cut and threshed the grain, clearing 20-foot-wide swaths on each pass. Grim, sun-toughened work crews baked on the parched, treeless plain. Tempers sometimes flared into horrific brawls. A field hand named Comfort had his nose bitten off and a cheek mutilated in a fight over seats at the chow table. In the fall, the men filled wagons with 120-pound sacks of grain that were shipped to England or milled into flour in the Lankershim mill, the largest in Los Angeles.

The Lankershim ranching stations were the only buildings for miles. Each ranch typically bore the name of the foreman. Clyman Ranch was at the east end, the Kester and Home were in the center, the Patton, West and Workman in the west Valley. Each compound was surrounded by windbreaks of eucalyptus and pepper trees. "There is a large dwelling house, one or two smaller houses with sleeping accommodations, a stable with accommodations for over 100 horses, a grain house, a blacksmith shop…a well, in this instance 40 feet deep, and a blindfolded mule doing duty drawing water," *Los Angeles Times* correspondent Jesse Yarnell wrote of the Patton Ranch (near today's Reseda) on September 11, 1882. "Plows, reapers, mowers, headers, horse-rakes, a thresher [and] wagons of every conceivable pattern…cover an acre of ground."

Van Nuys made another smart move and married the boss's daughter, Susanna Lankershim. After Isaac Lankershim died in 1882, the son-in-law shared ownership of the empire with his mentor's son, James B. Lankershim. While Van Nuys oversaw the wheat crop, younger Lankershim and a syndicate of investors jumped into the town boom with enthusiasm. They subdivided 12,000 acres on the east side of the family land (from today's Whitsett Avenue east to the Burbank city line), and near the center of this parcel they laid out a town they called Toluca. The main streets were San Fernando Avenue and Central Avenue (later Lankershim and Burbank boulevards respectively). This corner of the Valley has deep alluvial loam and a shallow water table, good for growing fruit trees. Ranchettes of 40 acres were sold to growers of vineyards and orchards of peaches, apples and apricots. Isaac C. Ijams, whose comment on the bones of perished livestock was so colorful, served for a time as justice of the peace in Toluca.

Elsewhere, the lower half of the Valley was mostly empty. Beside the dirt highway through the old *Rancho Encino*, Frenchman Jacques LaSalle operated a tavern frequented by the Basques who tended sheep at the ranch. Encino had been auctioned for back taxes in 1878; the buyer, Gaston Oxarart, paid $29,332 in gold currency. After his death the historic rancho went to his nephew, Simon Gless, and then into the Amestoy family. Further west along the highway, homesteaders just outside the boundary of the Lankershim lands organized the settlement of Calabasas.

To a stranger, the vast open country seemed available for the taking. New arrivals from the East and Midwest, where farms were small, could not

The bully of Calabasas

Calabasas was the scrappiest settlement in the Valley, a remote hamlet of homesteaders on the dirt highway that led west from *Rancho Encino*. Fights raged with fists and bullets over trespassers and squatters. Often the trouble swirled around a powerfully built Basque smuggler from the French Pyrenees whose girth and aggressive manner earned him the nickname of *"el Basquo Grande."*

Michel Leonis had shown up in Los Angeles in the late 1850s. Now going by the name Miguel, Leonis made his way to the west end of the Valley to work on the ranch of Joaquín Romero. Legend says Leonis had the strength to catch and rope a steer and toss it up into a wagon by himself. He was as devious as he was strong. He gained control of Romero's land, then in 1871 snagged title to historic *Rancho El Escorpión* by marrying Espíritu Chihuya, a widow whose father was an original Chumash grant holder.

Leonis ran his cattle herds onto lands all around Calabasas, deployed Mexican and Indian gunslingers to enforce his trespasses and filed numerous lawsuits in Los Angeles to bully anyone who resisted. In a gunfight through the rocks of today's Hidden Hills, a former Union Army major named Andrew Banks was shot defending his lawful claim against an intrusion by Leonis.

Hauled before a judge for roping two settlers with a lasso and dragooning them to Los Angeles, Leonis was ordered to pay $14,000 for malicious prosecution and assault. He always lost, and always paid up in gold.

On the day Leonis finally won a case in court, he met his end. He got sloshing drunk and fell out of his wagon while negotiating the treacherous trail through Cahuenga Pass. El Grande became the first known traffic death in the pass, on September 20, 1889.

His demise set off a bitter land fight. His will referred to his longtime wife as his housekeeper and left her only a token inheritance. Espíritu fell victim to unscrupulous schemers and lost title to her land, but she had the good fortune to attract the attention of some honest lawyers, including Steven M. White, a future United States senator. In 1905, the year before she died, Espíritu won her case before the California Supreme Court and regained some of her land.

The Leonis Adobe, a historic monument near Calabasas, is the home where she and El Grande last lived.

Ranch hands who worked the wheat fields and grazing lands on the Valley floor were a hardy crew. They included Mexicans, immigrants and possibly Indians. The date of this photo is unknown.

believe that all this unfenced land already belonged to someone. Their disbelief was fueled by promoters like the Land Settlers League, which told its members that the old Mexican land rights could be overcome in court by hardy individuals who squatted and worked the land. Critics called it the Land Suckers League, for its promises were dubious at best. But by 1890, some 1,200 squatters had filed claims, mostly on land that belonged to Van Nuys or the Porters, and ranchers often used roving gangs of gunmen to drive off the interlopers.

Eschewing violence, Isaac Van Nuys protected his land in court and won the case in a colorful way. Squatters were poring over his wheat fields, running surveys, building houses and sinking wells. His case, which eventually reached the U.S. Supreme Court, turned in part on a boyhood memory of Rómulo Pico, adopted son of the Valley's former landlord, Andres Pico. As a 15-year-old, Rómulo rode with the government surveyor on the first official U.S. map survey of the Valley.

He remembered a crucial oak tree being marked with a distinctive brand signifying a ranch boundary, but the lawyer for Van Nuys could not locate the tree. Rómulo rode out to the Valley with the lawyer and spotted the old tree, cut off some bark and found the official mark—"S.F. 39"—burned into the trunk. After they showed up in court with the piece of bark—which carried the branding in reverse on its inner face—the judge ordered the jury to side with Van Nuys. Squatters' rights were finally rejected.

As the end of the 19th century approached, the Valley remained a wild place, "nothing but cactus, brush, rattlesnakes and coyotes," in the words of resident Josephine LeRoy. Train robberies plagued the SP line, the boldest an armed takeover at the Roscoe flag stop on the night of February 15, 1894, that caused the deaths of the engine's fireman and a tramp who was riding on the cowcatcher when the locomotive derailed. But the region was edging closer to the modern world. At the first high school, in San Fernando, classes met from 9 a.m. to 4 p.m. (and the school board complained about teenage students dancing and kissing). Long-distance telephone service arrived in 1894. Toluca changed its name to Lankershim, and in 1898 the first motor cars appeared in the town, their drivers garbed in goggles and veils.

The smart money was no longer on the Valley remaining a domain of large ranches and scattered hamlets. A second Southern Pacific rail line veered west from Burbank and pierced across the plain to the subdivision of Chatsworth Park. Boring began on a rail tunnel beneath Santa Susana Pass that would open a coastal route to Santa Barbara and beyond.

The first automobile rolled into town two years after Toluca changed its name to Lankershim in 1896. This scene is in Laurel Canyon, between the Valley and Hollywood.

Thanks to flood-prone Tujunga Wash, the fertile loam around Toluca was ideal for growing peaches and other stone fruit. Picking the trees clean was a family activity, as seen here in 1895.

George K. Porter sold his last 16,200 acres of citrus groves and wheat fields to Los Angeles interests who planned to subdivide into small ranches and connect to Los Angeles with a grand trolley line. The 1,100-acre Hawk Ranch, once part of the Porter family lands, was sold in 1909 to more subdividers, mostly of Scandinavian descent from the upper Midwest. They laid out a 40-acre town site near an abundant well along the new railroad and named it Zelzah, for a biblical desert oasis. Stages still made the one-hour trip to Hollywood every day through Cahuenga Pass, but they began to share the winding road with automobiles. In the 1910 census, the Valley had 3,300 residents, including ranch hands and a few remaining Indians.

That year, the Lankershim-Van Nuys wheat empire harvested its most valuable crop ever. But Isaac Van Nuys felt too old to supervise the field operations, and he wanted cash to build a hotel in Los Angeles. He struck a deal with his friend Harry Chandler, business manager of the *Los Angeles Times,* who represented Los Angeles capitalists who saw gold in the Valley's land. The two men had a common bond besides friendship: Each had married the boss's daughter and become an officer in his father-in-law's affairs. As Van Nuys had married Susanna Lankershim, Chandler had taken Marian Otis, daughter of the *Times'* curmudgeonly publisher and editor, Gen. Harrison Gray Otis.

The biggest land transaction ever recorded in Los Angeles County was consummated by a single lawyer, Henry W. O'Melveny, and announced in a huge story on the front page of the *Times* on September 24, 1909. The syndicate Chandler represented paid $2.5 million for the entire 47,500 acres left in the Lankershim half of the former range of Mission San Fernando Rey. The price came to about $53 an acre and included everything west of the town limits of Lankershim and south of the old dividing plow furrow, excepting the Encino ranch— a swath 15 miles long and six and a half miles wide. The *Times* reported ambitious plans for new towns, highways and the eventual absorption of the Valley into the city of Los Angeles. The new owners acknowledged two motivations: "One, of course, is to make money. The other is to afford an opportunity for home-makers to secure desirable land close to Los Angeles at a reasonable price."

The newly formed Los Angeles Suburban Homes Company waited a year to take possession; then everything changed. On the first weekend of November 1910, ads in the *Times* proclaimed "The Sale of the Century." Everything to do with farming the Van Nuys lands was put up for auction: 2,000 head of horses and mules, including 400 brood

For many years, horses and motorized vehicles shared the same dirt streets, as here on San Fernando Road in Burbank in 1910. Skirmishes between the rural life and those desiring more urbanization continue today.

Saint of the Valley

The first American to be canonized as a saint of the Roman Catholic Church lived and performed some of her holy work in the Verdugo Mountains above Burbank, at a ``preventorium'' she established as a refuge for poor girls in Los Angeles.

Perhaps fittingly, the Valley's saint is the saint of immigrants. Mother Frances Xavier Cabrini was not a native-born American—she was born in Italy in 1850 and orphaned at the age of 13. When her request to become a nun was refused due to her frailty and small stature, she established her own order.

She sailed for New York in 1889 to work with Italian immigrants and came to Los Angeles in 1905 to serve the former pueblo's poor.

Finding scores of abandoned children on the streets, Mother Cabrini built an orphanage in Angelino Heights, northeast of downtown. But she wanted a haven where girls could grow up and learn without fear of tuberculosis. Her search for a piece of affordable land away from the city's slums brought her to the Valley in 1912, three years after she became a naturalized American citizen. Mother Cabrini and her Missionary Sisters of the Sacred Heart secured 475 acres in a fold of the Verdugo Mountains, between the towns of Burbank and Roscoe.

The sisters planted olive trees and grapevines and built a school and chapel. Mother Cabrini prayed each day in a one-room shrine to the Virgin Mary, built for her atop a hill overlooking the Valley by local members of the Knights of Columbus. After her death in 1917, the sisters pushed for her canonization and offered evidence of miracles attributed to her: a New York schoolboy who regained his sight and a Seattle woman who was cured of terminal cancer after Mother Cabrini appeared to her in a vision. She was declared a saint in 1946.

Her former compound in Burbank became the Villa Cabrini Academy, a school for girls and also served briefly as a campus of the California Institute of the Arts. The site now houses Woodbury University. The shrine where Mother Cabrini prayed was a visible landmark above Glenoaks Boulevard for many years. After being threatened by several wildfires, it was relocated to the grounds of St. Francis Xavier Catholic Church in Burbank.

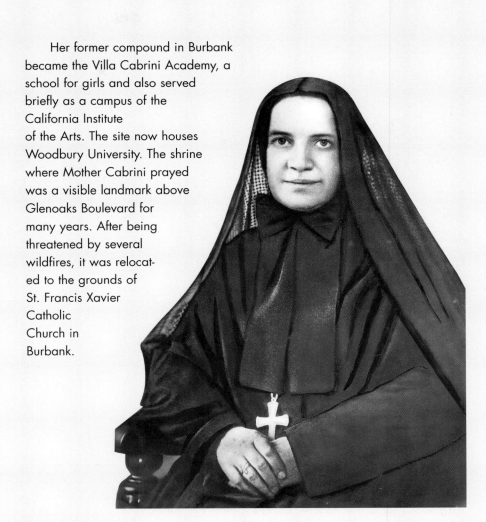

mares; wagons, Concord buggies, plows and harvesters, and four complete blacksmith shops. More than 2,000 buyers and curious came in special trains to the Kester Ranch, and six steers were slaughtered for a free barbecue. "It was a scene to stagger the imagination," the *Times* reported. On the following weekend the crowds moved west to the Patton Ranch to finish the job. Ranching on a large scale was finished in the Valley.

The *Times* reporter hit the mark when he called the auction "the beginning of a new empire and a new era in the Southland."

CHAPTER 4

Grand Ideas

Thousands looked on during the afternoon of November 5, 1913 as water from the far-off Owens Valley flowed near San Fernando for the first time, bonding the Valley's future to Los Angeles.

A simple brass plaque marks the unofficial birthplace of the modern San Fernando Valley, but the spot is no haven for quiet reflection on history. The blasting roar from the engines and tires barreling along 15 lanes of the Golden State Freeway smothers even silent thoughts. In more bucolic times, this hillside on the lip of Newhall Pass was a gently sloping natural amphitheater where, on November 5, 1913, thousands of expectant Southern Californians came to witness something extraordinary.

They bumped along rutted roads, hopped special excursion trains from Los Angeles or rode horses to the remote hillside five miles west of San Fernando—not certain what they would see, just that it would be momentous. "As all roads led to Rome, so all roads led yesterday to San Fernando," the *Times* reported the next morning, estimating—probably with some exaggeration—that 40,000 people made the journey. Churchwomen served up frankfurters and sandwiches washed down with tubs of lemonade and soda.

Everyone there knew the knotting fear of drought. They had seen the river vanish into dust in dry summers, and some had left open their water taps at night with buckets in place to catch stray drops. Now they were gathered to witness the promised arrival of an abundant new water supply from the distant eastern slope of the fabled Sierra Nevada—a river diverted an astonishing 233 miles across the Mojave Desert. The notion was fabulous, but if the reality came even close to the hype, the arid Valley would suddenly be good for growing much more than wheat.

To listen to the scheme's promoters, the prospects were without bounds. There were fortunes to be made, towns to build, a whole new population to lure—and who knew, maybe someday a million

PROGRAM

WEDNESDAY, NOVEMBER 5, 1913
AT CASCADES, SAN FERNANDO VALLEY

9:30 a.m. Official Party will leave Chamber of Commerce for Aqueduct.
11:00 a.m. to 12:00 m. Band Concert at Cascades.
12:00 m. Salute announcing arrival of Chief Engineer William Mulholland and other distinguished guests.
12:10 p.m. Exercises open with "America."
  The Catalina Military Band, fifty pieces.
12:15 p.m. Address
  Congressman William D. Stephens.
  Music—Vocal—*Ellen Beach Yaw.*
12:30 p.m. Address
  Arthur W. Kinney, President Chamber of Commerce
  Music—*The Band.*
12:45 p.m. Address
  Hon. George C. Pardee
  Former Governor of California.
  Music—*The Band.*
1:10 p.m. Address—Presenting Completed Aqueduct to the City of Los Angeles.
  Chief Engineer William Mulholland.
1:30 p.m. Opening of Gates of Aqueduct, upon signal from William Mulholland.
  Lieutenant-General Adna R. Chaffee.
1:45 p.m. Address formally accepting the Aqueduct on behalf of the City of Los Angeles.
  Mayor H. H. Rose.
2:00 p.m. Formal Transfer of Aqueduct Administration.
  Board of Public Works to Public Service Commission
  Exercises close with "Star Spangled Banner."
  The Band.
2:15 p.m. Leave mouth of Aqueduct for Lower Reservoir Dam, traversing bed of reservoir, into which the water has just turned, for three miles.
2:30 p.m. Reception and Luncheon to distinguished guests at residence of Fred L. Baruff, given by the host. Invitation. Admission by card.
7:30 p.m. Dinner to distinguished guests, Hotel Alexandria.

Take your drinking cups.
All programs free, through courtesy of the city banks.
Public comfort stations in Valley, free.
Report any charges to police promptly.

The official aqueduct dedication included, for the VIPs at least, a barbecue at a nearby ranch and, later, a dinner downtown.

people! two million! might inhabit this empty land of cactus and rattlesnakes.

Hail to the Chief

At 10 o'clock that November morning, a motorcade 40 cars long swung onto Broadway in downtown Los Angeles, escorting the hero of the moment. William Mulholland was the city's chief water engineer and the inventor of the aqueduct which that day would spill its liquid gold for the first time. Cheers and honking horns saluted him on the two-hour trip out of the city, then along the sandy Los Angeles River and across the eastern edge of the rural Valley on newly paved San Fernando Road. The *Times*, playing to the hilt its role as chief shill for the aqueduct, heralded "the culmination of a project daringly conceived, boldly executed and successfully completed." The payoff for Los Angeles, said the paper, was no less than "the assurance of metropolitan grandeur and future prosperity such as but a few cities of the world can hope to attain."

Mulholland's aqueduct was the longest working water conveyance in the world. Yet it was so simple and ingenious in design that it would remain an engineering triumph even in a world of microchips and space shuttles: a river of cool mountain snowmelt, collected in the distant Owens Valley, then delivered over the desert by a system of open culverts, steel pipes, inverted siphons and subterranean tunnels bored through hard granite. Not bad for a self-taught,

Mulholland's audacious vision

◆ Construction of the Los Angeles Aqueduct began in 1908 and lasted five years, as scheduled, despite engineering setbacks and bitter strikes among the 5,000 workers. Crews of mining roustabouts and Chinese workers battled smallpox, typhoid, rattlesnakes and 130-degree days. The most challenging feat was boring a five-mile tunnel through solid rock beneath Elizabeth Lake. It took crews 1,239 days just to dig the tunnel.

◆ The aqueduct plunges through nine major canyons and dips out of sight in 142 tunnels on its 233-mile journey from the Owens Valley in Inyo County across the Mojave Desert to the San Fernando Valley. In 1940 it was extended another 105 miles north to extract water from the Mono Lake Basin.

◆ The first water delivered by the aqueduct flowed into San Fernando Reservoir, constructed on the site of historic Lopez Station, the first stagecoach depot and post office in the Valley. The reservoir also drowned part of the Rinaldi ranch, site of the first producing orange groves in the Valley.

◆ A second, parallel aqueduct went into service in 1970. With it, the aqueduct system can deliver 500 million gallons of Eastern Sierra water daily. In a typical year,

75% of the Los Angeles water supply comes from the Owens Valley.

◆ The original cascade spillway that fascinated thousands when it opened in 1913 is barely visible today behind a fence next to Foothill Boulevard. On the same hillside, a higher 900-foot-long cascade connected to the second aqueduct has become a landmark, lighted at night and easily seen from many points in the Valley. Much of the time, however, both channels are dry—the water usually flows through pipelines into a power generating station.

William Mulholland became a folk hero for bringing water to Los Angeles.

Belfast-born runaway who walked across the isthmus of Panama to reach California and began his career as a *zanjero,* or ditch tender, along the Los Angeles River.

Reading voraciously and thinking grandly, Mulholland had made himself into an engineer. He first impressed the city fathers when he devised a way to capture the underground flow of the river through a system of filtration galleries sunk in the riverbed in the Narrows. His Los Angeles Aqueduct was far more visionary. Doubters called the venture $23 million worth of lunacy—or worse, a get-rich scheme manipulated by greedy land speculators. Some darkly predicted the water would carry typhoid and be undrinkable. Nevertheless, the newspapers had built up Mulholland as a genius—and he was a lucky genius at that. A falling block that killed a man at the city waterworks a few years earlier narrowly missed the chief. "My time had not come," Mulholland shrugged.

After five years of construction, it was time to show people the water. Soprano Ellen Beach Yaw inspired the hillside crowd and dignitaries spoke. Then came the 58-year-old Mulholland, not nearly as taciturn that Wednesday morning as his legend suggests. "This is a great event, fraught with the greatest importance to the future prosperity of this city," he began, according to the *Times.* "You have given me an opportunity to create a great public enterprise, and I am here to render my account to you. The aqueduct is completed and it is good. No one knows better than I

Gen. Harrison Gray Otis owned the *Times* and used the paper to promote development of his land in the Valley. He enjoyed a prominent seat at the aqueduct ceremony, shown here beside soprano Ellen Beach Yaw.

how much we needed the water. We have the fertile lands and the climate. Only water was needed to make of this region a tremendously rich and productive empire, and now we have it."

Mulholland unfurled a large American flag, the signal to open the aqueduct gates. Cannons boomed while all eyes stared up the spillway. For two or three minutes, nothing happened. Then a first gush tumbled from a concrete mouth in the hillside and toppled down the curved cascade, built of steps to fluff the stream into whitewater and slow the flow. As children and parents frolicked in the new river,

Mulholland turned to the mayor of Los Angeles and choked out his most-quoted remark, a sound bite for the ages: "There it is. Take it."

After celebrating with lunch at a nearby ranch, the city's most influential men gathered downtown at the Alexandria Hotel to fete their own foresight. Los Angeles had the water it sought to blossom into a major city. None of the bigwigs could have been more ecstatic than the downtown movers who four years earlier had committed $2.5 million to Isaac Van Nuys for his wheat empire in the Valley. Their Los Angeles Suburban Homes Co. owned half of the Valley—47,500 acres of dustbowl teased by a fickle river they could not touch, due to old Spanish water rights—and they had big plans for Mulholland's water.

Powerful men, thirsty men

Gen. Harrison Gray Otis, the combative anti-union owner of the *Times*, at age 76 was the patriarch of the Los Angeles Suburban Homes syndicate. Harry Chandler, the youngest partner at 49, was Otis' business manager and, eventually, his successor as publisher of the *Times* and scion of one of California's most powerful families. They were the influence men of the Valley land venture, along with two partners: Moses Hazeltine Sherman, 60, a streetcar mogul, and Otto Freeman Brant, 53, who was in the title insurance business.

The partner who knew most about developing

After crusading ferociously for public approval of the aqueduct, the *Times* treated its opening like an epic moment in history.

land was Hobart Johnstone Whitley, a 53-year-old Toronto native who had created new towns as he worked his way cross-country to California. While managing the subdivision of Hollywood, Whitley would drive through Cahuenga Pass with his family after Sunday dinner to gaze upon the wheat fields and vast emptiness of the San Fernando Valley and ponder the possibilities. Here was a basin of immense

size, located right next to a growing city. Whitley must have thought he had found a subdivider's Promised Land.

These five self-described capitalists—the syndicate's Board of Control—had their friends and admirers, but they also were controversial. This was especially true of Otis, who used the Times as his bully pulpit to rail against unions and anything liberal, and for favored projects like the aqueduct. The city's Socialists, a powerful bloc led by lawyer Job Harriman, assumed that Otis, their archenemy, exploited inside knowledge of the aqueduct to become even richer. Some even believed that Otis finagled the project's approval and construction in order to extract fortunes out of Valley land. This legend grew to mythic proportions even though the syndicate obtained the land two years after voters gave their approval for the aqueduct. From that point on, all of Los Angeles had openly anticipated the water and how their lives would change. "Mr. Chandler discussed this with me quite fully and quite frankly," Isaac Van Nuys acknowledged.

Still, if one were so inclined, there was plenty of reason to suspect the syndicate of shady dealings. Otis and Sherman were among the influential Los Angeles businessmen who had formed the San Fernando Mission Land Co. a few years earlier to purchase the 16,200-acre George K. Porter ranch, south and west of the mission. The investors, led by Glendale trolley car magnate L. C. Brand, intended to resell the Porter land in small plots and build a streetcar line to San Fernando from Los Angeles. This was the first big speculative subdivision in the Valley, and the group fashioned its purchase of Porter's ranch in secret, knowing almost certainly what the public did not yet know—that plans were afoot for an aqueduct.

They likely knew because of an insider who sat on the city water commission—Moses Sherman. He was privy to the secret that a former mayor of Los Angeles, Fred Eaton, had been acquiring water rights in the Owens Valley faster than farmers there could figure out his game. Eaton apparently bet that if he could deliver a reliable source of new water, Los Angeles would pay him dearly. Mulholland made a clandestine wagon trip to the Owens Valley with Eaton, his onetime mentor, and returned to advise the water board in July 1905 that the aqueduct idea was feasible. One day after the board privately gave its go-ahead, the secret Valley investors quietly claimed their option on the Porter land.

No proof has ever linked the Porter land deal to an insider tip from Sherman, but there also seems little reason to doubt the strong circumstantial case. He was eventually deemed too controversial to remain on the board, and with Otis was forced to publicly divest his stake in the Mission Land Co. subdivision. Nonetheless, the *Times* published the scoop of the young century on July 29, 1905, under the headline "Titanic Project to Give City a River!" Historian Remi Nadeau wrote later: "Copies of the *Times* were no sooner dumped on the depot platform at Burbank than valley property began to soar."

The town of Marian (later Reseda) was named for Marian Otis Chandler. The daughter of Gen. Otis, she married his lieutenant, Harry Chandler.

The murky Porter land deal seems almost trivial in scope compared with the Board of Control's ambitions for the southern half of the Valley. Their machinations have been scrutinized through the years, but never more thoroughly than by Catherine Mulholland, the engineer's granddaughter, in her 1987 book *Owensmouth Baby: The Making of a San Fernando Valley Town*. She dug through the personal papers of the principals, reconstructed meetings and documented the fervor they brought to developing the largest single subdivision ever filed in the county of Los Angeles, recorded officially as Tract 1000.

Each of the Board of Control partners put up $100,000; to raise additional cash they took in

leading members of the Los Angeles financial establishment, who put up $25,000 each as "participators." These investors got to select a small parcel of Tract 1000 land to keep or sell, while the main partners kept prime parcels for themselves. Otis, for example, took 550 acres at the base of the Santa Monica Mountains and built a hacienda and ranch, *Mil Flores,* on a site that later became the community of Tarzana. The rest of Tract 1000 was made available for sale and development.

A key to the strategy was the creation of three new towns, laid out across the Valley to lure buyers to the far ends of the tract. They called the first town Van Nuys, after Harry Chandler's old friend. The middle town was founded as Marian, named after Otis' daughter and Chandler's wife (later changed to Reseda). Otis himself dubbed the westernmost town "Owensmouth," a name he meant to conjure up the image of fresh, cool water from the Owens River, perhaps as an antidote to the dusty reality of the place. The name was a mouthful the townsfolk never quite mastered. "We are inclined to pronounce the name…with a little too much 'mouth,' " the editor of the *Owensmouth Gazette* gently chided a few years later. "For a little self-pride…and for the dignity of the town, let us practice up by putting the accent where it belongs, then we will pronounce it as though it were spelled 'Owensmth.' " Eventually, the town took the name Canoga Park.

Before a single board was nailed, the *Times*, doing its part to sell the boss' lands, proclaimed the nonexistent new communities "The Wonder Towns of the San Fernando Valley." The marketing strategy had a truly audacious element that commanded notice: a fine boulevard, extending 14 miles through the old wheat fields, would be built to connect the three towns-to-be. The *Times* lauded it as a "masterpiece of civil engineering...that ranks with the best hard-surfaced roads in the world."

Sherman Way began at the Board of Control's property line, west of the established town of Lankershim. It had a paved roadway for motor cars, an oiled track for horses and wagons, and a streetcar line laid on crushed rock. The route was lighted at night, and its shoulders were planted with more than 8,000 shrubs and trees so passersby could not see the bare landscape that stretched for miles. Signs posted the speed limit at 100 miles an hour, an invitation to sporting motorists to put the roadway to the test.

Declaring the existence of new towns was simple, but convincing people to come live on a dying wheat field posed more of a challenge. To sell Van Nuys, the Board of Control turned to William Paul Whitsett, a Pennsylvanian whose mother was related to patriotic flag-sewer Betsy Ross. A marketer by nature, Whitsett incited buzz about Van Nuys by calling every person with a telephone in the Los Angeles region and inviting them to the opening day barbecue on February 22, 1911. Travelers in Los Angeles hotels also found tags on their luggage offering free transport to the new town. Whitsett's ads invited "the businessman, the mechanic, the gardener, the farmer,

Sherman Way, the grand boulevard

Modern commuters know Sherman Way as a reliable, if monotonous, traffic artery that scribes a straight line across the Valley floor from Burbank Airport to the community of West Hills. But in 1912, Sherman Way was a renowned and most pretentious highway, a tourist attraction said to be inspired by the famous *Paseo de la Reforma* in Mexico City.

It curled through the wheat fields like a snake, with long straight-aways that enticed drivers to open the throttle. The name Auto Speedway was even considered, but the boulevard was named instead for Moses Sherman, one of the partners in the Tract 1000 subdivision. Though expensive to build, the boulevard served its purpose of luring curious motorists—and prospective land buyers—to the new towns of Van Nuys, Marian and Owensmouth.

Sherman Way was not just a blacktop highway. Beside the fresh pavement ran streetcar rails and a separate oiled road for horses and tractors. Rows of trees and electric lights lined the 14-mile route. Rose bushes and other shrubs were planted to hide the motorists' view of the barren fields between towns.

Even today, a discerning eye can trace the original route. In the community of Valley Village, follow Chandler Boulevard west from Whitsett Avenue, noticing the mature trees and dirt median strip that are remains of the original. Today's Van Nuys Boulevard was the north-bound leg of old Sherman Way. Where Van Nuys Boulevard meets Vose Street, the old roadway curved west and shot through the fields for nine miles, following the current route of Sherman Way through the communities known today as Reseda and Canoga Park.

Then, as now, speed was a danger. The road was barely opened when the first fatal crash occurred on July 23, 1912.

Sherman Way, shown here in the late 1910s or early 1920s, was long and flat. Note the photographer's shadow in the foreground.

the retired professional man or woman, or the astute investor" to buy in Van Nuys—"the largest opportunity on the entire Pacific Coast today."

Never mind that the place was bone dry and that opening day was carefully timed to avoid stifling heat or blowing dust. Prospective buyers who came by train from Los Angeles found sidewalks being paved, wells being dug and homes being finished—the activity all staged by Whitsett. Home lots began at $350, business property at $660; $39,606 in cash down payments the first weekend ensured that a town was born.

The first baby, Whitley Van Nuys Huffaker, arrived on October 18, 1911. Two months later, on December 16, flags and bunting greeted the first trolley cars connecting Van Nuys to Lankershim and Hollywood, clattering and swerving along tracks carved into the east side of Cahuenga Pass. The Pacific Electric Red Cars were a crucial cog in the sales strategy. Though the 18-mile ride was slow and at times unnerving, settlers could reach Hill Street in the shopping district of Los Angeles for a quarter (40 cents round trip). Youngsters in Van Nuys rode into Lankershim for Saturday lessons at Miss Ruth Wilson's Dancing School. In a few months Van Nuys boasted of 200 homes and 40 businesses, including a factory manufacturing Johnston organs.

Owensmouth, nine miles to the west, opened for sales on March 30, 1912, with the now-traditional barbecue and an auto race on Sherman Way featuring champion driver Barney Oldfield, the most

Trains from Los Angeles brought visitors to the dusty town site of Van Nuys for the first day of land sales on Washington's Birthday in 1911. Empty fields extended for miles, but business was good.

Three years later, Van Nuys had the look of a real town. The main street, known as North Sherman Way in 1914, had electric lights and sidewalks and today is Van Nuys Boulevard.

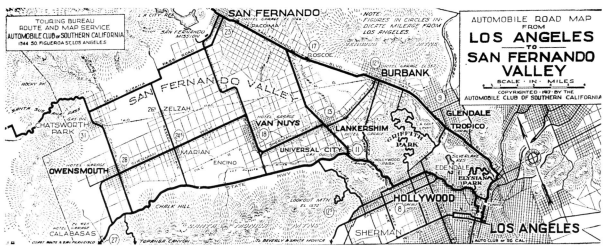

This early touring map from the Automobile Club of Southern California shows the Valley's towns with the names as they existed in the late 1910s.

famous racer of the day. The first land auction at Marian was held on July 20. Some 18,700 acres of Tract 1000 had been divvied up, taking in more than $5 million—double the original investment. Almost 29,000 acres remained to be sold and developed; the partners often fretted that the land was not selling fast enough, and battled among themselves over tactics and money.

Many buyers came from out of state, their moves west subsidized by low train fares. From Winnipeg came a Mr. St. Johannes, who paid $20,000 for 40 acres near Van Nuys and planted fruit trees. Rev. Truman A. Hull brought his family from Lincoln, Nebraska, to Owensmouth, followed by his son, who became the first doctor in town. The newcomers cul-

tivated, built and did constant battle with the elements. Winter floods inundated large sections of the Valley, including the center of Van Nuys, and freezes ruined citrus growers.

By 1913 the PE Red Cars reached west through Marian to Owensmouth, 29.1 miles from downtown Los Angeles. The trip took 80 minutes, if the erratic power supply across the Valley cooperated, but settlers curious to see the city didn't seem to mind. Catherine Mulholland's mother, Addie Haas, even rode the wooden Red Cars from Owensmouth to high school in Hollywood. Across the Valley, town rivalries were stirring. Whitley referred privately to San Fernando as "a den of thieves and wharf rats." Cecil M. Wilcox, the editor of the *Lankershim Laconic*

newspaper, took regular potshots at the upstart Tract 1000 towns and their controversial godparents. And Van Nuys, Marian and Owensmouth competed for desirable buyers—the Board of Control didn't seem to care which sibling won, so long as the land kept selling. A Valley baseball league formed with teams from each town.

San Fernando reigned as the biggest town. Lankershim was the peach-growing capital of the region. Across the Valley, Chatsworth had a few hundred residents and two hotels. The Norwegian immigrants who settled Zelzah built a wood-frame Lutheran church and sprouted a colony of small ranches alongside the Southern Pacific tracks. Menton Neggen was 8 years old when his family arrived from Minnesota to begin their new life in Zelzah. First they had to lug their belongings up the dirt lane that became Reseda Boulevard. "There was a barbed wire fence on either side, and it was about six inches deep with dust," he said. "Most everybody kept a cow or two, a flock of chickens and a few hogs." Even with Burbank and the settlements of Roscoe, Sunland and Hansen Heights beginning to populate on the flanks of the Verdugos, fewer than 10,000 people lived in the Valley.

William Mulholland continued to live in the city, but he joined in the rush to the Valley by acquiring land between Zelzah and Chatsworth—notably, in the northern half of the Valley, not the southern half being marketed by the Tract 1000 moguls, with whom he had his differences. His son Perry worked

Automobiles and horse-drawn stages shared an unpaved road on the left side of the Cahuenga Pass headed into the Valley; Pacific Electric trolleys kept to the right.

BURBANK REVIEW

VOL. 4   BURBANK, CALIFORNIA, FRIDAY, SEPTEMBER 22, 1911   NO. 12

Progress   -   -   -   Prosperity
Opportunity

Pacific Electric Railway Co. Completes Its Line To

BURBANK

We are now
forty-five minutes
from Broadway

Our Soil, Scenery
and Society
are A No. 1

Local newspapers did their best to boost the fortunes of their towns, as in this *Burbank Review* front page from Sept. 22, 1911. At left, in a photo from the same year, is tree-lined Olive Avenue, in Burbank looking toward the Verdugos.

the ranch, planting hay and beans, and later citrus and walnuts. Mulholland remained the most respected civic dignitary in the West. A portion of Pacoima, hoping to enjoy some of his glory, briefly changed its name to Mulholland. On the ridges of the Santa Monica Mountains, engineers carved a sinuous 25-mile scenic drive from Hollywood to Calabasas and christened it Mulholland Highway; cowboy star Tom Mix performed at the celebration marking its opening. Plans were made to extend the scenic route around the entire Valley, and for a time the road that became Foothill Boulevard through San Fernando

and Sylmar was known as Mulholland Street.

The precious water flowing through the aqueduct lubricated the Valley's dreams of prosperity. Most land was selling to small-time farmers and ranchers who, if they had a reliable supply of cheap water, could produce lucrative crops like oranges, apricots and lima beans. But getting access to the aqueduct water was a problem. The City of Los Angeles owned it, and the city limits stopped on the far side of the Santa Monica Mountains. The Valley had no fair claim to any of the water.

Knowing that the aqueduct supplied far more

than Los Angeles needed at the time, some Valley landholders offered to buy the surplus flow. But the city's biggest powers had another idea and put it in the form of an ultimatum to the Valley: agree to be annexed by Los Angeles or stay dry. Some Valley ranchers with good wells resisted, saying they preferred independence. Residents in Burbank, San Fernando and, initially, Owensmouth and Lankershim declined to be annexed.

But on March 29, 1915, by a lopsided public vote of 681-25, some 170 square miles of the Picos' old range became part of Los Angeles. The newly

Small beginnings

Burbank, founded in 1887, finally incorporated as a city on July 8, 1911, with 600 residents. The city was small, less than three square miles. Neighboring Glendale snatched up territory that was left out of the new city, helping to explain today's erratic boundaries.

One of early Burbank's most colorful figures was an eccentric apricot grower who rode in a carriage drawn by high-stepping horses and was usually accompanied by a matched pair of Dalmatians. Joseph Fawkes liked to tinker with machinery. He patented an aerial trolley that resembled a propeller-driven cigar, designed to whiz along at 60 miles an hour on rollers suspended from a trolley wire. Fawkes promised that his "Aerial Swallow" would ferry passengers to Los Angeles in 10 minutes.

But on its debut run through his orchard in 1907,

the sheet aluminum contraption fell apart. From then on, the whole idea was called Fawkes' Folly. Fawkes became more unpopular for another reason: He opposed Burbank's existence as a separate city and led a move to make the community part of Los Angeles. For this he was hanged in effigy outside his home at 110 West Olive Avenue.

Joseph Fawkes vowed his aerial trolley would bring mass transit to Burbank, but it didn't even survive a test run through his apricot grove.

annexed section, including Mission San Fernando Rey itself, more than doubled the city's land area. The destinies of the city and the Valley were now inextricably joined. Faced with the inevitable, Owensmouth soon capitulated and voted to annex, followed by Hansen Heights and Lankershim, and later Tujunga. Of the early settlements, only San Fernando, Glendale, Calabasas and Burbank remained forever outside the borders of Los Angeles.

In the distant Owens Valley, a way of life was transformed by the loss of water to Los Angeles. Farming gradually vanished, towns with names like Laws and Aberdeen withered away, and the once-navigable Owens Lake dried into a vast dust bowl that spawns noxious alkali clouds. Vengeful Inyo ranchers on occasion sabotaged the aqueduct with shotguns and dynamite. They drew moral support from writers such as the humorist Will Rogers and from Morrow Mayo, an East Coast journalist who popularized a dark theory: that Otis and others conspired to "buy up worthless San Fernando Valley land, acquire control of the Owens River and then frighten the taxpayers of Los Angeles into paying for a huge aqueduct…and, incidentally, to use a great portion of the water to irrigate the San Fernando Valley and thus convert that desert region into a fertile farming section." Mayo's conspiratorial version of events is still embraced by some, but many historians dismiss it as exaggerated.

"The St. Francis is gone"

Mulholland's aqueduct could deliver up to 258 million gallons a day, but its weak link was a subterranean crossing of the San Andreas Fault. As a hedge against a disabling earthquake—and against sabotage—he sought to build a dam massive enough to hold one year's supply of water. In 1925-26

Mulholland supervised construction of his largest edifice, the St. Francis Dam in San Francisquito Canyon northeast of Newhall. A colony of dam keepers, power station workers and their families grew up around the towering concrete structure, which had a nagging propensity for small seeps and leaks.

In farm towns downstream, friends used to jest, "I'll see you later, if the dam don't break." But Mulholland always insisted the seepage was routine. After the reservoir was filled for the first time, portentous new leaks erupted in the dam face.

Mulholland came out on March 12, 1928, to inspect the latest trouble. His son Perry rode along and remarked that there did seem to be an alarming flow of water through the structure, but the chief engineer reassured dam keeper Tony Harnischfeger that all was fine and returned home to Los Angeles.

Just before midnight the great dam shuddered and broke apart with a roar. A wall of water 10 stories high plunged down the canyon, scouring out everything—homes, power plants, trucks, huge slabs of soaked concrete—and racing toward sleeping farm towns on the river plain below. The flood wave and its load of tumbling debris hit the Santa Clara River at 18 miles an hour and veered west, washing out railroad and highway bridges as it sped through the dark toward Castaic. Lights that flickered out alerted light sleepers that something was amiss, and telephone operators called frantically ahead, trying to awaken as many people as they could downriver. In Los Angeles, Mulholland's assistant telephoned the chief's house on St. Andrews Place to deliver the grave news: "The St. Francis is gone." Catherine Mulholland writes that family lore recalls her grandfather mumbling, "Please God, don't let people be killed."

The rampage swept into Ventura County, churning through the citrus groves of Piru and Fillmore and leaving parts of Santa Paula underwater. Finally it reached the coast at Ventura and spilled into the Pacific Ocean. In five and a half hours, the flood had traveled 54 miles.

Winding through the Santa Monica Mountains, Mulholland Highway is the grandest remaining monument to the aqueduct builder. The dirt road was dedicated on December 27, 1924.

St. Francis Dam, seen here in 1926, was William Mulholland's largest public works project. He originally sought to put the dam in Big Tujunga Canyon—a move that would have averted tragedy.

Defending Owens Valley

Columnist Will Rogers, one of America's most popular and respected figures, helped publicize the plight of Owens Valley ranchers who felt victimized by the Los Angeles Aqueduct. In a column that ran nationwide in 1932, he wrote: "Ten years ago this was a wonderful valley…but Los Angeles had to have more water for the chamber of commerce to drink more toasts to its growth, more water to dilute its orange juice and more water for its geraniums to delight the tourists.… So now, this is a valley of desolation."

Mulholland was driven to the site and waited, like everyone else, for the night to end. Sunrise exposed a tragedy of grotesque extremity. A tall obelisk of jagged concrete was all that remained of the dam. The colony of families that lived at the dam—74 people—was utterly gone. Harnischfeger, the dam keeper, and his 6-year-old son were never found. Downstream, bodies lay encased in a thick layer of muck and debris. The remains of one victim were washed out to sea and later found on a San Diego beach, more than 150 miles away. Survivors and livestock clung to trees or were snarled in fences. At least 450 people perished, including 140 workers in a Water and Power Department work camp and half of the pupils enrolled at Saugus Elementary School. An unknown number of migrant farm workers who had been camped along the quiet Santa Clara River also died. The actual toll possibly rivaled the more than 700 believed dead in the 1906 San Francisco earthquake and fire, the only worse disaster in California. Across the swath of destruction, 1,200 homes were demolished.

Arguments over who or what was to blame for the dam's collapse began almost immediately. Many suspected Inyo ranchers who had bombed the aqueduct seven times in the previous year. Other theories focused on earthquake faults or blasting by road workers. But out in the muck, where troops helped slaughter and burn animals to avoid a typhoid outbreak, much of the rage was aimed at the dam's builder. A woman who lost her entire family posted a sign in dripping red paint: "Kill Mulholland!" Some newspapers demanded his resignation; the Los Angeles district attorney vowed to bring manslaughter charges against whoever was responsible, and left no doubt whom he meant.

Looking sad and broken, Mulholland testified at the coroner's inquest just after a widower who described losing his wife and three daughters. District Attorney Asa Keyes gave Mulholland no quarter, frosting his questions with sarcasm and hammering at the record of leaks. When he showed a grainy home movie of the devastation, Mulholland sobbed and muttered, "I envy the dead."

After deliberating for two weeks, the inquest jury ruled that no prosecution was warranted, but it blamed deference to Mulholland's reputation for errors in judgment that had led to the collapse: "The construction of a municipal dam should never be left to the sole judgement of one man, no matter how eminent." Mulholland had not consulted any geology experts before choosing the site himself. The chief slumped in his chair, weeping into his hands. His career was over. He resigned seven months later at age 72, suffering from Parkinson's disease and apparently mired in depression.

Modern engineers have taken steps to clear Mulholland of blame for the greatest American civil engineering catastrophe of the 20th century. The dam

Dam break survivors, some of them newly orphaned, lived for weeks in Red Cross relief camps. These children are trying on donated shoes.

was indeed seriously flawed. It lacked basic drainage features, and the cement was too porous. But a new inquiry published by the Association of Engineering Geologists in 1992 concluded that design shortcomings did not cause the tragedy. Simply, the dam was built in the wrong place, although Mulholland and the most learned geologists of the time could not have known this. The eastern dam abutment was anchored not to solid rock but in the rubble of an ancient and still moving landslide. This condition was undetectable in 1928, the report concluded. The old slide probably began to shift on the night of March 12, causing the St. Francis to rupture.

By the time Mulholland passed away on July 22,

Damaged vehicles were pulled from the muck that covered the flood plain along the Santa Clara River. Soldiers and an army of volunteers retrieved corpses, burned livestock carcasses and kept away sightseers.

Not much of the giant dam remained after the March 12, 1928, failure, as seen in this view looking downstream in San Francisquito Canyon. Concrete remnants still remain.

1935, the city had mostly forgiven him. Thousands filed through the rotunda of City Hall, where the chief's body rested in a flag-draped open coffin, surrounded by notes, photographs and flower wreaths, including one from President Franklin D. Roosevelt. At 2 p.m., the city stopped working for 10 minutes of silent tribute. Out in the desert, the aqueduct's flow was stilled.

During his lifetime, Los Angeles had grown from 10,000 to 1.5 million residents. And the San Fernando Valley had been transformed from a wind-blown pasture for the longhorned cattle of Andres Pico to a magnet for dreamers from every state.

CHAPTER 5

Dreamers and Schemers

Irrigation turned the Valley into a farming paradise. This Cross aerial photo looks over Encino and the Santa Monica Mountains.

Adding water to the fertile soil let the parched San Fernando Valley bloom. Between the towns and subdivisions, fields of tomatoes, grapes and lima beans thrived, and orchards of walnuts, oranges and lemons flourished. Soon 75,000 acres were in irrigation, including a continuous sea of sugar beets for 10 miles from the town of Owensmouth to the slopes of what later became Sherman Oaks.

Agriculture became the culture of the Valley in the 1920s. Farmers met over coffee to stew about prices and politics and squired their families to square dances and western-theme parades. The sons of William Mulholland and Otto Brant became pillars of the farming community—Perry Mulholland planted citrus groves west of Zelzah, Alfred Brant introduced walnuts and David Otto Brant bred the world's largest herd of Guernsey cattle where the Topanga Plaza shopping mall is today. Historic *Rancho El Escorpión,* the land grant made by Governor Pío Pico in one of the last acts of Mexican rule, became Platt Ranch, an outpost in the dairy empire of Los Angeles Creamery Co. impresario George Platt.

Stores nationwide sold Sylmar brand olives, plucked from a 2,000-acre grove reputed to be the world's largest. Packing plants in San Fernando and Owensmouth shipped oranges and grapefruits to points east. Lankershim claimed the world's largest apricot tree and advertised itself as a classy town: "No saloons—no mud." By one count, there were 750,000 citrus trees and more than a million laying

The Petit family farmed land along the Los Angeles River that historically had been part of Rancho Encino. These fieldworkers are sowing onions.

hens, most of them white leghorns, providing eggs to Los Angeles and fertilizer to the Valley's farms and gardens. Most everyone grew something, even if it was just roses or honeybees.

"Everywhere in this broad, flat valley are farms, orchards, gardens and typical California homes set amid gardens…or clinging to the hillsides or overlooking several golf courses," gushed a 1928 driving guide, "The Romantic Southland of California." "The [spring] air is deep with the aroma of growing things and of budding flowers, and in the early fall the scent of ripened fruits and grains permeates the valley."

The Valley's new status as a district of municipal Los Angeles promoted another kind of exploitation of the land. Men itching to make a name—and some money—for themselves had come into the area and left their marks on the map in the form of new subdivisions. Dr. Homer Hansen, who came to Southern California to restore his health, had driven up into the northern foothills of the Verdugo Mountains in the early 1900s and built the settlement of Hansen Heights, "a little paradise in itself, nestled in the north hills where it supports a thriving citrus industry," an editor wrote at the time. What remains of Hansen Heights now carries the name Shadow Hills. Nearby, "Pep" Rempp took advantage of the boulders strewn by centuries of flooding in Tujunga Wash and developed the peculiar subdivision of Stonehurst, which grew to include dozens of houses and a community center constructed of boulders. A 1924 pamphlet promotes Stonehurst as the future home of

The San Fernando Fruit Growers Assn. ran the Valley's oldest citrus packing house, active from 1903 until 1951.

movie stars, a place "where life's worth while." Stonehurst and its remaining boulder houses are now part of Sun Valley, and the old community center is a city historical monument.

William Hamilton Hay was already an accomplished subdivider when he took on the task of selling off the 4,460-acre Amestoy Ranch, the final incarnation of the historic Los Encinos rancho. Domingo Amestoy had come to Los Angeles from France in 1846 and amassed great tracts of land, including the Encino rancho. The *Times* in 1915 called it "the largest body of land ever put on the market at one time within the limits of Los Angeles." To make the lots more appealing to prospective buyers, Hay plant-

ed more than 700 live oak trees. Today those trees and their progeny shade million-dollar estates and help give Encino a distinctive arboreal feel. Hay's own 50-acre estate, Hayvenhurst, gazed over the Valley from atop a knoll south of Ventura Boulevard and gave its name to a street that extends the width of the basin.

Happiness on an acre

Two dreamers who preached the goodness of a frugal existence close to the land did not stay long in the Valley, but they left behind a visible legacy.

Today, in the heart of Tujunga upslope from Foothill Boulevard toward the San Gabriels, a neighborhood of stone houses centered along Commerce Avenue and Summitrose Street is a reminder of an unusual colony begun in 1913 by William Ellsworth Smythe. When he arrived, the former *Rancho Tujunga* was populated by a few hundred homesteaders and the small community of Sunland, which had grown out of the settlement of Monte Vista. The main road through the area was Michigan Avenue, though many locals still called it "Horsethief Trail."

Smythe, born to a wealthy Massachusetts family, had passed up Harvard to become a newspaperman in Nebraska. After watching the Midwest suffer through a drought, he crusaded for organized irrigation. It became a personal philosophy—he founded *Irrigation Age* magazine, lectured widely and came up with his creed that an American family could support itself on an acre of well-irrigated earth, a goat for milk, and some chickens and pigeons for eggs and meat. The key, he said, was working in concert with other families.

Smythe established his first cooperative utopia at San Ysidro, on the Mexican border south of San Diego. For his second community he ventured into the small upland valley wedged between the Verdugo and San Gabriel Mountains. A few miles east of Sunland, he teamed with Marshall V. Hartranft, a local subdivider, and they founded the townsite of Tujunga on March 17, 1913, and began the Little Lands Colony. Prospects were enticed to join the fledgling *Ciudad de los Terrenitos*, its Latinized name, with promises that members would pool their earnings, buy land cheaply (typically in one-acre lots) and help each other out. The Little Landers, as believers called themselves, built houses of stone taken from hills and washes.

When the cornerstone for a community house was laid April 12, 1913, there were 209 people present to sign the register. Bolton Hall, built on a hillcrest surrounded by nothing but open land, became the spot for weekly meetings held before the huge boulder fireplace. Little Landers would socialize and exchange tips on growing oranges or getting rid of gophers. In a bit of a pun, Smythe named the building for Bolton Hall, a New York writer whom he admired.

Michigan Avenue served as the main highway through Sunland and Tujunga, linking the San Fernando Valley with Pasadena.

Today a museum in Tujunga, Bolton Hall was built by members of the Little Lands colony with boulders gathered from nearby washes.

The ``Millionaires Club of Happiness and Contentment,'' shown here in 1921, was the name a group of men took after deciding to go into the banking business.

Milestones

Just over 21,000 people lived in the Valley at the time of the 1920 census. San Fernando (3,204) and Burbank (2,913) were the most populous towns. The Valley also had 2,240 registered cars.

Dial telephone service reached the Valley in 1926. Residents could reach Dr. Axel Swenson at Van Nuys emergency hospital by dialing 101.

Unfortunately for the Little Landers, the air might have been sparkling and the mountain scenery dramatic, but the Tujunga soil was ill suited to farming. The sandy ground so close to the mountains was lousy with boulders and gravel. Cactus was easier to grow than citrus trees—not good news for a colony that was intended to thrive on what it produced. "It was so barren, so unfriendly and so unlike the rolling, green hills of our native Michigan," a long-time resident, Mabel Hatch, later described those first days. "And the rocks. Always and always the rocks." As for the acre that her aunt and father took over in 1913, "it was about the roughest, toughest looking piece of land I ever saw."

Shortly after Smythe left in 1914 to establish a new colony at Hayward in northern California, the Little Lands colony counted about 500 residents, a post office, electric lights, a phone system and some 6,000 fruit trees. But the end was near. World War I took away the able-bodied young men needed to work the fields. Foothill Boulevard opened up the area to more outsiders, and some of the Little Landers began selling off their farms. By 1925 only one Landers family remained. Tujunga, however, continued to attract settlers. That year the town incorporated as a city, and Bolton Hall served as the city hall and jail. In 1932 Tujunga gave up its independence and agreed to be annexed to Los Angeles, lured by the promise of more water and other resources. Bolton Hall housed city offices for a time.

Meanwhile, the San Fernando Valley in the 1920s was making a reputation as a major poultry center. Runnymede Farms, one of the largest chicken operations in the nation, almost surrounded the town of Marian and had its own colony of resident workers. At the intersection of Sherman Way and Sepulveda Boulevard, the Holly Hatchery sometimes offered as many as 200,000 baby white leghorns for sale. The town of Roscoe, which was growing alongside San Fernando Road, compared itself to a famous northern California poultry capital, billing itself "Another Petaluma!"

Charles Weeks, on the other hand, preferred to think small. He preached a self-proclaimed gospel that careful husbanding of an acre of land with 2,500 hens would lead to prosperity. He had a track record as a community builder who had founded Winnetka, Illinois. In the Valley, Weeks bought up more than 600 undeveloped acres west of Marian. He built a model one-acre farm at the southwest corner of Saticoy Street and Winnetka Avenue, and moved in with his family.

Weeks cultivated grapes, put in a small trout pond and placed ads in the Los Angeles papers inviting visitors to ride the Pacific Electric Red Cars out to the Charles Weeks Poultry Colony, where every Sunday he lectured for anyone who showed up. "I have a far greater work than the mere subdivision of land," a 1923 ad in the *Times* read. "I am building an ideal community made up of successful people who wish to live this natural healthy life close to Nature in a neighborhood of uniform, symmetrical, harmonious garden homes."

Weeks sold the first acre to Jenja Beckman of Los Angeles in 1922, when the lots went for $1,250. By the end of the year, 41 families had established their acre plots in the tract bounded by Winnetka and Oso avenues and Leadwell and Lanark streets. Weeks emphasized the importance of the arts and led residents on outings to Hollywood Bowl. He also played violin in the Weeks Colony Orchestra, which gave concerts in the community center on the northwest corner of Sherman Way and Winnetka. His magazine, *Little Farms*—"published every little while"—kept members up to date on techniques and methods.

The Weeks Colony became a Valley institution, listed on maps and well known in the surrounding towns. Weeks deeded five acres at Winnetka and Roscoe Boulevard to the city for an elementary school. The colony grew to more than 500 families and had its own egg co-op, warehouse and packing plant. The stock market crash in October 1929 and the ensuing Depression pummeled Weeks financially, and when he left California in 1934 the colony was essentially finished. Some residents who stayed to raise chickens the Weeks way founded the community of Winnetka, between Reseda and Canoga Park.

Weeks himself was living in comfort in West Palm Beach, Florida, pursuing his daily hobby of underwater spearfishing, when he spoke to the *Valley Times* in 1951 about his old colony. "I am now 78 years old and still firmly believe that a little land highly fertilized and developed into a productive garden affords the very best environment for the highest development of man."

If Weeks' sentiment could be read as applying to the larger Valley, a lot of people seemed to agree with him. The Valley population doubled during the 1920s. Investors acquired 450 acres around a swampy wetland,

The Weeks Acre

A successful Charles Weeks Acre was planned to the foot. The first shelter was to be simple and set back from the street, so it could become the garage when a main house was built. At each corner of the lot, Weeks urged planting a palm tree to create a tropical feel. On the right side of the property was to be a long egg-laying house with room for 2,500 hens and a feed shed.

Behind the residence Weeks recommended planting a kitchen garden, with rows of crops such as Swiss chard and beets, then alfalfa and barley. The selection was important as feed for the chickens. Fruit trees were trained to grow on espaliers along the fence line. Finally, there should be a clover lawn to attract pollinating bees. Large lots with remnants of the old Weeks design can still be found amid the suburbs in the original tract.

The colony's community center was at the northwest corner of Winnetka and Sherman Way.

Every ranchette in the Weeks Poultry Colony featured a long house for laying hens. The colony was located in present-day Winnetka.

In the 1920s, this stretch of the original Sherman Way was renamed Van Nuys Boulevard.

Laurel Canyon Boulevard, looking southeast, was a country lane in 1929.

Sorting out the streets

The 1920s saw the Valley's street map begin to resemble today's. A wholesale renaming of major thoroughfares occurred. Saugus Avenue became Sepulveda Boulevard, Pacoima Avenue became Laurel Canyon Boulevard, Diaz Avenue became Coldwater Canyon Avenue and North Sherman Way became Van Nuys Boulevard.

The road later called Foothill Boulevard was known in parts as Michigan Avenue, Tujunga Valley Avenue and, through Pacoima and San Fernando, Mulholland Street. Victory Boulevard was christened in honor of World War I veterans.

When Burbank would not pay for a boulevard connecting his subdivision of Magnolia Park with Cahuenga Pass, developer Earl L. White paid to grade and pave Hollywood Way. "One can hardly drive into the valley without becoming aware of streets recently paved or under construction," a University of Chicago master's thesis noted in 1928.

A comprehensive paper called the "Major Traffic Street Plan for Los Angeles" recommended modernizing the Valley's infrastructure, among other things by widening the narrow, winding

highway through Cahuenga Pass to eight lanes and opening a truck highway in the Los Angeles River channel. Neither occurred, but the city's inspector of public works reported in 1926 that "Cahuenga Pass has become one of the most heavily traveled roads in Southern California and also one of the most congested."

After Ventura Boulevard was widened to 70 feet—from soft shoulder to soft shoulder—between Lankershim Boulevard and the rural outpost of Calabasas, the *Times* called it "one of the great major boulevards of Los Angeles."

Pacific Electric ``Red Cars'' rattled the length of the Valley. This car waited at the Kester Junction station on south Sherman Way, now Chandler Boulevard.

institutions did begin opening across the Valley: Olive View tuberculosis sanitarium and a U.S. veterans hospital in Sylmar, St. Charles Borromeo and Our Lady of Lourdes churches in 1921. The first traffic signal went up at Ventura and Lankershim boulevards in 1927. "The whole valley has the well kept appearance of a yard," Gladys Lillian Brandt wrote in a 1928 master's thesis at the University of Chicago. "Weeds are hard to find. Everywhere carefully cultivated fields, and small bungalows with lawns, flowers and shrubs emphasize the appearance of prosperity."

Developer Victor Girard did his part to improve the appearance of the far west Valley—and his legacy remains on the winding streets south of Ventura Boulevard in Woodland Hills, where thickets of tall eucalyptus and pepper trees provide some of the densest shade in the Valley. Girard's subdivision in the barren west end of the Valley needed to be dressed up, so he planted 120,000 shade trees and shrubs—seven varieties of eucalyptus, five kinds of acacia, Arizona elms, Monterey pines. On the corner of what today are Ventura and Topanga Canyon boulevards, he built false storefronts and garish

put up a dam and welcomed the official opening of the Toluca Lake development with a fly-casting tournament. The town of Granada appeared on the lower fields of the Sunshine Ranch, which was headquartered on Shoshone Avenue north of Rinaldi Street. Actress Mary Pickford was an investor, and actor James Cagney had a spread nearby. The first home in Granada ("Hills" would be added to the name later), at the southwest corner of White Oak Avenue and Kingsbury Street, was occupied by the retired police chief of Los Angeles.

Burbank made a bid to sweeten its future and offered 209 hillside acres of the former Stough ranch for a southern branch of the University of California, but UCLA was placed in Westwood instead. Lasting

This police station and realty office was at San Fernando Road and North Sherman Way in Pacoima.

Turkish-style towers to make the community look more established.

The town of Girard was born on February 4, 1923, on 2,000 hilly acres broken off from the Brant dairy. Its founder, born Victor Girard Kleinberger, had come to Los Angeles from Louisville about the turn of the century as an ambitious 18-year-old who would develop towns all over the county. He was called a "devious genius…a natural dreamer and big spender." His dream for the west Valley was possibly loony. There was no streetcar access to Girard, as there was to other Valley towns; to reach the 6,000 lots that Girard hoped to sell, motorists were expected to negotiate Cahuenga Pass and a dozen miles of twisty Ventura Boulevard, passing a gauntlet of other beckoning real estate ventures.

Among the more conveniently located competitors, Hazelhurst, a quarter-mile outside North Hollywood, advertised itself as "truly a dream spot…[with] freedom from all pools, mud, washes or flood conditions." The Hollywood Country Club, south of Ventura where Coldwater Canyon Boulevard now rises into the hills, called its neighborhood around the Valley's first grass golf course "America's Most Beautiful Suburb." Adjacent was Holly Heights, "one of the scenic beauty spots of the San Fernando foothills." Clearly, free barbecues wouldn't be enough

Girard was barren and distant, making it difficult for the promoters to sell lots in the area that later became Woodland Hills.

Name game

As the Valley's farming settlements and new subdivisions began to grow into towns, many assumed new identities. In 1927, Lankershim renamed itself North Hollywood and Mission Acres took the name Sepulveda. Marian became Reseda and Zelzah became North Los Angeles, before later changing again to Northridge. Owensmouth assumed the made-up name of Canoga Park in 1931. Soon after, Cahuenga Park evolved into Sherman Oaks, honoring the memory of Moses Sherman, who had subdivided the land after receiving it as his share of the massive Tract 1000 development.

to get people out to Girard.

To lure prospects, Girard ran ads emphasizing that his town was closer to the beach than any place in the Valley—since there was a winding road through Topanga Canyon. He published the Girard News, built stables and a riding club, and opened the Girard Country Club and golf course with a championship-size pool and tennis courts. "Sucker buses" brought potential buyers out to the far end of the Valley, where teams of sales agents put on the pressure.

The Girard subdivision did not work out, the victim of its geography and suspicions that its developer's tactics were unethical, if not illegal. Choice pieces of land were reportedly sold over and over in a bait-and-switch scheme, and the subdivision was financed by a lien on the properties that proved a burden to the early buyers. After the 1929 stock market crash, many who could escape Girard did so, and by 1932 there were fewer than 100 families left.

Flowery ads in the Los Angeles newspapers fought to lure prospects to the new Valley subdivisions. The competition was fierce, as seen in these examples from the *Times* of February 4, 1923.

Lord of the Tarzana Ranch

Unlike the other men in this chapter, Edgar Rice Burroughs came to the Valley and remained. Already a prolific best-selling author, he used the money from his first successful adventure story, *Tarzan of the Apes,* to relocate to Los Angeles from Chicago. His Tarzan books sold 2 million copies in the United States in 1919-20, and he paid $125,000 for *Mil Flores,* the estate that Gen. Harrison Gray Otis, the late *Times*

owner, had established west of Encino. Burroughs received 550 acres of rolling grassland and rugged canyons climbing from Ventura Boulevard to the crest of the Santa Monicas.

Before his death in 1917, Otis had planted an extensive grove of exotic trees from Africa and Asia on a hill overlooking the Valley. Atop the knoll Otis built a 20-room hacienda with a lookout tower that offered a panoramic view of the Valley. Nestled in the foothills was a log house that Otis called the

Koonskin Kabin, and that Burroughs later rented to film crews.

When Burroughs moved onto his new estate on March 15, 1919, the *Times* proclaimed him "the newest addition to the ever-growing literary colony of the American summerland." He renamed his new holding the Tarzana Ranch. He often rose early in the morning, dressed in breeches and boots, strapped on a Colt .45 automatic and went riding on the property. At his direction, ranch hands dug a large swimming

The first art colony

Park Moderne, an artist colony-cum-subdivision in the hills above Calabasas, opened in 1927 on the onetime homestead of Sam Cooper Jr. The development was the idea of Los Angeles arts patron William Lingenbrink, who wanted a bucolic community in the chaparral where artists could live and work in small cottages on lots decorated with stylish fountains and rock waterfalls.

Some of the cottages were designed by noted modernist architect Rudolph Schindler, a friend of Lingenbrink. Plans called for a community clubhouse, a swimming pool and more than 150 cabins, but the stock market crash of 1929 spoiled the dream.

Remnants of the original colony remain in the Mulwood section of the city of Calabasas, including the original street names: Blue Bird Drive, Black Bird Way, Hummingbird Way, Sparrow Dell and Wren Crest Drive.

pool from which it was possible to overlook the Valley—possibly the first residential pool in the future pool capital. In his garage were two Packards, a roadster and a sedan, and a Hudson roadster. Burroughs "led the quiet, dignified life of the Lord of the Rancho," biographer Robert W. Fenton wrote.

He kept the Otis goat herd and brought in champion Berkshire hogs, intent on becoming a real hog farmer between books. The venture went badly. After he ended 1920 some $17,000 in the red, the hogs were put up for auction. Burroughs also sowed alfalfa, baby limas, barley and corn and tried growing apricots, but with mixed success—he joked later that he planted an acre of potatoes and 12 years later not a one had come up. More than the ranching itself, Burroughs enjoyed the rolling chaparral terrain and the wildlife—deer, bobcats, coyotes, mountain lions—though he complained in a letter to a friend that his goats kept disappearing—"things come down and carry the kids out of the corrals in broad daylight."

Each Friday night he extended a standing invitation for anyone who lived nearby to come up the hill for movies in his private theater and ballroom. Sometimes, his daughter Joan recalled, there would be upwards of 150 people, since there were no movie houses within miles. Burroughs was both host and projectionist. Diana Serra Cary, who began acting in films in 1921 as "Baby Peggy," remembers that when her family moved adjacent to the Tarzana ranch, her parents attended parties at the Burroughs estate.

Often the guests played a salacious game called "Murder." With all the lights in the house dark, and inhibitions loosened with bootleg liquor, guests groped their way through the house in search of the game's victim and perpetrator. Some fell into the ponds or pool, and Cary wrote in her book, *What Ever Happened to Baby Peggy?*, that when the lights came on at the end of the game naked couples were sometimes found in trysts in beds or bathtubs.

Shortly after Burroughs occupied the ranch, a stranger appeared with an ambitious plan for a new town at the base of the property. It would have banks, a school, a city hall and a movie theater and would

The writer Edgar Rice Burroughs, then 59 years old, eloped in Las Vegas with his second wife—former actress Florence Gilbert Dearholt—in 1935.

be called the city of Tarzana. Burroughs sneered that the name "sounds like a steamboat" and sent the stranger away. But in 1922, sensing the time was right, Burroughs himself announced plans to offer for sale lots of nearly an acre for a colony of artists. Potential buyers were required to apply to Burroughs for his approval and were expected to share his love of the hills and the Valley—"of our gorgeous sunsets, of the flowers and birds, and of all outdoors," he declared in a full-page ad in the *Times*. The colony would be called Tarzana.

He promised to hand everyone who came to look personal copies of his pamphlet "The Story of Tarzana." Interest was scant. He later admitted that the tone of the ads turned off buyers. In the fall of 1923 he dropped the artist colony conceit and turned over the promotion of Tarzana to a local real estate agent. Ads promised a big barbecue with the movie Tarzan, Elmo Lincoln, in attendance and the giveaway of a new Ford. But Lincoln didn't show up, and Burroughs grumbled that "the guy who won the Ford didn't buy a lot." While the subdivision enterprise languished, Burroughs offered the ranch to studios as a movie location.

In need of money, Burroughs sold 120 acres to help establish El Caballero Country Club, and he became the club's managing director. His former hilltop residence, the old hacienda of Gen. Otis, was to be the clubhouse. Burroughs wanted El Caballero with its two courses and polo field to be the most exclusive club on the West Coast, but interest lagged.

He resigned his involvement and lived for a time in Los Angeles; then, in 1926, he built a seven-room English-style cottage at 5046 Mecca Avenue, back on his old ranch but at the foot of the knoll where his former hacienda stood.

Burroughs became an avid booster, coining the optimistic slogan "Tarzana, Gateway to the Sea," which referred to the hopes of the community's promoters to pave Reseda Boulevard through the mountains to Sunset Boulevard as quick access to the beach. On December 11, 1930, the community secured its own post office under the name Tarzana. His other cause, besides promoting Tarzana, was to protect the deer, rabbits and birds on his land from hunters. He published anti-hunter diatribes in his *Tarzana Bulletin* under the nom de plume Normal Bean.

When he returned from an overseas tour as a World War II correspondent, Burroughs moved to 5565 Zelzah Avenue in Encino, where he died in bed on March 19, 1950, while reading the

In the 1922 pitch for his Tarzana art colony, Burroughs turned off would-be buyers by demanding they share his idyllic vision.

The Tarzana pitch

Writer and rancher Edgar Rice Burroughs pitched his subdivision of Tarzana with a different appeal than the other colonies around the Valley. His promised the freedom of nonconformity, as long as you fit in with him.

"Let me tell you the sort of colony I hope to see grow up around my home," he wrote in an ad. "A colony of self-respecting people who wish to live and let live—who will respect the rights and privileges of their neighbors, and mind each his own affairs… a colony of artists, whether they express themselves through the medium of pictures, books, flowers or vegetables; furniture, drugs, plumbing, poetry or the screen. If you are such an artist… I will be glad to receive your application."

Sunday comics. More than 40 million *Tarzan* books had been sold—yet the branch city library in Tarzana refused for years to carry his books, declaring that they were not literature. Nonetheless, during his memorial service, every business in Tarzana closed its doors from 2 to 3 p.m. His ashes were buried beneath a black walnut tree in the front yard of the Burroughs family offices, which remain at 18354 Ventura Boulevard.

CHAPTER 6

Hooray for Valleywood

Film legend D.W. Griffith directed battle scenes in *The Birth of a Nation* in the foothills on the Valley side of the Santa Monica Mountains. The film opened in 1915.

84

The first filmmakers to come to the Valley, soon after the turn of the 20th century, were attracted by its versatile terrain and authentic-looking western locations. The weather was also a plus: Compared with New York or even Hollywood, it was more predictably sunny, a crucial advantage since every frame of film had to be exposed in natural sunlight.

Directors especially favored the crumbled-down mission near San Fernando as a backdrop for their productions. When D.W. Griffith brought Biograph Pictures to Los Angeles in January 1910—with a company that included future film stalwarts Lillian Gish, Mary Pickford, Mack Sennett and Lionel Barrymore—he used the mission ruins and surrounding grassland for *Over Silent Paths,* the story of a pioneer miner and his daughter who journey to California by covered wagon. The following year, Griffith's company returned to "the San Fernando desert," as his wife Linda complained, to camp out with cowboys for *The Last Drop of Water.* They built a mock western town on the Valley floor for *The Battle at Elderbush Gulch,* a two-reeler about pioneers doing battle with Indians and sandstorms.

So long as the actors and crew could withstand blazing summer days without natural shade, the

This film crew was part of the Famous Players-Lasky production company, one of the first to shoot movies in the Valley. The Lasky ranch sprawled along the river between Burbank and the mouth of the Cahuenga Pass.

Valley could pass for prairie or savanna, old Rome or, especially, the American West. Plenty of real cowboys and ranch hands were around and willing to work a few days as extras. Directors liked hiring sun-darkened Mexicans and Japanese to add realism to scenes, although ranchers groused that the easy money paid by the film companies made it more difficult to get workers to do hard field labor after the cameras departed.

Over time, the movies came to define the Valley as much as new towns and agriculture did. Many of the biggest early screen stars made the Valley their home. Thousands of films were shot on location in the hills and among the ranches and neighborhoods. On the list are classics like *Casablanca* and *It's a Wonderful Life,* as well as hundreds of B-movies, none more forgettable than a World War II western made by Republic Studios and worth mentioning for two reasons. It featured popular cowboy singer Roy Rogers' first onscreen kiss—to Jean Porter, not his future wife, Dale Evans—and it had a catchy title. From Variety's review on August 23, 1944: *"San Fernando Valley* will be pleasant entertainment for Roy Rogers fans…but it is just about time for somebody to give screenwriters an ultimatum to turn out decent material or get out of town."

The early days

The first established studio in Valleywood opened its doors in December 1912 on the Oak Crest Ranch, in a crook of the Santa Monica Mountains at the mouth of Cahuenga Pass. The Los Angeles River flowed through the studio lot. Universal, as it came to be called, included numerous makeshift stages and a herd of long-horned cattle, and it provided work for hundreds of silent-film actors and extras. The studio, which grew to absorb the Taylor ranch and other nearby spreads, took the name Universal City on July 10, 1913. The German-born film distributor who headed Universal, Carl Laemmle, said the studio would operate as an unofficial municipality, with residents voting for a mayor and other officials. In the first election, more than 700 people cast votes, electing actress Laura Oakley as the county's first female chief of police. She carried badge number 99 issued by the Los Angeles Police Department, according to film historian Marc Wanamaker.

Universal City opened formally on March 15, 1915, with a boisterous party and barbecue attended by upwards of 10,000 people. A poster declared it the "world's only movie city…the strangest place on earth…an entire city built and used exclusively for the making of motion pictures." It was a new kind of studio, with dozens of stages and theme sets plus barracks, shops, commissaries, hospitals, tennis courts, a school and a menagerie of wild lions, tigers, bears and pythons. The residents lived in cottages or in teepees on the grounds. The public was invited to pay 25 cents for a bleacher seat to watch movies being made. As years went by, passersby got used to seeing impromptu stunts performed outside the Universal gate by would-be actors hoping to be noticed. Cowboys did horse tricks, others showed off their fast draw and all comers displayed their knife-throwing prowess. "It was all for a purpose," veteran cameraman Karl Brown noted in his autobiography. "Someone might see them from a front-office window—even Uncle Carl himself—after which a bored assistant might step out, crook his finger at the lucky one, say 'You,' and that lucky someone would be sure of a day's work and a free lunch."

Movie history of another kind had already been made a mile or so downriver, on a wide slope where the Forest Lawn Hollywood Hills memorial park is now. There D. W. Griffith had filmed his silent Civil War epic, *The Birth of a Nation.* The movie was far longer than customary—three hours instead of 15 or 30 minutes—and broke the rules for how to shoot action scenes.

Money was tight, but Griffith dreamed large. He was the first director to place cameras in trenches beneath stampeding horses. He staged big battle scenes among the scrub trees and grass along the river, and lit bonfires to film some of the mock warfare at night. The cast included John Ford, the future Oscar-winning director, who portrayed a Ku Klux Klansman. Presidential assassin John Wilkes Booth was played by Raoul Walsh, a future director and Valley landowner.

When *The Birth of a Nation* premiered in February 1915, it was hailed as a breakthrough that established cinema as art and Griffith as the art's first master. It was also embroiled in controversy. Griffith was a Southerner, and the film became his personal attempt to spin the historic record on the Civil War and Reconstruction—"only the winning side in a war ever gets to tell its story," he had told the company one night, swearing them to secrecy. He chose to treat the Klan as a heroic outfit saving the South's gentlemen and belles from the indignities of life with freed slaves, rather than as terrorists hiding behind white sheets and hoods. Today the film is a classic, which makes it widely available as a video rental to anyone curious to gaze at the Valley landscape of the era.

Griffith himself became smitten with the Valley, and he bought a ranch against the foothills of the San Gabriels, northeast of San Fernando. The spread became a hangout for Lillian Gish and other old friends, who gathered on Sundays under the fruit trees or on the screened-in patio, reading Shakespeare and Dickens and musing about the issues of the day.

Cecil B. DeMille, another cinema legend in the making, came to the Valley in January 1914 to shoot wild West scenes for *The Squaw Man,* released the following month as the first full-length motion picture made in "Hollywood." A rock quarry near the town of Roscoe provided the location. "There wasn't a house anywhere," DeMille wrote in his notes, according to film historian Wanamaker. Later, DeMille's Lasky-Famous Players company leased several hundred acres along the river east of Cahuenga Pass, a site that became known in Valleywood as the Lasky Ranch. On location there, DeMille began to wear his trademark high leather boots "as a protection against snakes, scorpions, cactus or poison oak," he later explained. It was also there that DeMille glanced at a rubbish fire started by workmen and saw an official-looking document in the flames. He pulled out and saved what turned out to be a lost copy of the first U.S. census of the city of Los Angeles, taken in 1850.

Cecil B. DeMille, shown here in 1914, came to the Valley that year to film scenes for *The Squaw Man.*

Mogul refuges

After Cecil B. DeMille died in 1959, his Paradise Ranch in Little Tujunga Canyon was donated to the Hathaway Home for Children. Since 1968, the old hangout where the director entertained his friends has housed Hathaway Children's Village for emotionally disturbed and abused youngsters.

D. W. Griffith's ranch tucked in the hills of Sylmar met a different fate. In the 1940s and 1950s, the land supported a herd of reindeer belonging to local developer Fritz B. Burns. After the herd was sold off or donated to zoos, the ranch was developed as an industrial park adjacent to San Fernando Airport, a small airstrip that was also a popular spot for weekend swap meets. The airport and the ranch are long gone, and the only remaining evidence of Griffith's hangout is a plaque mounted at 12841 Foothill Boulevard.

The Warner Brothers studio in Burbank, seen here in 1941, began as First National Studios. Beyond the river is the filming site for *The Birth of a Nation*.

In 1916 DeMille sent his attorney ahead to check out a remote ranch for sale in Little Tujunga Canyon. The lawyer was driving back down the canyon when he ran into DeMille. Go back, his lawyer advised, "there's nothing there but sagebrushes. It's the wildest, most terrible place you ever saw in your life." But DeMille relished the isolation, purchased the ranch and named his haven Paradise Ranch. He built cabins and a redwood guest house in which the limbs of two giant oaks served as pillars in the living room. An expensive Wurlitzer Hope-Joacs pipe organ, the largest organ for home use ever built at the time, was later installed so composers could work on movie scores, beginning with *The Ten Commandments.* Paradise Ranch became DeMille's retreat from Hollywood. He rendezvoused there with his mistress, actress Julia Faye; other visitors included H. G. Wells, Gary Cooper and Charlton Heston. Male guests who accepted DeMille's weekend invitations to the remote canyon were expected to bring black trousers and to dress for dinner in cummerbunds and silk Russian shirts he had placed in their closets.

Motion pictures fast became the Valley's third big industry, behind ranching and subdividing. First National Studios moved in 1926 onto farmland that had belonged to David Burbank, the town's founder. Within a few years the studio became Warner Brothers. Also in 1926, work began on converting a lettuce ranch along Ventura Boulevard into a studio for Mack Sennett, who had made his reputation on the Keystone Kops comedies, and producer Al

Many western scenes were shot at the rugged Iverson location ranch in the Santa Susana Mountains near Chatsworth.

Christie. Studio City, as the developers called it, would cover almost 500 acres and include residential subdivisions and businesses. Maxwell Terrace, at Ventura and today's Laurel Canyon boulevards, became the first housing development in the area. The Sennett studio lot later turned into Republic Pictures, home of the movie cowboys Gene Autry and Roy Rogers, as well as of John Wayne—and remains today a busy TV production studio. Columbia Pictures opened a location ranch near Warner Brothers in 1936. Walt Disney moved his small animation studio into Burbank in 1938, constructing the main building oversized so that, some said, if the studio venture failed the property could

be turned into a hospital.

With land plentiful, filming ventured off the studio lots to large location ranches. Warner Brothers' ranch in Woodland Hills and Calabasas grew to cover 2,800 rugged acres of oak trees and rocky grassland. Harry Warner, one of the studio chiefs, used a corner of the ranch to raise thoroughbred horses. No location was busier than the Iverson Ranch, set amid the rocks of Santa Susana Pass. More than 2,000 motion pictures and perhaps hundreds of early television episodes were shot on Karl Iverson's spread after its craggy canyons and picturesque boulder fields were discovered by location scouts.

Chatsworth Reservoir stood in as the Sea of Galilee in the 1950s, while Paris' Notre Dame cathedral was re-created at the RKO location ranch in Encino.

The Iverson was notorious among the actors for heat and dust—and for rattlesnakes. Lillian Gish said that in the spring actors were given a vial full of poison antidote in case they were bitten. "I'd say about 90% of all the cowboy movies were made on this ranch," Sunset Carson, who performed in 60 westerns, told the *Times* at a reunion of stunt men in 1985, after the construction of the Simi Valley Freeway through the ranch had virtually shut down filming. Roy Rogers, who made his first and last films at the ranch, and the family of former child actress Shirley Temple each offered to buy the Iverson, but much of the acreage was subdivided. Townhouses cover the old main entrance off Santa Susana Pass

Road. The Garden of the Gods, a remarkable grove of rock outcroppings where hundreds of film scenes were shot, was preserved by the efforts of the Santa Susana Mountains Conservancy.

Another location ranch covered 110 acres of farmland in Encino west of Balboa Boulevard and south of the river. The RKO studio ranch, opened in 1929, had New York streets, mock mansions, an airplane hangar and a Moroccan marketplace. A herd of black-faced sheep grazed on the open fields between sets and kept the grass in check. No film ever required disguising the Valley as much as the production at RKO's ranch of *It's a Wonderful Life,* the Frank Capra Christmas classic with Jimmy Stewart as

a suicidal banker who rediscovers the joy of life. Craftsmen worked for two months to build Bedford Falls, the film's mythical town, on the lot. The town's Main Street was planted with 20 large Encino oaks. For autumn in Bedford Falls, the leaves were knocked off the trees. Before winter scenes, crews coated the trunks and limbs with white plaster. The famous snow scenes where Stewart, as George Bailey, runs in the snow were filmed outside on a hot June day in 1946. The entire "town" was covered in artificial snow, using gypsum, plaster and crushed ice. The ranch closed down in 1953—the site is now suburban homes and soccer fields.

A young Howard Hughes tries filmmaking

Dozens of stunt pilots and daredevils found their way to the San Fernando Valley in 1928 to work on an audacious film project for a novice producer barely old enough to buy himself a drink. Howard Hughes knew almost nothing about making movies, but he had one quality even the gruffest sky jockey could admire in a boss: He was a free-spending multimillionaire, having inherited his family's Texas tool business.

Hughes spent the unprecedented sum of $4.2 million on *Hell's Angels,* a tale of World War I aviators. Insisting on strict authenticity, he assembled the world's largest private air force—a fleet of 87 Sopwith Camels, Fokkers and other biplanes that had seen combat over Europe. He hired "practically every stunt flyer and ex-war ace in America," American Cinematographer magazine said. No film had ever been attempted on such a grand scale, but as Hughes told his longtime confidant Noah Dietrich, "I'll do whatever it takes to be the greatest movie producer in Hollywood history."

After more than a year of shooting, the young director's inability to complete the film amused Hollywood. *Hell's Angels,* reported Photoplay magazine, "has had the cinema industry gossiping, scoffing, laughing up its sleeve…doubting, amazed, astonished, goggle-eyed and simply flabbergasted."

The climactic scene required the simulated crash of a German bomber. Pilot "Daredevil Al" Wilson agreed to fly, and a mechanic named Phil Jones volunteered to lie inside the fuselage releasing smoke. At 7,000 feet over Pacoima, Wilson put the big Sikorsky into a dive as the cameras rolled. Pilots in the camera planes watched in horror as the bomber failed to pull up. Wilson parachuted safely, but Jones was still on board when the

The German base in *Hell's Angels* was built—and bombed —in the hills near Chatsworth.

plane slammed into an orchard near Terra Bella Street and Haddon Avenue. Two pilots also died in crashes during the production.

Hughes neared completion in March 1929, but while he had shot *Hell's Angels* as a silent film, the talkie era had begun. Rather than work with his leading lady's Norwegian accent, Hughes reshot all the dramatic scenes with an unknown actress, 19-year-old Jean Harlow. He exploited her youth and sexuality with skimpy clothes and provocative lines such as, "Would you be terribly shocked if I slipped into something more comfortable?"

Hell's Angels finally premiered on June 30, 1930, with a festive spectacle that Hollywood talked about for years. A formation of warplanes flew in from the Valley and staged dogfights over Grauman's Chinese Theatre, while uniformed Marines kept the large crowds in check. When the last reel ended, the audience stood and applauded.

Hughes, then 24, was the Hollywood player he wanted to be. But his wife had left him, he suffered a mental breakdown and began drinking heavily, a crash had left him disfigured—and according to Noah Dietrich, the movie lost $1.5 million. Hughes came to rue his obsession, telling a magazine in 1932 that "making *Hell's Angels* by myself was my biggest mistake."

He made more movies, but his passion switched to designing fast airplanes. He established Hughes Aircraft in a Glendale garage and set numerous flight records. His company became the mainstay of an empire that later included Trans World Airlines and RKO Pictures, with Hughes as the world's richest and most mysterious globetrotting recluse until his death in 1976.

Young Valleywood couples in the 1940s congregated at the Chatsworth ranch of Lucille Ball and Desi Arnaz.

The Valleywood colony

Stars in the early days of Hollywood tended to work for a single studio, so it was convenient for actors connected to Warners or Universal or Republic to reside in the Valley. Others were drawn to the Valley for its plentiful ranches, polo fields and open land. Actor Gary Cooper lived on 10 acres in Van Nuys. Cowboy star Tom Mix had a ranch at Canterbury Avenue and Osborne Street in Arleta.

Until John Wayne moved to Orange County after contracting lung cancer, his family lived on five lush rolling acres at 4750 Louise Avenue in Encino. Laurel and Hardy, the comedy duo, had a neighborhood theater where they tried out material, the Fun Factory at 14155 Magnolia Street in Van Nuys.

The Valleywood colony, then as now, mostly attracted young families who favored a life filled with backyard barbecues and babies outside the swirl of Beverly Hills. Lucille Ball was 28 and Desi Arnaz, her bandleader husband, just 23 when they paid $16,900 for a ranch house and five acres behind a white plank fence at 19700 Devonshire Street, in orange groves between Northridge and Chatsworth. They dubbed it Desilu Ranch, bought a station wagon and adopted a pack of dogs and six cats. Desi planted fruit trees and built an extra suite for parties that also served as his home in exile when the couple fought, which they did often. One morning, Lucy got up at dawn and in a rage used a hammer to smash every window in the station

Francis Lederer at his Canoga Park stable in 1963.

Mayor Dracula

Francis Lederer was born in Prague in 1899 and starred in his first American film, *The Pursuit of Happiness*, in 1934 with Charles Ruggles and Joan Bennett. He played romantic leads and took a turn as Dracula in *The Return of Dracula* in 1958. In the 1930s Lederer built an ornate hacienda atop a ridge on his ranch west of Canoga Park, the community where he served as the honorary mayor for many years. The house and his former stable built of rocks along Sherman Way have been designated as Los Angeles cultural heritage landmarks. When he died in 2000 at the age of 100, Lederer was still teaching acting part time in the Valley.

wagon. They also made up with style. On her thirtieth birthday, Desi sent Lucy to town to do some shopping. When she returned in late afternoon, she traversed the long driveway off Devonshire to find a Latin combo leading 40 friends in "Happy Birthday." Floating white gardenias covered the pool.

Chatsworth and Northridge were still fairly remote outposts in the early 1940s, and socializing centered around quiet evenings at home. The regulars for bridge and gin rummy at Desilu included neighbor-actors such as William Holden, Gordon McRae and Francis Lederer, a matinee idol who reigned over a corner of the west Valley from his hacienda atop a ridge beside Sherman Way. Desi's musicians often showed up for a good time as well. "We celebrated Halloween, birthdays, new puppies, salary raises: anything was pretext for a party," Ball wrote in her autobiography, "Love, Lucy."

After-dinner talk often turned to the nuances of planting and irrigating. Many Valleywood land barons fancied themselves real dirt-under-the-fingernails ranchers, but the results seldom matched the image. When World War II began, Desi brought in 300 baby chicks, roosters named Saint Francis, Saint George and Saint John, a pig and a heifer. The chickens all died, despite Lucy keeping them warm in the den on cold nights, and the calf was sent away after crashing through a window. The orchard contained 250 orange trees, but the fruit was too sour to eat. Lucy calculated that the vegetables they grew ended up costing about nine dollars a serving in water, fer-

A lost masterpiece

The most extensive private art collection in the Valley—as well as one of its most architecturally celebrated homes—belonged to an eminence of the 1930s movie colony. Josef von Sternberg, the Austrian-born director of such films as *The Blue Angel* and *Shanghai Express*, owned a ranch in citrus country between Northridge and Chatsworth with a house fashioned of glass and steel and surrounded by a 16-foot moat with drawbridge.

Modernist architect Richard Neutra designed the house in 1935 so that the master bedroom opened onto a rooftop pool stocked with tropical fish, and a drip system cooled the living room with "artificial rain." Von Sternberg could look from his bedroom through glass to the open living room below, and enjoyed views of the Santa Susana Mountains and across the orchards and horse ranches of the west Valley.

He cluttered his home and 36-acre estate with paintings, drawings, sculptures and lithographs. When his collection later went on display at the Los Angeles County Museum of Art, it included works by Picasso, Matisse, Modigliani, Renoir, Seurat and Gaugin.

The "Von Sternberg Home" at 10000 Tampa Avenue became one of Neutra's most admired local works. The home was purchased in 1944 by the writer Ayn Rand, whose novel *The Fountainhead* had an outspoken architect as its protagonist. She lived there while in Hollywood for the making of the movie based on her book and while writing *Atlas Shrugged*.

Two years after Neutra's death in 1970, the home was demolished to make way for a subdivision.

Of all his works in the Valley, Richard Neutra's Von Sternberg home is missed the most.

Glamorous alums

Two of the most celebrated movie sex symbols of the 1940s and 1950s began storied romances while they were students at Van Nuys High School.

Before Howard Hughes cast her as Rio in the "sex western" *The Outlaw,* Jane Russell grew up a tomboy, roaming her family's La Posada ranch on Sherman Way near Woodman Avenue. At Van Nuys High she caught the eye of football star Bob Waterfield. In her autobiography, Russell describes how she resisted his urgings to make love until her graduation night—and 18th birthday—when she took her man to the dairy barn where she had played in the haystacks as a girl. By the time they were married five years later, Waterfield was known as the star quarterback for UCLA and was on his way to becoming the city's first homegrown pro sports hero, leading the Los Angeles Rams to their only championship in 1951.

Hughes exploited Russell's busty, ravenhaired appeal so much that censors held up release of *The Outlaw* for several years. Even now, the uncut version is unavailable. Later, in *Gentlemen Prefer Blondes,* Russell played the brunette alternative to another sensation out of Van Nuys High, Marilyn Monroe. As a teenager named Norma Jeane Baker, she lived with a fos-

ter parent on Odessa Avenue. To avoid being sent back to an orphanage, she accepted the courting of a neighbor, Jim Dougherty, a night-shift fitter at Lockheed who took her on outings to Pop's Willow Lake. They were married on June 19, 1942, three weeks after Baker turned 16. The couple moved into a studio apartment at 4524 Vista del Monte in Sherman Oaks.

After Dougherty signed on with the Merchant Marine, Baker took a job inspecting parachutes at Radioplane, a war plant in the Valley. An Army photographer under the command of Capt. Ronald Reagan snapped a sexy picture of her at work that caught an agent's eye. An American icon was born. Dougherty was soon out of the picture, and Marilyn Monroe left the Valley behind.

tilizer and tending. Lucy and Desi had two children and lived on the ranch until 1955, well into their television fame as the stars of the "I Love Lucy" program, before moving to Beverly Hills.

Another pair of stars who tried their hand at ranching were Clark Gable and Carole Lombard. After he finished shooting *Gone With the Wind* in 1939 and received a divorce, they were married and moved onto a 25-acre ranch in the Encino hills that had been a weekend retreat for director Raoul Walsh. The neighbors included studio mogul Darryl F. Zanuck and singer Al Jolson. Gable and Lombard were

Marilyn Monroe and Jane Russell, rivals in *Gentlemen Prefer Blondes,* left their marks in cement at Grauman's Chinese Theatre in Hollywood.

Clark Gable and Carole Lombard enjoyed riding horses on their Encino Ranch—and cheering on the ponies at the Hollywood Park race track. After *Gone With The Wind*, they were Hollywood's glamour couple.

Hollywood's most glamorous It couple, the hottest male lead in the country and a female comedic star nominated for an Oscar for *My Man Godfrey*.

The ranch came with a two-story Connecticut-style house, stables for nine horses, a hay barn, workshop and garage, 250 citrus trees and shady eucalyptus and peppers. The lovebirds gave each other horses—a sorrel show horse called Sonny for Gable and a bay polo pony named Melody for Lombard. She wore pigtails and grubby clothes to work on the property, and took shooting lessons so she could go hunting with the boys. But nights were elegant—linen napkins, Waterford crystal and antique flatware were her style. She also enjoyed driving the yellow Cadillac Gable had given her.

Gable bought a Caterpillar tractor and joined the citrus association, but after three poor seasons he gave up on the notion of turning a profit. They also tried raising hens, but the eggs cost about a dollar apiece to produce. If he couldn't succeed at growing, at least he could defend the castle. One afternoon a burglar managed to get into the house by bluffing the cook, took a pistol and hid overnight in the garage. The next morning, Gable caught the intruder inside the house and they scuffled. Gable came out on top, and the Van Nuys police were called. They arrived well after studio security officers.

Valleywood's celebrated marriage ended in tragedy on January 16, 1942. Lombard was returning from a war-bond promotion visit to her home state of Indiana when her TWA DC-3 crashed near Las Vegas,

A colony of Valleywood entertainers, among them Bing Crosby and Bob Hope, built homes at bucolic Toluca Lake, shown here in 1924.

Their Honors

In the 1930s and '40s, nearly every community in the Valley boasted of a resident celebrity who served as honorary mayor. The job usually meant appearing at parades and ribbon-cuttings and little else, though some took the post more seriously. Singer Al Jolson, the longtime honorary mayor of Encino, was active in founding the chamber of commerce and in other community affairs. Actor Jack Oakie at one time did double duty, in Northridge and West Van Nuys. Andy Devine, a gravelly voiced sidekick who acted in more than 150 films, presided for many years in Van Nuys.

The make-believe civic duty was thought

Jack Oakie, in his Northridge study in 1971, served as honorary mayor for two Valley communities.

to be good publicity for the actors and an image booster for the communities, even if some towns were forced to dig pretty deep for their brush with glamour. In a desperate act in 1939, faltering Girard anointed a Hollywood mystic and prophesier, Rev. Violet Greener, but after a few embarrassing months she begged off by mutual agreement.

The tradition continues today in communities with sizable celebrity populations. Asked about the rewards of his tenure as the honorary mayor of Encino, the late writer-performer Steve Allen quipped that it amounted to one thing: "free food."

decapitating Lombard and killing everyone on board, including her mother. The *Van Nuys News* ran an unusual front page tribute, saying: "Down deep in their hearts, those who had chatted with her over the back fence or across a garden row knew that Carole Lombard wanted more than anything else to be a model housewife and a good neighbor. And she was just that. She was a loveable person, just as much at home in blue denims and ginghams as she was in furs and jewels."

Gable seemed devastated. He began racing his motorcycle on the country lanes that crisscrossed the Valley, sometimes with actor friends Keenan Wynn, Andy Devine and Ward Bond, but often morose and alone. Lucille Ball feared that her friend was recklessly flirting with death. He would skid to a stop on her long driveway off Devonshire and pour out his grief for hours. "Carole and Clark did everything together," Lucy marveled. "That was a marriage." Gable joined the Army, then remarried and lived in the Encino house until his death on November 16, 1960; his widow, Kay, lived there into the 1970s.

The Golden age

In the 1930s and 1940s the Valley became widely known as a playground for celebrities. Many played cricket or polo—studio boss Zanuck had his own field in Encino—but the pursuit of choice was golf. Lakeside Country Club was the unofficial colony course, and the adjacent neighborhood of

Toluca Lake became for many the most chic address. Tales were told of the elusive Greta Garbo being sighted through hedges and a tipsy W. C. Fields battling swans while rowing from his rented quarters across the lake to the country club for his daily round of golf. Bing Crosby, who built a house at 4326 Forman Avenue, reigned for years as the Lakeside champion. He used to joke that Fields sat in his arbor by the lake sipping bourbon and practicing his comedy and juggling routines. He gave it up, Crosby said, because the geese hissed him.

Crosby later moved into Beverly Hills, but Bob Hope, his longtime film partner and golf rival, remained to become the dean of the Toluca Lake colony. Hope's compound on Moorpark Street looks no different than other suburban estates in the area, save for high hedges and iron gates. Behind the fence is a sprawling house with separate wings for Hope and his wife Dolores, a small golf course and offices for his archives and legendary computer catalog of jokes. The Hope compound was a center of parties and activity; Dolores prayed daily at St. Charles Borromeo Catholic Church on Lankershim and Moorpark, and there were often priests or dignitaries at the house working with her on projects.

Stars favoring a more rural existence put down stakes farther west. Northridge, which called itself the Horse Capital of the West, boasted dozens of working ranches and attracted celebrities who liked to ride or to breed horses. When she became estranged from her first husband, Frank Fay, 28-year-old Barbara

Bob Hope—entertainer and eminence of the Toluca Lake film colony—at one time was a major Valley landowner.

Stanwyck fled Brentwood for the hills of Northridge and went into the thoroughbred breeding business with her agent Zeppo Marx, one of the Marx Brothers comedy team. Their Marwyck Ranch covered 140 acres of pasture and barns along north Reseda Boulevard, on a gentle hill near where the pavement in the late 1930s ended at two-lane Devonshire Street. On a neighboring knoll lived actress Janet Gaynor and her husband, the designer Adrian. Stanwyck began dating actor Robert Taylor, a young rising star for MGM who enjoyed Saturday barbecues and swimming parties at the ranch. He soon joined the rush to the land and built his own house on a hill nearby.

After Stanwyck and Taylor married, they gave up the Valley for Beverly Hills. In 1940 she sold her share of the ranch to Marx and her Paul Williams-designed house at 18650 Devonshire Street to Jack Oakie, a comic actor who was nominated that year for the supporting actor Oscar for his role as the dictator Napolini in Charlie Chaplin's *The Great Dictator*. Oakie planted orange trees, raised Afghan hounds and hosted celebrity parties around his hilltop swimming pool, which enjoyed a view to the south across orchards and horse ranches. "Ah, those bacchanalian Sunday binges at your baronial manor—Northridge's last stand against civilization—the most palatial rabbit hutch west of the Picos," writer Seaman Jacobs scribed in a scrapbook presented to Oakie on his 70th birthday. The west Valley show business colony included gossip columnist Louella Parsons and even labor racketeer Willie Bioff, who controlled the Hollywood unions and who used a $100,000 payoff from the president of United Artists to purchase an 80-acre horse and alfalfa ranch, the Laurie A, at Shoup Avenue and Oxnard Street in Woodland Hills.

The heyday of Valleywood before World War II also included a bevy of important novelists who tried their hand at screenwriting. William Faulkner worked on *The Big Sleep* and *To Have and Have Not* at Warner Brothers. Nathanael West and F. Scott Fitzgerald toiled as studio writers in the late 1930s, and both resided in the Valley at the end of the decade. West crafted scripts for Republic Pictures, and later RKO, while writing his Hollywood novel

The Day of the Locust. After he married Eileen McKenney in December 1940, the couple moved into a brick house on two acres of walnuts and pears at 12706 Magnolia Boulevard in North Hollywood.

Fitzgerald's Valley months were more tortured. Already renowned for *The Great Gatsby* and *Tender Is the Night,* Fitzgerald did jobs for MGM while struggling to write his novel about Hollywood, *The Last Tycoon.* He rented a guest house at Belly Acres, the Encino realm of comic actor Edward Everett Horton. From his manor house on a little rise on Amestoy Avenue, Horton kept a suspicious eye peeled on his famous alcoholic tenant in the white guest cottage. After Horton was seen poking through the discarded gin bottles, Fitzgerald gave his secretary an unsavory task: She hid his bottles in burlap sacks, then once a week drove up Sepulveda Pass and dropped the bags into a ravine. Fitzgerald memorialized her furtive forays in a story, "Pat Hobby's College Days," published in Esquire.

The young secretary, Frances Kroll Ring, became the troubled writer's caretaker and confidante. He dictated and drank in his upstairs bedroom, often still in bed, while she typed in the office downstairs. At times, when he wanted to give up his ritual straight gin, Fitzgerald would try to drown the urge with Cokes, cigarettes and fudge, but he could never stay dried out for long. The Pat Hobby stories and piecework for Hollywood kept him in gin and paid Ring's $35-a-week salary. After a coronary scare, Fitzgerald left Encino for an apartment on Laurel

The boys club

After his service in World War II, director John Ford wished to honor 13 colleagues who did not return from overseas service in the Naval Field Photographic Reserve. The unit, which Ford commanded, was made up mostly of cinematographers, actors and writers such as Garson Kanin and Budd Schulberg who traveled the world chronicling the war on film.

Valleywood war veterans and their families enjoyed the backyard pool at the Field Photo Memorial Farm in Reseda.

Many others, including Ford's good friend John Wayne, tried to get in but were turned away.

Ford raised the money to purchase a 20-acre ranch at 18201 Calvert Street in Reseda for the use of Field Photo veterans and their families. Field Photo Memorial Farm and its bar, the Starboard Club, became their private postwar drinking hole and a center of Valleywood socializing around the pool and horse barn. The Christmas parties for Valleywood children were legendary.

Actor Harry Carey lay in state at the farm after his 1947 death. Funerals were common; John Wayne gave the eulogy at the 1960 service for Ward Bond.

Each Memorial Day, members dressed in their old Navy uniforms, stood in formation and recited the names of the fallen, muttering after each name, "died for his country." The farm closed in 1965.

Avenue in West Hollywood to be near his lover, gossip columnist Sheilah Graham. As his health deteriorated and climbing steps became an effort, he moved in with her.

On December 21, 1940, at the age of 44, Fitzgerald dropped dead of a heart attack on their floor. *The Last Tycoon* sat only half finished. The next day, Nathanael West and his new wife were driving home from a hunting trip in Mexico when he neglected to stop at an intersection outside El Centro. They were both killed in the crash, leaving the Magnolia Boulevard home full of unpacked moving cartons. West was 37, McKenney 27.

The golden age of Valleywood is memorialized at local cemeteries. Forest Lawn Hollywood Hills, built on the former Lasky movie ranch, is the final resting place for Lucille Ball, Bette Davis, Buster Keaton, Dorothy Lamour and Stan Laurel, among others.

The original Forest Lawn in Glendale contains the graves of many Valleywood personalities, among them Clark Gable and Carole Lombard, Humphrey Bogart, Mary Pickford, Spencer Tracy, W. C. Fields, Jack Oakie and Walt Disney. Engineer William Mulholland also is interred there.

Oliver Hardy, the stout half of the Laurel and Hardy comedy team, is buried at Valhalla Memorial Park in North Hollywood. Fred Astaire and his dance partner Ginger Rogers were laid to rest at Oakwood Memorial Park in Chatsworth. Walter Brennan and William Frawley are buried at the San Fernando Mission cemetery in Mission Hills.

Even the animals of Valleywood stars have their own place to be remembered. The Los Angeles Pet Memorial Park opened on a hillside pasture in Calabasas in 1928, and its grounds now contain 40,000 remains. Some of the more famous inhabitants include Scout, the Indian Tonto's horse in the "Lone Ranger" television series, and Petey the spotted dog from the *Our Gang* comedies. In Evelyn Waugh's satirical novel of Los Angeles funeral customs, *The Loved One*, the pet cemetery was dubbed the "Happier Hunting Ground."

CHAPTER 7

Happy Times, Troubled Times

This fly-in of Curtiss bombers at United Field, now Burbank Airport, was a crowd pleaser on Memorial Day in 1930. The Verdugo Mountains are in the background.

In 1930 the Valley reached a population of 51,000 and began a decade of enormous upheaval. Half of the people lived in North Hollywood, or in Van Nuys; Chatsworth had just 961 inhabitants, Encino merely 935. City folk in Los Angeles thought of the Valley as a place for enjoying weekend drives on country roads, gawking at movie sets and visiting odd roadside attractions like Monkey Island in Cahuenga Pass, which advertised that it had a thousand monkeys on display. At Bird Wonderland, a one-acre compound at 15640 Ventura Boulevard in Encino, one could buy a tropical bird or a python. At the top of Topanga Canyon, motorists who paid 10 cents could scan the width of the Valley through binoculars and telescopes.

Those with money played on lush golf courses and polo fields strung along the foot of the Santa Monica Mountains. Holly Heights Polo and Hunt Club, at Ventura Boulevard and Fulton Avenue, had two first-class polo fields, stables for 200 ponies and a two-story clubhouse with swimming pool. The Hollywood Cricket Club—headed by noted Anglophile actor Charles Aubrey Smith, with a membership that included movie stars Laurence Olivier, David Niven and Boris Karloff—played where the Los Angeles Equestrian Center is located today in Burbank. Weekend outings included boating at Glover's Twin Lakes park in the hills at the north end of Chatsworth, or at Lancaster's Lake in Sunland, or outdoor dances at the Garden of the Moon pavilion in Tujunga. In 1931 James A. (Pop) Gautier opened

Small lakes and fishing ponds provided recreation in the 1930s. This scene from a postcard shows Twin Lakes Park near Chatsworth.

Pop's Willow Lake alongside Big Tujunga Wash, in the area of today's Lake View Terrace. The resort had a spring-fed lake, canoes for rent, a dance pavilion, cafe, swimming beach and bathhouses.

The presence of movie colony glamour masked the real human toll of the Great Depression. Studios racked up huge losses, which at Warner Brothers meant directors and actors were pressured to churn out features on the cheap. The Johnston Organ and Piano Co. plant, the first factory in Van Nuys, became a Civilian Conservation Corps warehouse, maintained by the Army for supplying 23 youth camps in the Angeles National Forest. Relief camps opened at Roger Jessup County Park in Pacoima and in Griffith Park, and by 1934 an estimated 7,500 Valley men were working in some kind of public assistance job. In welfare offices and packing houses, Communist Party organizers were repeatedly arrested for handing out literature.

In Griffith Park, land beside the Los Angeles

The Van Nuys municipal building, a smaller version of the landmark Los Angeles City Hall, was built as a public work during the Depression.

River—originally a municipal prison farm and later a boys' camp—was rebuilt as a CCC base. Crews assigned to public works built trails, bathrooms and flood control channels and planted golf courses. On October 4, 1933, a crew at work on the Valley side of the park was trapped by a fast-moving wildfire, and an estimated 36 men died.

The era saw some progress as well. The eight-story, art deco municipal office building dubbed "Van Nuys City Hall" was designed by Peter K. Schabarum and erected in 1932 by the Works Progress Administration. Burbank's city hall was built and the Canoga Park post office on Sherman Way rose with a mural, *Palomino Ponies*, painted under the federal arts project by Maynard Dixon, an artist whose Depression works "represent a high point in the art of the mural," historian Kevin Starr wrote in *The Dream Endures*. Helen Lundeberg, another New Deal artist, designed large murals on the Canoga Park High School assembly hall tracing the progress of science through the ages. A mural by Barse Miller in the Burbank post office on Olive Avenue saluted the movies and the Valley's newest major industry—aviation.

Small airfields had sprouted amid the orchards and tomato fields as early as 1912. Grand Central Air Terminal opened in 1923 beside the river on the Valley side of Glendale with an air rodeo starring a young aviatrix named Amelia Earhart. Metropolitan Airport, the field that became Van Nuys Airport, opened in 1928 and attracted a factory of the Bach

Aircraft Co. Two years later United Airport opened in Burbank with a factory under the auspices of Boeing. For most of the rest of the century, the Valley would be a center of aircraft design and manufacturing.

In the middle of the 1930s, a highway carved through Sepulveda Canyon put the beaches and clubs at Ocean Park and Santa Monica in easy reach of the Valley. The road, long a dream of Valley boost-

The future looked bright for the contenders for San Fernando Valley Queen in 1939, including the future actress Jane Russell, second from left.

ers, featured a 655-foot-long tunnel bored under Mulholland Drive. The canyon that Portolá had climbed to discover the Valley now had a scenic highway that linked Van Nuys and San Fernando to the coast, but it had the effect of making Sepulveda

The Valley takes off

The first organized airfield in the Valley was a rutted, cactus-strewn dirt runway called Griffith Aviation Park, which opened May 12, 1912, on land Avenue and Sherman Way.

Grand Central, in Glendale, was the hub for airlines into Los Angeles in the 1930s. Its former

aerial daredevils, hobbyists and entrepreneurs who guessed that airplanes were more than a fad. Private investors opened Metropolitan Airport, the predecessor to Van Nuys, on December 17, 1928, with two intersecting grass runways and big plans. "Two and a half months ago this port was just a bean field, but we are not only building a permanent location for an airport but an airport city with industries, with homes for employees, with stores for their wants, with a hotel," Waldo Waterman, a noted flier who was the airport manager, told the crowd.

Metropolitan Airport, in 1930, was rejected as the first site of Los Angeles International. Today it is Van Nuys Airport.

land now occupied by the parking lot for the Los Angeles Zoo. Some early landing strips appear on old maps but leave no other traces—places such as Lloyd's Airport at the north end of Lankershim Boulevard, or Wilson Field at Vine-

terminal still stands in an industrial park off San Fernando Road.

The modern Valley's two busy airports, Van Nuys and Burbank, came into existence near the beginning of the Great Depression. They lured

United Field opened in Burbank on Memorial Day 1930 with a huge fly-in. Unique among local fields, United had five runways that radiated in varying directions, each 300 feet wide and 3,600 feet long, and soon attracted airline service. Boeing built planes on the field. Lockheed Aircraft had its own nearby airfield, but it took over the larger United field in 1940 and renamed it Lockheed Air Terminal. The facility is now known officially as the Burbank-Glendale-Pasadena Airport.

After the death of Jim Jeffries, his Burbank boxing barn was moved to the Knott's Berry Farm amusement park in Orange County.

Boulevard a busy truck route across the Valley. "Great double trucks rumbled down over Sepulveda from Wilmington and San Pedro and crossed towards the Ridge Route, starting up in low-low from the traffic lights with a growl of lions in the zoo," Raymond Chandler wrote in one of his Los Angeles detective stories.

The Valley remained a mostly peaceful place— on Labor Day weekend in 1936, not a single crime was reported. But the Valley was growing a residential culture. High school rivalries developed. In the

last football game of 1935, Van Nuys faced heavily favored North Hollywood. A senior halfback named Dale "Buck" Gilmore came through for Van Nuys, and the underdogs won 28-0. Gilmore, a champion track runner, went on to UCLA and played football in a backfield with future baseball great Jackie Robinson. "Buck was the first of the outstanding athletes from the San Fernando Valley," Pete Kokon, the ultimate local sports authority, said many years later. Also a graduate of Van Nuys High, Kokon began in 1937 to write about local sports for the *Van Nuys*

News and the *Valley Times*. He chronicled bowling tournaments, softball leagues and holes-in-one at the local golf courses in his "Kookin' with Kokon" column. He especially liked to write about the Thursday night fights at Jeffries Barn, a tradition begun in 1931 by the Valley's most famous sports celebrity in the first half of the century.

Jim Jeffries had retired as the undefeated world heavyweight boxing champion in 1904 to grow alfalfa in Burbank. But he returned to the ring to try to stop a black Texan, Jack Johnson, who had won the world heavyweight belt. Johnson didn't act like many whites thought blacks should—he was cunning and intelligent, and he enjoyed humiliating his opponents. Perhaps most threatening, he had married a white woman. In the blatant racism of the day, the call went out for a Great White Hope to defeat Johnson. "Jim Jeffries must emerge from his alfalfa farm and remove the golden smile from Jack Johnson's face," implored the author Jack London.

When the boxers met in Reno on July 4, 1910, Jeffries was three years older and 15 pounds heavier than the champ, and he had been out of the ring for six years, but he was the betting favorite. Unimpressed, Johnson toyed with his older rival, then knocked him out. The arena crowd stood mute, "readjusting things in their minds," an Associated Press writer observed. The news was flashed to 30,000 people waiting in Times Square in New York and to several thousand in front of the *Los Angeles Times* building. Anti-black riots erupted around the

Amelia and George

Amelia Earhart was the Valley's preeminent aviation celebrity, nearly as well known a flier as Charles Lindbergh. She was the first woman to fly the Atlantic as a passenger, and at the age of 34 she became the second person—after only Lindbergh—to pilot solo across the ocean, landing in Ireland. She held speed and altitude records, was a guest at the White House and received the Distinguished Flying Cross and France's Cross of Knight of the Legion of Honor.

Her marriage to George Palmer Putnam, the son of a New York book publisher, was anything but traditional. She accepted his proposal reluctantly, informing Putnam that there would be no "medieval code of faithfulness" between them and insisting, "Let us not interfere with each other's work or play." They moved into a ranch-style cottage her family purchased at 10042 Valley Spring Lane in the Toluca Lake film colony.

Attempting her most ambitious exploit, a circumnavigation of the globe in a Lockheed Electra, Earhart vanished in the South Pacific with navigator Fred Noonan on July 2, 1937. Putnam set up his own

search base in the Burbank hangar of stunt pilot Paul Mantz, Earhart's rumored lover, but the mystery of her disappearance has never been explained. The best guess is that her

Aviator Amelia Earhart struck a domestic pose in 1935, serving breakfast to her husband, George Palmer Putnam, at their new home in Toluca Lake.

plane simply went down in the ocean.

Putnam was to figure in a mystery of his own. In 1938 he published *The Man Who Killed Hitler*, by an anonymous author, then reported to police that he was being threatened by local Nazis. On May 12, Putnam later recounted, he was jumped in his Toluca Lake garage by two German-speaking men who slipped a sack over his head and drove him to a construction site in Bakersfield, where they dumped him with a warning to withdraw the book. After authorities became suspicious of his story, a grand jury found that "police have no evidence of a crime." Eventually the episode was dismissed as a publicity stunt, and Putnam quietly remarried and left town for the Eastern Sierra Nevada mountains. At the time of his death in 1950, the former publishing scion operated a motel in Death Valley.

Sepulveda Boulevard, shown here looking south from Magnolia Boulevard in 1939, was a heavily traveled state highway that helped link the two halves of California. A winding road and tunnel connected the Valley with the coast.

The numbers game

Several main boulevards across the Valley carried highway designations in the 1930s, before the freeways were built. Ventura Boulevard was U.S. 101, and San Fernando Road was known both as U.S. 6 and as state route 99. The other state routes were 7 (Sepulveda Boulevard), 118 (Devonshire Street), 159 (Lankershim Boulevard) and 134 (Alameda Avenue).

North Los Angeles in 1938 took the name Northridge, hoping to create a new identity and avoid confusion with North Hollywood. Girard changed its name to Woodland Hills in 1941.

country, killing 10 people. On his way back to Los Angeles, Jeffries conceded graciously that "I couldn't have beaten Johnson on my best day."

Jeffries retired again to his Burbank farm and, in 1931, converted his dairy barn at 2500 Victory Boulevard into a boxing arena. He acted as a trainer to young boxers and refereed the Thursday night fights.

War clouds

By 1940 the Valley's population had doubled again, to more than 112,000. The plain was still occupied mostly by small ranches and farms, with widely spaced country towns. But as the likelihood of another world war grew, aviation activity mushroomed. Factories began to spew out airplanes, and jobs became plentiful for designers and assemblers and welders.

Lockheed Aircraft, builder of the Electra, had moved from Hollywood to Burbank and established its own airfield at Five Points, where five major thoroughfares met. In 1938 Lockheed received its first defense order—from the British for Hudson bombers—and began adding to its force of 2,300 workers. Lockheed expanded and bought the original United Field, then known as Union Air Terminal, and renamed it Lockheed Air Terminal. It would remain the company's home base for more than four decades. By 1941 Lockheed and its sister Vega plant were serving 60,000 hot meals a day to workers in Burbank.

Lockheed assembly lines in Burbank geared up for war, working around the clock to turn out planes like these Lodestar transports for the Army. Lockheed also produced the famed P-38 pursuit plane.

On Friday, December 5, 1941, 25,000 people lined Van Nuys Boulevard to view the annual Van Nuys Christmas parade. A lazy weekend of holiday shopping was at hand, or so people thought. Around noon on Sunday, radios broadcast the shocking report that Japanese planes had bombarded Pearl Harbor in Hawaii, yanking America into World War II. By sundown, all private planes were grounded and an Army observation post with spotlights was in place at Metropolitan Airport in Van Nuys.

With hostilities declared against Japan, Germany and Italy, the Valley went into war mode. More than 3,000 volunteers turned out to join the Civilian Auxiliary Police, starting with Lou Costello, half of the Abbott and Costello comedy team. A call went out for men of "exceptional courage" to volunteer for a bomb squad, and Boy Scouts older than 14 were summoned to Van Nuys Elementary School to take training in first aid and fire suppression. The West Van Nuys Civic Club offered instruction in fighting fires, warning its members: "What Will You Do When an Incendiary Bomb Lands on Your Roof? Your House May Be a Japanese Target!" More than 100 station wagon owners, among them entertainers Buster Keaton and Robert Young, formed up as the First Evacuation Regiment. They met Tuesday nights at Warner Brothers and trained on weekends at the Warner movie ranch.

Airplanes groaned overhead on incessant training flights, and the occasional crashes into fields and mountain ridges made the war seem real. The 1st

Pursuit Group, which guarded Valley airspace, flew the Lockheed P-38, the fastest and, some would say, loudest planes in the Army Air Corps. Ranchers griped that the fighters disturbed horses and chickens, and studio moguls complained about the hindrance to filming. But after the squadron arrived at Grand Central in February 1942, crowds gathered beside the runway to watch pilots return from training missions. As part of the war effort, the 115th Observation Squadron of the California Air National Guard, housed at the dirt Griffith Park airstrip since 1927, shifted to Metropolitan Airport, which was redesignated Van Nuys Army Airfield, a training base for P-38s and P-61 "Black Widow" night fighters.

Camouflage netting painted to confuse enemy pilots was strung in Burbank over the Lockheed and Vega plants, which now employed more than 90,000 workers—nearly half of them women recruited out of kitchens and high schools for their first paying job assembling warplanes. These Rosie the Riveters worked in all the major plants and included a teenaged Van Nuys wife named Norma Jeane Baker, who was on the job at Radioplane when a photograph of her in sexy shorts launched her on a new career as Marilyn Monroe. As the Army draft stripped the plants of male workers, Lockheed also recruited high school boys who went on the "four-four plan"—four weeks of school, then four weeks of day shifts on the assembly line. School hours in the Valley were staggered so that buses could be used to ferry both plant workers and students.

The war was excruciating for families with loved ones in combat, but for many the most hurtful impact was the rationing of tires, gasoline, sugar, meat and butter. Due to the limits on tires and gas, Adohr Milk Farms apologized to customers that it

Blackout

On the night of December 10, 1941, three days after the Japanese attack in Hawaii, sirens and radio broadcasts signaled the first full blackout of Los Angeles. State troops and police patrolled Valley streets, ordering merchants to shut down their businesses. Opportunists tried to sell supposedly official "blackout cloth" for windows, until officials advised residents that any dark or heavy material would do the job.

War jitters made people a little crazy. Singing radio cowboy Stewart Hamblen, who lived on Valleyheart Drive in Studio City, went out one night and shot out a half-dozen streetlights on Coldwater Canyon Boulevard, explaining later, "I was afraid I was going to be bombed." Unmoved, the Department of Water and Power billed him $49.12.

had to drop daily home delivery and go to alternate-day service. "Mrs. Adamson and I started Adohr [her name, Rhoda, spelled backwards] out here in San Fernando Valley back in 1916. Now we have 3,500 cows producing milk for a lot of folks who depend on us," owner Merritt Adamson said in ads.

The front page of the *Van Nuys News and Green Sheet* reflected the remoteness of the war to daily life. The March 27, 1942, page downplayed war news but listed the breed, sex and markings of nine stray dogs, and also reported that a North Hollywood tailor who cursed in the presence of women and children had been booked for disturbing the peace. The "Meet Your Neighbor" feature introduced actors Don Ameche (4875 Encino Avenue) and Dana Andrews (14527 Killion Street). The previous week, featured neighbors had been comedians Stan Laurel (20213 Strathern Street) and Oliver Hardy (14227 Magnolia Boulevard).

The paper warmed up, though, to the hysteria over residents of Japanese, German or Italian ancestry. "Enemy aliens" were required to surrender shortwave radios and cameras, be home by 8 p.m. and stay away from airports and other sensitive areas. Suspicions ran high. A Japanese gardener who threatened his employer in a dispute was booked not for assault but on suspicion of espionage. The Campagna brothers, who ran a cafe on San Fernando Road, were arrested even though one had moved here from Italy 38 years and the other 20 years before.

Half or more of the 3,177 people of Japanese

The February 19, 1942, order incarcerating so many Valley families did not merit a big headline in the *Van Nuys News,* but the paper bannered state Assemblyman Everett G. Burkhalter's demand to reduce the $50 to $94 a month in subsistence pay promised to those Japanese Americans who lost their homes and farms. "In my opinion these enemy aliens

Hoping to mislead enemy bombers, camouflage netting was hung above Valley war plants—even parking lots as here at Lockheed Air Terminal in Burbank. The top was painted to resemble farm fields.

descent in the Valley were American citizens. Some had worked vegetable and flower farms or picked oranges as trusted employees for decades. (In World War I, the list of dead from Pacoima included a Japanese immigrant named Ito Osugo.) After Pearl Harbor, foreign nationals and Japanese Americans alike were urged by authorities to continue farming to assist the war effort. But official surveyors visited every Japanese-run farm in January 1942 and took note of all residents, their histories and crops being grown. The original reports, discovered in dusty archives in 1999 by *Times* reporter T. Christian Miller, show that many Japanese had been farming in the Valley for decades and willingly cooperated with the war authorities.

After President Franklin D. Roosevelt signed Executive Order 9066, authorizing the rush military "evacuation" of all 112,000 Japanese Americans and "enemy aliens" on the West Coast, the Valley farms were emptied. Families were sent to live in inland internment camps with only the possessions they could carry. Children left behind friends and treasured toys, and their parents were forced to abandon homes and stores. It was war hysteria fueled by racism: There was no mass internment of American citizens of German or Italian heritage.

Before the 1942 internment order, authorities questioned farmers of Japanese descent, including those employed at the Valley ranch of *Times* publisher Harry Chandler.

should be paid no more than an Army private—$21 a month," Burkhalter fumed. He also urged that plans be scrapped for recreation facilities at Manzanar, the Eastern Sierra camp where enough locals were held to field a baseball team called the San Fernando Aces.

With the Japanese gone and huge numbers of men and women in military service or assembling airplanes, alarms went out for help picking crops. Housewives and boys over 16 were urged to work a few hours a day in the field, and office workers were pressured to spend their vacations helping the harvest "where they will find the work not only profitable, but healthful and invigorating." The 1943 tomato crop and the 1944 apricot crop were saved by housewives, high school girls and Mexican nationals housed in barracks in Reseda and San Fernando.

The war's reality became more visible after February 28, 1944, when the Army opened a sprawling hospital for maimed troops in the fields west of Van Nuys at Vanowen Street and Balboa Boulevard. Birmingham General Hospital, named for a veteran of the Spanish-American War, had beds for 1,000 wounded in single-story wooden wards linked by board sidewalks. Casualties came in waves off hospital ships docked in San Pedro, ferried to the Valley by train or in ambulance convoys. Desi Arnaz, the entertainer and husband of Lucille Ball, served his Army hitch at Birmingham, leading the morale effort there. Lucy and Desi staged their vaudeville act for patients, and celebrities such as Spencer

Women filled many traditionally male jobs during the war. These new gas jockeys worked at the Lockheed garage in 1942.

Tracy, Jack Benny, Gregory Peck and Fred MacMurray made appearances.

The first soldier to enlist from the Valley, Walter Stone of Roscoe, was also the first to be discharged when the war ended in Europe on May 8, 1945. As children sang "Holy God We Praise Thy Name," the original bell of Mission San Fernando Rey was rung on a live national radio broadcast. When the war ended on August 14—following the dropping of atomic bombs on Japan—shops closed and celebrations erupted in the streets. Church bells and honking horns announced the news. "I'm celebrating V-Day. My boy is coming home," slurred an intoxicated man as he pleaded not to be arrested. On Craner Avenue in North Hollywood, it took six LAPD officers and an M.P. to subdue a drunken couple who couldn't believe they would spend the end of the war in the lockup. The military policeman did his celebrating at Birmingham Hospital, thanks to a kick in the groin from the woman.

Ranchettes and ranchitos

The Valley at war's end remained more country than suburb, even though the population had swelled to 176,000. "I had no idea I even lived in Los Angeles," author and food writer Charles Perry recalled in a piece for the *Los Angeles Times Magazine* in 1990. "My home was a little farm town called Van Nuys. Whatever else they might have done, everybody on my street raised a couple of acres of wal-

nuts." But suburbia began to take hold. Commuters returning in the afternoon from downtown rode the Red Cars—the 5:10 Limited took 63 minutes to reach Van Nuys and Sherman Way—or sped along a new wide expressway through Cahuenga Pass, then onto Ventura Boulevard and home.

Raymond Chandler wrote: "There was nothing lonely about the trip. There never is on that road. Fast boys in stripped-down Fords shot in and out of the traffic streams, missing fenders by a sixteenth of an inch. Tired men in dusty coupes and sedans winced and tightened their grip on the wheel and ploughed on north and west towards home and dinner, an evening with the sports page, the blatting of the radio, the whining of their spoiled children and the gabble of their silly wives."

A 1945 article in the Atlantic Monthly by Gordon Kahn was even more scornful of this new Valley life. Kahn acknowledged something faintly exotic about the Valley—he reported seeing an elephant stacking wood on Sepulveda Boulevard—but he took issue with the conceit of real estate hucksters and other boosters.

"Every plot of ground that nourishes four walnut trees is called a ranch. Two trees and a patch of lawn, in the language of the San Fernando realtor, is known as a ranchette. One with a back yard, a barbecue pit, and a rabbit hutch is a ranchito," Kahn observed. The inhabitants of the Valley live well, "in a hedonistic sort of way. They are kept beautiful by 140 beauty salons, cosmetologists and scalp

POWs

Camp Griffith Park (on the site of today's Travel Town museum) held German, Japanese and Italian prisoners of war in 1942 and '43. Later some 350 German prisoners of war were brought to the Valley and assigned to help pick fruit. The head of the San Fernando Fruit Growers Assn. said they were good workers, "fast and efficient."

At least two of the POWs never got home—they died in 1945 when a truck driver speeding in thick fog overturned at Devonshire Street and Zelzah Avenue, throwing 30 prisoners to the pavement.

The prisoners' presence inspired a fad among schoolboys in the Valley: They began to wear jackets and sweaters with the letters "P.W." stenciled on the back, flouting the warnings of local officials that they could be shot by mistake.

Birmingham hospital

Birmingham Army Hospital was named for Brig. Gen. Henry Patrick Birmingham, a Brooklyn-born veteran of the Indian wars and of Spanish-American War campaigns in Puerto Rico and the Philippines.

After the war, the hospital provided the setting for actor Marlon Brando's first film, *The Men.* He played an angry, paralyzed veteran, alongside Jack Webb of "Dragnet" fame. The hospital's closure in 1950 was controversial since its population of 1,323 recovering Army veterans, many of them paraplegic, was transferred to Long Beach, far from family and friends in the Valley.

The abandoned site was considered for a state college, but instead the southern end of the grounds became the home of Birmingham High School. The northerly portion along Vanowen Street later became William Mulholland Junior High.

The final wartime medal ceremony at Birmingham Army Hospital drew a crowd in August 1945. The hospital faced Vanowen Street.

masseurs. They keep their skin and muscle in tone at 17 Turkish baths, five of which specialize in a rare miasma known as eucalyptus steam."

He counted only one branch library, but 59 liquor stores, 24 nightclubs and 43 interior decorators. Kahn reserved his greatest disdain for the rising popularity of the wood-paneled family rumpus room. "No home is too humble for one of these Ping-Pong shrines."

But Kahn held a decidedly minority view. The Valley had basked in some notoriety during the war; Birmingham was reputed to be the Army's poshest hospital, and movie stars were said to be everywhere. GIs especially had a pleasing image of the place, due more than anything to a Bing Crosby record that hit number one on the Billboard chart on April 29, 1944. "San Fernando Valley" was written by Gordon Jenkins, a Sherman Oaks composer who wrote many popular songs that he liked far better. "One night I had the hives and couldn't sleep," Jenkins recalled many years later in the *Times.* He got up, wrote the tune and sold it the next day. "It was a melody, if you can call it that, that people liked. Made more money than it really deserved."

For troops overseas it held out the promise of a happier life in an almost mythic place back home. "The strange thing is that in the song lyrics I never say anything good about the San Fernando Valley. All I say is, I want to go…. It could be a sewer," Jenkins said, after he had moved to Malibu.

In a national radio broadcast on June 29, 1944,

Suburbia began to appear during the war years. In this photo of the Sherman Woods development in Sherman Oaks, the view across the Valley takes in Newhall Pass, center.

Crosby clowned with fellow Valley resident Roy Rogers, joked about actor Andy Devine and his "big spread" out in the San Fernando Valley, then crooned the words that hundreds of thousands of Americans would take to heart:

Oh I'm packin' my grip and I'm leavin' today, cause I'm taking a trip California way

I'm gonna settle down and never more roam, and make the San Fernando Valley my home.

I'll forget my sins, I'll be makin' new friends where the West begins and the sunset ends.

'Cause I've decided where yours truly should be, and it's the San Fernando Valley for me.

CHAPTER 8

Welcome to Suburbia

Swimming pools fit in with the backyard lifestyle that grew in the postwar Valley. These models were on sale on Ventura Boulevard in Sherman Oaks in the late 1940s.

At the end of World War II a population spigot suddenly opened wide, splashing young couples through Cahuenga Pass to take root and germinate in the fertile Valley soil. They came from all over the country looking for a temperate climate and the promise of prosperity, as they did in every Southern California suburb. But the lure of the San Fernando Valley was different.

Nobody sang songs about Lakewood or Westchester. The Valley had studios, orange groves and the optimistic aura of a place where a soldier and his sweetheart could make up for lost time. No other place had film stars as the "honorary governor"

(Edward Everett Horton) and "honorary sheriff" (cowboy rider Montie Montana).

There was a glimpse of the future in the news that within a week of Japan's surrender, Fleetwater Pools finished its first custom swimming pool and began digging six others. "We are in the Valley to stay," the proprietor declared triumphantly. CBS and NBC praised the new suburb to their nationwide radio listeners, saying GIs liked the San Fernando Valley because, as NBC's Sam Hayes gushed, "it reminds them of their own hometown." Magazines joined in hyping the image. In the Valley one could ride horses, mingle with stars at the local Piggly

Where stagecoach riders used to eat dust, the Cahuenga Pass Parkway, shown here in 1948, made the Valley easy to reach. The Hollywood Freeway follows this route now—minus the streetcar tracks.

With veterans and their families sleeping outside due to a housing shortage, Basilone Homes opened in converted Army barracks on Glenoaks Boulevard near Pacoima.

Wiggly grocery and enjoy the good life that a Coronet writer called "the dizzy, ubiquitous mixture of Fifth Avenue and Main Street." On Ventura Boulevard, "one may find a glamour starlet in imported gabardine chatting earnestly with a chicken farmer in jeans."

So the writer exaggerated a bit. Malodorous dairies and turkey ranches still raised a stink beside new homes, and tractors threw up dust all day long. There were no sewers or freeways, and not many streetlights, hospital beds, police cars or fire trucks. Six hundred miles of roadway were still dirt, most of

the paved roads were narrow and the few wide boulevards were blocked with annoying frequency by long freight trains that rattled to a stop to unload lumber—or by herds of cattle and sheep on the move.

A solid job was required in order to join this new middle-class enclave, but the aircraft plants were cutting back, not adding on. Union tension ran high in the studios; violent rioting erupted on the streets outside Warner Brothers. Moreover, the suburban dream made no room for the 3,000 internees of Japanese ancestry who returned to the Valley to find their old lives extinguished. Not only had they lost their homes and possessions, but in some cases the land they had worked no longer existed as a farm. With housing extremely hard to find and the war's racial wounds an open sore, they were refugees in their own country. "It was very frightening. We didn't have any place to go, and we were broke," Harold Muraoka recalled in the Times in 1986. Where many landed first was in government trailer camps in Burbank (at Hollywood Way and Winona Avenue) and Sun Valley (at San Fernando Road and Olina Avenue).

Veterans without means didn't have it much better. Homeless veterans lived in tent cities in Burbank and in Big Tujunga Canyon, or in a village of surplus Quonset huts erected on the site of the decommissioned National Guard air base in Griffith Park. Rodger Young Village, named for a war hero who died in the Pacific, accommodated 1,500 families at 40 dollars a month for a furnished unit. Another subsidized housing project, using surplus barracks shipped in from Washington state, opened on Glenoaks Boulevard near Hansen Dam. Basilone Homes were named for Marine Gunnery Sgt. John Basilone, who held off a Japanese regiment before dying on Iwo Jima.

Still, a real estate man came back from Europe and reported breathlessly that Lloyd's of London regarded the San Fernando Valley as the best real estate investment market in the world. And perhaps it was, if you played the game right. Isaac Van Nuys had gotten $53 dollars an acre for half of the Valley in 1909. Heirs of Benjamin F. Porter sold the last 4,150 acres of untouched Porter Ranch land in 1962 and received $4,819 per acre. Six years later, Aetna Life and Casualty paid $48,000 an acre for Harry Warner's old thoroughbred ranch in Woodland Hills and turned it into the lucrative Warner Center development.

Growing pains

Full of postwar optimism, young newlyweds scraped together a few hundred dollars for down payments on two-bedroom, one-bath tract houses and spent their weekends planting greenery to distinguish their rectangle of suburbia from next door. Neighbors shared gardening tips and rotary lawn mowers, got together for bridge games and barbecues, and formed lifelong friendships.

Throngs filled the aisles and cash registers of the modern Valley Market Town when it opened in 1947 on Sepulveda Boulevard near Oxnard Street. The shopping center, first of its kind in the Valley, offered free baby-sitting and sterilized dog kennels with plenty of free parking, and the stars shopped alongside ordinary people. There was a quirky innocence to it all. Holiday magazine reported that Ventura Boulevard had become a "vast mechanized midway, part thoroughfare and part bazaar, whose weird miscellany epitomizes the valley." The boulevard had Mildred Alexander's Motel for Cats, each feline housed in a little bungalow and provided with a customized menu that might include lobster or ice water in crystal goblets. A gourmet grocery, Meadowlark Farm, kept Encino stocked in caviar and fresh fish. The best-known Chinese restaurant on Ventura was run by renowned cinematographer James Wong Howe. Nearby, actress Maureen O'Hara ran a dress

Instead of crowing roosters, residents of the new suburbs often awoke in the postwar years to the sound of hammers and saws as new subdivisions sprouted weekly across the Valley floor.

shop and Ruby Keeler operated a dance academy.

In the five years after the war, the population more than doubled to 402,538 residents—the pastoral San Fernando Valley was suddenly the ninth-busiest urban area in the nation. Valley society was a mix of young suburbanites, older families who had come west to try their luck as engineers, animators or pioneers in the new field of television, and ranchers trying to hang on in the face of the new hordes. Traffic snarls worsened each year on the two-lane streets—Vanowen, Sherman Way, Saticoy—that crossed the basin. It was worst for those who left the Valley in the morning for jobs in Hollywood and downtown Los Angeles. The roadway through Cahuenga Pass, upgraded to freeway status in 1947 and later to become the Hollywood Freeway, carried so many rush-hour commuters between the Valley and town that in two years it surpassed the San Francisco Bay Bridge as the most heavily traveled highway link in the state.

Growing pains abounded. The state health director warned of "shockingly unhealthy conditions" due to lack of sewers, but builders could not throw up new tract neighborhoods fast enough to satisfy demand. Telephone companies fell a year behind in hooking up new service. Meanwhile, ranchers who could see the future began selling out and moving west to Ventura County or north to Saugus and beyond.

There wasn't much entertainment for those who stayed—scattered movie theaters, a community play-

Fiery end for canyon cult

The crash of a Standard Airlines C-46 in the Simi Hills above Chatsworth on July 12, 1949, gave the outside world its first look at an unusual cult that lived in nearby Box Canyon. The New York-to-Burbank flight went

Khrishna Venta and his followers in the Fountain of the World cult met the press in 1953. WKFL stood for Wisdom, Knowledge, Faith and Love.

down near today's Mesa Drive and Lilac Lane, killing 35 people. Fourteen survived, including an actress who was Judy Garland's stand-in in *The Wizard of Oz*.

Among the rescuers were curious-looking men dressed in cotton robes and sandals with long, stringy hair—followers of Khrishna Venta or, as the law knew him, Francis Pencovic. Fifty-three men, women and children lived in his canyon compound, where he preached world peace, universal love and the pursuit of knowledge. "I may as well say it, I am Christ," he once informed his flock. Venta declared that humans came to Earth in spaceships and ruled that smoking was a healthful and desirable habit.

He had run-ins with authorities over bad checks and nonpayment of child support, but his final dispute was with two vengeful ex-members who suspected he was having sex with their wives. On December 10, 1958, Venta died in an explosion that rumbled across the Valley from the direction of Box Canyon and touched off a brush fire that scorched 150 acres. People feared it might have been an accident at the nearby Rocketdyne test lab, but it was a blast of 20 sticks of dynamite at the cult's compound. The ex-devotees and six others died in the explosion.

house or two, a Valley symphony. For a few spring seasons, the St. Louis Browns played a dozen or so games at Olive Memorial Stadium in Burbank, but the Brownies were the worst team in baseball. Children could find adventures in the many orchards and home construction sites, but the amusement calendar was especially bleak for teenagers. A good Friday night might involve a high school football game followed by burgers and malts and maybe an amorous interlude in the backseat of someone's car.

"In his parents' blue Chevy or my mother's green Pontiac we perched at night on the rim of Mulholland Drive, the great plain of twinkling lights below us like an endless airport, oblivious of the mating couples in cars parked around us, pursuing our own pleasures," the writer Susan Sontag wrote in the New Yorker of her bored teens in the late 1940s. She found North Hollywood High an intellectual desert where Reader's Digest served as a textbook for tenth-grade English, the Bible Club led a boycott that forced the banning of a biology text, the campus lawn was littered with condoms and the students included armed robbers and drug pushers. Her favored escape was to hop the Red Car on Chandler Boulevard and ride into Hollywood to haunt bookstores and record shops.

Soon even that became impossible. The last Red Car left the Valley on December 29, 1952—dubbed "the Streetcar Called Expire," a play on the year's hit movie. The Pacific Electric trolleys had made the Valley livable when they arrived in 1911, but they

By 1948, orchards had vanished and a sea of new homes covered the fertile land beside Tujunga Wash in North Hollywood. The Santa Monica Mountains are in the distance at right.

were an annoyance to the new suburbanites, who preferred automobiles and thought nothing of making a 20-minute trip for a hamburger. This mobile culture gave rise to some peculiarly Valley institutions, among them Bob's Big Boy, Gelson's Markets, DuPar's Coffee Shop, Cupid's Hot Dogs and the International House of Pancakes.

Devonshire Downs, an institution of another sort, opened in the mid-1940s as a track for training racehorses. Its location, at Devonshire Street and Zelzah Avenue in Northridge, was deep in horse ranch country. In 1946 the San Fernando Valley Trotting Assn. began Sunday afternoon harness racing there; quarter horse races were also staged. The state bought the site in 1948 to be the home of the San Fernando Valley Fair, an annual tradition that gave local breeders and farmers a place to show off their prize stock and keep hold of the fast-vanishing rural life. The track and barns remained, as a training ground for racehorses, for another three decades. Another institution grew from a Dust Bowl refugee's idea to fill a pressing need at the hundreds of Valley construction sites. Massena Gump's portable privy, fashioned in his Mission Hills garage, became a $7-million-a-year business. Each wooden shed bore his nickname and slogan: "Another Andy Gump."

Competing visions

The Valley today looks a lot like an amorphous, interlocking mass of tract home communities with no

Preserving the rural way

Northridge Farms, in 1957, was the kind of West Valley rural idyll Purcell hoped to preserve.

Former movie cowboy Robert M. Purcell was among the first to sound the alarm that encroaching suburbs were destroying rural tradition. He made a bold suggestion in 1949 for retaining a colorful piece of Valley lore.

Purcell proposed setting aside land in Chatsworth for an authentic western town, without cars or modern comforts—a kind of Colonial Williamsburg of the rural Valley. "Modern industrial progress has crowded the cowboy, his horse and his ranch out of all but a small corner of Los Angeles," Purcell railed. "The west end of the San Fernando Valley is now our last refuge." His dream of a final refuge was soon forgotten.

real distinctions between, say, Canoga Park and Winnetka. But if the official vision in force at the end of the war had been followed, the Valley might yet have real towns with greenbelts of orchards and ranches around them. That was the goal of the city's planning director, Charles B. Bennett, who preached that farms and horse ranches made the Valley special.

The term "urban sprawl" would not be coined for another decade, but Bennett warned in the 1940s of "the indiscriminate scattering of subdivisions

throughout the valley." He proposed a master plan in which each of the existing communities would evolve "all the amenities of a country town" but remain separated by crops and open space. He proffered a new type of Los Angeles neighborhood, part suburban and part country, where raising rabbits or horses in backyards would be permitted. Ringing these residential-agricultural zones would be small farms. The rest of the Valley, 50 square miles, would be devoted to large farms, including breeders of "alligator, ostrich, mink or fox." Bennett's ideal also called for planting native trees and opening bridle paths along the flood washes, extending Mulholland Drive into a pleasure drive circling the entire Valley, and carving high-speed parkways across the Valley floor to relieve the overburdened grid of country roads. Riverside Drive was to be one of those parkways; an odd bit of divided road in Burbank and North Hollywood called Whitnall Highway is a fragment of the system that Bennett urged.

Bennett's plan may have been visionary, but it was not very politic. Though the Valley still had 12,000 dairy cows, 75,000 turkeys and 60 farms breeding thoroughbred racehorses, pressure was immense to let new subdivisions rise up wherever the developers could coax a rancher to sell. Bennett argued that his plan would save the Valley from itself and still allow the population to reach 900,000 by the year 2000. For the growth-minded, even that was too limiting. The *Times* editorialized in favor of letting the Valley stay largely rural only "until population growth requires further urban development," and suggested there was room for possibly 2 million people.

Ferdinand Mendenhall, whose family ran the *Van Nuys News*, sat on the city planning commission and with his newspaper helped make sure the Valley continued to populate unfettered. Developers were allowed to skip over the land closest to established centers in Van Nuys, San Fernando and North Hollywood and to target the cheaper, more expansive

A boom for classrooms

The Valley's first institution of higher learning, Pierce College, opened in 1947 as an agricultural school amid rolling pasture-land in Woodland Hills. Valley College, another two-year junior college, opened in Van Nuys in 1949. The Valley later gained a third community college, Mission College. San Fernando Valley State College, now California State University Northridge, opened to undergraduate students on a new campus in Northridge in September 1956. Its focus at the time was the training of teachers.

As the post-war Valley swelled with children, new public schools opened each February and September when semesters began. Unlike in the rest of Los Angeles, schools were built on spacious acreage, usually as sprawling one-story campuses, and often in the open style exemplified by modernist architect Richard

Neutra's design for Kester Avenue Elementary, built in 1951. He positioned the buildings to take advantage of natural light and breezes, and opened the rooms onto patios and tree-shaded lawns. South walls are shaded with colonnades to keep rooms cool. Neutra also designed the land-mark fine arts building at San Fernando Valley State that was badly damaged in the 1994 earthquake and torn down.

Pierce College students, such as these inspecting a heifer in 1952, learned agricultural skills at the campus overlooking the still-rural western end of the Valley.

The community of Panorama City was the idea of innovative Valley land developer Fritz B. Burns, center.

acreage farther west toward Canoga Park and Woodland Hills. Soon a patchwork of construction projects and vacated ranches covered the Valley, and boulevards were extended wherever the builders chose to go. The old towns began to blend together.

Builders were king, and no developer saw the boom coming more clearly than Fritz B. Burns. Before World War II he had introduced the notion of tract housing in the Toluca Wood subdivision, on the North Hollywood border with Burbank. Two-bedroom cottages with a garage there cost $3,690. Burns standardized the floor plans and fixtures, and targeted buyers who might not yet be considered middle class, but would be soon. Sales pitches advertised the development's proximity to good jobs in the Lockheed and Vega aircraft plants in Burbank. A real-

estate marketing prototype was born.

On May 9, 1945—one day after the cessation of war in Europe—Burns and industrialist Henry J. Kaiser announced a grand venture to build tens of thousands of mass-produced homes on the West Coast. Their foothold in the Valley would be Panorama City, a subdivision that took its name from the Panorama Ranch, a dairy north of Van Nuys. Kaiser Homes paid $1 million for about 400 acres of dairy barns and alfalfa fields and in 1947 began erecting homes in the area bounded by Van Nuys and Roscoe Boulevards, Woodman Avenue and Osborne Street. The roads were either two-lane or dirt, but not for long.

Panorama City soon had schools, playgrounds, churches, a Kaiser Permanente hospital, a movie theater and a bowling alley. It was the first planned tract in the postwar Valley. Just to the south, a Chevrolet assembly plant rose, the second largest in the General Motors empire. A Joseph Schlitz brewery opened on Woodman Avenue, and a Carnation Research Laboratory—where food engineers invented Coffee-mate and improved on powdered milk—rose on Van Nuys Boulevard. These plants meant that buyers in

Homes in Panorama City were affordable—especially for veterans on the GI Bill—and more varied in style than usual.

Living south of Ventura Boulevard was desirable in part because of shady suburban scenes such as this 1957 view of Cantura Street in Studio City. Lots were small, but many streets were attractive.

shopping destination. Parking lots alone covered 18 acres. Robinson's followed, then Montgomery Ward, Orbach's and more than 100 smaller stores. Each Christmas, families came from across the Valley to line up by the hundreds and see live reindeer from Burns' own herd. Panorama City's biggest competition came from Valley Plaza in North Hollywood, which by 1959 billed itself as "the largest suburban shopping center in the West." Meanwhile, fewer shoppers patronized local stores on the main drags of Van Nuys, San Fernando and North Hollywood.

Panorama City would have good paychecks, and never mind that when they dug pools in the backyard, they sometimes encountered the skeletons of dairy cows that had died of hoof-and-mouth disease.

Ads for Panorama City proclaimed "25 miles of sidewalks…18 miles of sewers…2,236 men at work." Vets could move in for as little as $500 down plus loan fees, and get two bedrooms with 800 square feet, a garage and street trees for less than $10,000. A third bedroom added about 200 square feet and $1,000. To reduce the monotony of such a

large tract, Burns curved the streets, altered rooflines, varied the placement of garages and used vibrant colors. Director Terry Gilliam, whose resume includes the movies *Brazil* and *The Fisher King* (and who was the lone American member of the British comedy troupe Monty Python), vividly remembers homes of mustard yellow and pistachio green when his family moved to Panorama City from Minnesota in 1952.

After a Broadway department store opened in 1955, Panorama City also became a preeminent

The sandy beach at Hansen Dam, here in 1950, gave the Valley its own strand until floods in Tujunga Wash filled the lake with debris.

Bad guys

As the Valley suburbs grew, so did their reputation for being the Los Angeles home of the mob. Burbank was singled out in 1952 by the California Crime Commission as a hangout for Mafia figures who held sway with key city officials: "The people of Burbank are virtually without protection against the inroads of organized crime."

Reformers opposed to gambling and prostitution formed the Burbank Citizens' Crime Prevention Committee and drove out several suspect officials, including the police chief and the city manager. Other targets included the Sica brothers, Mafia members who ran the Champ Café, and Mickey Cohen, a hoodlum who operated a gambling casino at the Dincara Stock Farm.

Ostensibly a legitimate haberdasher on the Sunset Strip, Cohen was the quotable favorite mobster of Los Angeles newspapers. He lived in Brentwood but often got into trouble at mob-favored nightspots along Ventura Boulevard. In one early morning incident in the 1950s, Cohen, his lawyer and their wives brawled at Charley Foy's Supper Club, then at 15463 Ventura Boulevard in Sherman Oaks.

Cohen got into a more serious pickle at Rondelli's, a cafe of notorious repute at 13359 Ventura. On the night of December 2, 1959, someone put a bullet between the eyes of Jack "The Enforcer" Whalen, thought to be the biggest bookie in the Valley. Los Angeles police had been trying to shut down Rondelli's as a mob hangout, and Police Chief William Parker took personal charge of the murder investigation.

Cohen told detectives he was sitting opposite Whalen when the gunfire erupted: "I just ducked." Nonetheless, he was taken to Van Nuys headquarters and booked on suspicion of murder. Later, guns linked to Cohen and his late bodyguard, Johnny Stompanato, turned up in a trash bin behind Rondelli's. (By then, Stompanato had been stabbed to death in the boudoir of Lana Turner, reportedly by the actress's daughter.)

A Cohen associate took the fall for the Whalen murder, but two years later Cohen was indicted on new evidence. Witnesses at his trial included comedian Joey Bishop, who said he was supposed to meet one of Cohen's codefendants for dinner that night but canceled because he was too tired. Jurors deadlocked 9-3 for acquittal. Cohen, who lived for a time in a rented home at 13841 Wyandotte Street in Van Nuys, beat those charges. He soon went to prison on tax charges. He died in 1976 at the age of 62 of stomach cancer.

Steely eyed gangster Mickey Cohen, right, awaits a 1950 court date with bodyguard Johnny Stompanato.

The Valley style

Casual became the defining feature of Valley living. Entertaining took place mostly at home with friends, often around the barbecue and swimming pool. *Times* columnist Bill Henry in 1952 tantalized readers with images that appealed to people still recovering from the Depression and harsh winters back east. "The heat has ripened the luscious tomatoes, the blushing but juicy late peaches, [and] has fattened the rapidly maturing navel oranges…. Some just grow flowers, some raise horses and dogs and cattle and goats. Thousands of us commute to town to earn our living and then hurry back to the Valley to enjoy the sort of living we think makes the trip worthwhile."

The Valley was a "major spawning place for what is now universally recognized as the Southern California way of life," commentator Art Seidenbaum wrote. Sports cars, backyard pools and basketball hoops were ubiquitous. Yards were bigger than elsewhere in Los Angeles, garages and driveways more roomy. Kids played baseball in fields, not on streets, and felt safe wandering far from home even if there were hazards like abandoned wells and quarries.

Those who didn't have pools spent summers at the water-skiing lake, with sandy swimming beach, behind Hansen Dam, or drove to the ocean. Before freeways made Santa Monica easily reachable, Valleyites took Topanga Canyon to the beach or motored through Malibu Canyon and up the coast to

Sports heroes

The roster of celebrated athletes who hailed from the Valley includes quarterback John Elway, who played football at Granada Hills High; basketball star Gail Goodrich of Francis Polytechnic High in Sun Valley; ice skater Tai Babilonia of Mission Hills; boxer Bobby Chacon of Pacoima; and baseball Hall of Famers Don Drysdale, of Van Nuys, and Robin Yount, who grew up in Woodland Hills and played at Taft High School.

One of the most surprising was Bill Johnson of Van Nuys, who upset all expectations at the 1984 Winter Olympics in Sarajevo and became the first American to win a gold medal in downhill skiing. Two decades earlier, a pair of local champions had scored big in the Tokyo Olympics. Mike Larabee, a math teacher at Monroe High School, won the gold medal in the 440-meter race and also earned gold as a member of the 1,600-meter relay team. Swimmer Cathy Ferguson of Burbank won the gold medal in the 100-meter backstroke event.

After bringing home the gold in 1964, math teacher Mike Larabee got a hero's welcome from the students at Monroe High School in Sepulveda, now North Hills.

The Rev. Erling H. Wold, leading the drive-in service at Emmanuel Lutheran in North Hollywood in 1965, could have asked worshipers to ``honk if you love Jesus.''

Finding a place to worship

Growth came so fast in the postwar years that churches met in homes, school cafeterias and other improvised quarters while money was being raised to erect permanent sanctuaries. Prince of Peace Lutheran Church met for two years inside the Anheuser-Busch brewery in Van Nuys. Services for the "Valley Visual Church" were held in the Encino movie theater, with almost the entire service—including the sermon—conducted via films projected on the screen.

St. Jane Frances Catholic Church began in a parishioner's barn, then moved into a tent before construction started on a permanent home on Victory Boulevard in North Hollywood. A neighborhood boy who rode his bike to the new church still visits on occasion. He is now Cardinal Roger M. Mahony, the spiritual leader of Southern California Roman Catholics.

Zuma, as "Valley" a stretch of sand as could be found.

Fine restaurants were scarce; the big dinner houses were the Smoke House and the Castaway in Burbank, the King's Arms in Toluca Lake and Queen's Arms in Encino, Tail O' The Cock in Sherman Oaks. At Sportsmen's Lodge in Studio City, children could catch their own fish in ponds on the grounds. About the most exotic fare was offered at Phil Ahn's Moongate, a Panorama City landmark with Chinese cuisine and a Korean family as proprietors. (Ahn was a character actor who often played the Japanese villain in patriotic World War II movies, but it was his siblings who operated the restaurant.)

For adult entertainment there were supper clubs along Ventura and numerous bowling alleys with cocktail lounges and piano bars. Small community stages had thrived since the Valley Playhouse opened in 1938 in a remodeled church building in North Hollywood. The San Fernando Valley Symphony began performing in 1947 and presented guest conductors like composer Henry Mancini, a Northridge resident. Two radio stations, KGIL and KVFM, broadcast in the Valley and geared their programs to suburban listeners.

After the Dodgers came to Los Angeles in 1958, families in the Valley began driving into the city to see games, first at the Memorial Coliseum in Exposition Park, and after 1962 at Dodger Stadium in Elysian Park. The team's biggest stars lived in the Valley—Sandy Koufax in the hills of Studio City, and Don Drysdale, a graduate of Van Nuys High School,

They came by car, foot and bike to the 1957 grand opening of this Dairy Queen in North Hollywood.

Freeways eased traffic but ravaged many neighborhoods. Here, in 1957, the Alameda Avenue interchange on the Golden State Freeway, now Interstate 5, is being carved into the Burbank landscape.

in Hidden Hills. Thousands of boys listened to the World Series on transistor radios and played organized baseball on fields sprinkled across the Valley, and in 1963 the national Little League champions came from Granada Hills. Although the Los Angeles football team, the Rams, practiced for a while at Olive Stadium in Burbank (and counted Van Nuys High grad Bob Waterfield as one of their stars and later as a coach), the lone pro team the Valley could almost call its own was the L.A. Braves. They went to war on Thursday and Friday nights at the Valley Garden Arena on Vineland Avenue in North Hollywood. The Braves' stars were Ronnie Rains and Marge Forrest, and their sport was roller derby.

Thunder on the mountain

While times were mostly good, Valley people felt the threat of the Cold War in their bones. How could they escape it? Air raid sirens wailed at 10 a.m. on the last Friday of every month, just like in the war movies. Nike missile batteries were visible on Oat Mountain and beside busy Victory Boulevard in the Sepulveda Dam basin, while a missile-spotting station sat beside Mulholland Drive above Tarzana. Students dropped under desks in classroom drills a couple of times a year, in preparation for nuclear attack. Sonic booms from experimental planes rattled windows and nerves.

The most dramatic evidence of all was the growl of rocket engines being test-fired in the Simi Hills behind Chatsworth. When Rocketdyne ran tests at night, the sky over the west Valley glowed orange. A ditty sung to the tune of "My Darling Clementine" became part of the local lore:

> When there's thunder
> On the mountains
> Every evening just at nine,
> And your walls begin to tremble
> It's not God
> It's Rocketdyne.

At the end of the 1950s, nine of the 10 biggest manufacturers in the Valley were largely in the service of the Defense Department. Defense plants with more than 1,000 employees included Lockheed and Rocketdyne, Litton Systems and Ramo-Wooldridge in Canoga Park, and RCA, Marquardt and Radioplane in Van Nuys. High fences and signs prohibiting photography gave the plants a foreboding feel, and plenty of dads never could talk at home about their work.

"I figured that an analyst for Soviet intelligence in Moscow probably knew more about my Skunk Works projects than my own wife and children," wrote Ben Rich, the former chief of Lockheed's secret Burbank facility. The Skunk Works would have been high on the list of Soviet targets for missiles and espionage. The Advanced Development Projects section, its official name, began after World War II in Building 82, a huge hangar on the Lockheed side of Burbank Airport. The unit later moved to a windowless concrete blockhouse within sight of departing airliners.

Mr. Skunk Works

The founder and creative heart of the Lockheed Skunk Works, Clarence (Kelly) Johnson, handpicked its elite force of engineers and talented shop jocks. Clipped and no-nonsense, Johnson's motto was "Be quick, be quiet, be on time." He designed 40 airplanes before he retired and was well known in the corridors of the Pentagon and the Capitol.

The Skunk Works' assignment to build the U2 spy plane, which gave the U.S. an edge in the Cold War, came directly from President Dwight D. Eisenhower, who wanted a plane to fly high enough to evade Soviet radar and missiles yet still take useful photos. The U2s flew secret spy missions for four years, unknown to the world and the Russians until May 1, 1960.

On the last scheduled U2 overflight, Soviet missiles scored a hit. The wreckage and the startled pilot, Francis Gary Powers, were paraded on Russian television. Many at the Skunk Works called Powers a traitor for not committing suicide, but after he was swapped in 1962 for a Soviet bloc master spy, Kelly Johnson gave Powers a job as a flight test engineer. He worked for Lockheed for eight years before going into local traffic reporting. Powers died in the crash of his KNBC-TV helicopter in Encino on August 1, 1977.

The Skunk Works and the rest of Lockheed—at one time the Valley's largest employer—left Burbank in the 1990s. All that remains is a large swath of vacant land where Lockheed's original Burbank factory stood, now the site of a major environmental cleanup.

Clarence (Kelly) Johnson, beside a 1981 version of the U2, made the Burbank Skunk Works a legendary, if officially secret, outpost of the Cold War.

Nighttime engine firing at Rocketdyne's Santa Susana Field Lab, such as this test on May 21,1961, regularly lit up the west end of the Valley and could be heard for miles.

134

Even some Lockheed employees never knew the Skunk Works location or grasped its extensive role in the Cold War.

Skunk Works designers, fabricators and test pilots produced many of the nation's Cold War secret weapons: the F-104 "Starfighter," America's first supersonic interceptor; the U2 spy plane that flew in secrecy over the Soviet Union; the P-80, the first American jetfighter; the SR-71 "Blackbird," which flew at three times the speed of sound; and eventually the first stealth fighter, the F-117A, which Americans watched bomb with precision on television during the Gulf War. "We functioned as the CIA's unofficial toy-makers," Rich wrote in his autobiography.

Rocketdyne, the Valley's other large Cold War installation, had a plant in the flats of Canoga Park but was best known for its sprawling Santa Susana Field Laboratory at the top of Woolsey Canyon Road above Chatsworth. Opened in the late 1940s by North American Aviation to improve on the V2 rocket that the Nazis had unloosed on London, the lab drew on famed German engineer Wernher Von Braun. After the Rocketdyne subsidiary was formed, "Santa Sue" became one of the most advanced rocket test facilities in the world.

Huge engines were bolted onto steel scaffolds and fired up, their exhaust shooting into water-cooled "flame buckets" sunk in the rocks. On busy days, a half-dozen liquid-fuel rockets might be lit, their roar echoing off the cliffs. America's first orbit-ing satellite, Explorer 1, was launched January 31, 1958, with a Rocketdyne engine. Engines tested at Santa Sue launched the first American in space, Alan Shepard—as well as the first to orbit, John Glenn—and powered the Apollo rockets that flew Neil Armstrong and Buzz Aldrin to the moon in the summer of 1969.

Less known is that the lab also became a nuclear experimentation facility. After 1957, Atomics International operated more than a dozen reactors on The Hill, plus a "hot lab" for processing old irradiated fuel rods. A reactor accident in 1959 caused 13 uranium fuel rods to rupture or partially melt, forcing the reactor to be shut down and releasing radioactivity in the building. "It was a messy accident" but did not endanger the public, one evaluator of the incident said. At the peak, more than 9,000 people worked up on the hill inside the high-security facilities; some of them today blame their work at the lab for cancers and other ailments. A costly environmental cleanup is underway at the lab.

After the Soviets won the race into space with the Sputnik satellite launch on October 4, 1957, fear of a nuclear attack escalated. Backyard bomb shelters began to appear, the most ambitious an $89,000 elevator-equipped accommodation for 30 people sunk by car-rental magnate John D. Hertz on his Amarillo Ranch in Woodland Hills. Hertz bred champion thoroughbreds—including three Kentucky Derby winners—at Oxnard Street and Shoup Avenue on acreage he had purchased from

The ultimate Red

In the midst of heated Cold War fears over Soviet belligerence and supremacy in space, the most hated Communist of all dropped in on Granada Hills.

Soviet Premier Nikita Khrushchev arrived in Los Angeles on September 19, 1959, under the city's tightest security ever. He lunched at 20th Century-Fox with more than a hundred stars, among them Bob Hope and Frank Sinatra. "I feel this is a historic occasion for the nation and for the film industry," Marilyn Monroe told the *Times*.

After lunch, Khrushchev wanted to visit Disneyland but authorities deemed it too risky. Instead he was driven to the Valley to inspect a new subdivision in the 16200 block of Rinaldi Street. Model homes on nearby Sophia Avenue were cleared for Khrushchev to walk through, but he was so miffed at not being allowed to see Disneyland that he never left his car.

Large crowds, more curious than hostile, lined the routes that Khrushchev's motorcade followed.

This Reseda woman showed off her backyard fallout shelter to the local civil defense officer in 1959.

Hollywood labor racketeer Willie Bioff.

In truth, a greater threat to the Valley way of life may have been the sheer number of people flooding in. The population had doubled again in a decade, reaching 840,000 in the 1960 census. New housing tracts sprouted every month, and new schools opened twice a year, sometimes full from day one. Enrollment surged at the local two-year junior colleges, Pierce and Valley, although the presence of a new four-year college, San Fernando Valley State in Northridge, took some of the pressure off.

As Charles Bennett had feared, the Valley was choking on itself. Schoolchildren went back to tem-porary classrooms after lunch with burning eyes and lungs from the smog. There were no storm drains, so roadways flooded every rainy season. And with only the beginnings of a freeway system, automobiles had to share most surface streets with heavy trucks haul-ing between Los Angeles and anywhere north. "In essence, a community the size of San Francisco is trying to make out with country roads," historian Remi Nadeau said of the Valley in 1960.

That year, the Ventura Freeway finally opened—until then, traffic had crawled over Cahuenga Pass on the Hollywood Freeway, only to spill onto the Valley's outdated streets. The San Diego Freeway opened in 1962 through Sepulveda Pass, where the Portolá expedition had walked into the valley of the Tongva. Freeways ruptured dozens of neighborhoods, but the streets loosened up, at least temporarily. *Times* columnist Paul Coates was lukewarm on the new inventions: "The freeways are wonderful…they take all the little traffic jams and combine them into one big traffic jam."

Once the freeways arrived, the old Valley seemed to fade away more quickly. Platt Ranch—the old *Rancho El Escorpión*—sold for $6.1 million to devel-opers with plans for 6,000 homes. Warner Brothers had already sold its 2,800-acre location ranch for a reported $10 million. G. Henry Stetson, of the cow-boy hat family, sold his 250-acre *Rancho Sombrero* in Sylmar to the Mormon Church. The rancho had the largest privately owned swimming pool in America, measuring 325 feet by 100 feet at its widest point.

On Plummer Street just east of the new college in Northridge, Art Record gave up being a walnut grower after 36 years and sold out to subdividers. "I almost know each tree by name," he sighed. "I planted them myself."

CHAPTER 9

Borders

Until suburbanites turned the Valley into a white enclave, there was a history of ethnic diversity as seen in these faces of children playing together at the San Fernando grammar school in 1930.

To the casual observer, the Valley looks like one giant place—but the singularity is an illusion. Invisible borders are recognized by the locals. They know where Sun Valley stops and North Hollywood begins, or where Mission Hills fades into Granada Hills. Streets south of Ventura Boulevard are generally more desirable than those in the flats. West of the San Diego Freeway is more conservative and Republican, the East Valley more blue-collar and Democratic, if only somewhat more liberal.

In the postwar boom, the most glaring borders strove to keep the Valley a thoroughly white domain. Racism has been a Valley tradition. As early as the original subdivision of Tract 1000 lands, deeds on town lots specified that the property could never "at any time be sold, conveyed, leased or rented to any persons of African, Chinese or Japanese descent." In early Owensmouth, this also meant that the Mexican immigrants who worked in the fields and packing-houses were confined to a section called Cholo Town.

A 1933 master's thesis at the University of Southern California found 1,500 Mexican families in the Valley. Their children mostly attended separate elementary schools until the seventh grade, and then were thrown into mainstream high schools, welcomed or not. Health and attendance problems were common, the paper said. At Lemona Avenue School, a Mexican PTA met once a week to help families adjust. After a short business meeting in Spanish, an "Americanization" teacher gave lessons in sewing,

cooking and child care. The USC thesis reported on a high school meeting for parents conducted almost entirely in Spanish. The program included singing of the Mexican national hymn and Mexican folk songs performed by the Spanish class.

The thesis, entitled "The Problems Which Confront the High Schools in Regard to the Mexican Girl Pupils in the San Fernando Valley," by Laura Lucile Lyon, was mostly patronizing in tone. But it did acknowledge the poverty of many Mexican immigrants. Lyon noted that since many of the girls did not bring lunch or money to school, one high school arranged for them to take cooking class in the final period before lunch. This way they could be assured of something to eat and a glass of milk. At another school, the cooking class was held in first period so the girls would have an adequate breakfast, and they were given jobs in the school cafeteria at lunch.

Japanese also have a long history in the Valley. A count in 1905 found 23 Japanese in the San Fernando area and more than 300 in the Tropico district, a strawberry-growing area beside the Los Angeles River that became part of Glendale. The San Fernando Valley Japanese Language Institute, which still operates in Pacoima, opened in 1924 for Nisei children of vegetable farmers and flower growers. In 1935 a survey by the Japanese-American Citizens League found 435 U.S.-born and 431 foreign-born Japanese in the Valley. The community included a baseball team, the San Fernando Nippons, which played teams of white players around the Valley.

In most sections of the Valley, minorities were unwelcome. The lack of color was stark in the first postwar census of 1950. While the black population of Los Angeles County swelled that year with the sons and daughters of the segregated South drawn to California by jobs and freedoms they had discovered during the war, of 402,538 Valley residents, only 2,654 were black and 2,189 were other nonwhites. Most of those lived in and around Pacoima, the Valley's unofficial minority district.

Pacoima has always stood out among the Valley's communities. A high-end subdivision and summer resort in the 1880s, it boasted the Valley's first concrete sidewalks. Since it was built in alignment with the Southern Pacific tracks, Pacoima's main streets run at a diagonal to the strict rectangular grid found elsewhere in the Valley. The majority of residents in the 1950s were white and blue-collar, but the area had enough minorities that many of the new suburbanites avoided it. Many streets remained unpaved, the tuberculosis rate was high and the city's chief of building and safety described the district as "a jungle of tents, broken-down trailers, rusty iron huts and run-down shabby houses." That was the outside view. If you grew up there, as Mary Helen Ponce did, Pacoima was simply home.

Pacoima days

Pacoima and its neighbor, San Fernando, were the center of a thriving Mexican American popula-

Early farmers could be of Japanese, Mexican or, like this asparagus grower tilling a field near San Fernando in 1917, Chinese descent.

More than other Valley towns, San Fernando accepted Mexican Americans in community life. The Higuera family was photographed outside their home in 1909.

The writer Mary Helen Ponce grew to love Pacoima's Mexican barrios so much that she authored a memoir that told of lives foreign to most Valley suburbanites.

tion. San Fernando, the first city of the Valley, had plenty of Lópezes and Picos and other families with roots in an earlier century. Inhabitants of Pacoima tended to be newly arrived and poorer.

As a youngster in Pacoima, Mary Helen Ponce rode her bike on Van Nuys Boulevard, hiked in the hills behind Whiteman Airpark and chased baseballs in the street with the boys. Her childhood was a happy one, she recalls in "Hoyt Street: An Autobiography," her memoir of the time. "We knew everyone; everyone knew us….Ours was a secure world. We were free to play in the streets, climb trees and snitch fruit off a neighbor's tree without fear."

Ponce was an anthropology and Chicano studies major at Cal State Northridge in the 1970s when she began to probe her memories and her family's experiences for a research paper in folklore. The result is a body of written work that includes a collection of short stories and "Hoyt Street," which author John Rechy called "as engaging as a novel…a wonderful book brimming with genuine love for her culture." Ponce richly describes street and family life in an enclave of the Valley that few white suburbanites ever saw.

"On summer nights old ladies sat on front porches to swap gossip and tales of la llorona—the legendary weeping woman—while small kids chased stray dogs," she wrote in an article for the Times. The abuelitas kept herb gardens in old coffee cans and vegetable crates, so there would always be some rosemary or peppermint for tea if someone took ill. Spanish was spoken at home and forbidden in school. "My birth name, like those of my friends, was anglicized by teachers; María Elena gave way to Mary Helen." She remembers that during the 1950s at San Fernando High School, the Latinos and blacks were not invited to join clubs or attend the right parties. But they made their mark on the field: "During football games, the best (and best-looking) players were named López, García, Sierra."

On weekends, Pacoima teenagers rode the bus to the movies in San Fernando or went to Hansen Dam. "El dam," she wrote for the Times, was "where poor folks from the Pacoima and San Fernando areas went swimming…. It was free, close to home and, for

teenagers, a great place to meet guys and show off a bathing suit…. Boys from all over the San Fernando Valley came to Hansen Dam; a few came to swim but most were there to check out the chicks."

Pacoima fared badly in competition with the white suburbs for new parks, sidewalks and city services. It took a tragedy to spark outrage over the lack of a hospital. On the last morning of January in 1957, a new DC-7 undergoing final tests before delivery to Continental Airlines was flying at 25,000 feet when it collided with an F-89 fighter jet. People watched in helpless horror as the wreckage of both planes rained down.

The F-89 fell in remote La Tuna Canyon. But the four-engine airliner plummeted into the yard at Pacoima Congregational Church on Laurel Canyon Boulevard. An explosion showered hot shrapnel and flaming fuel on the adjacent athletic field at Pacoima Junior High School, where 220 boys were just being called indoors.

Most of the boys ran to safety as the sizzling debris sprayed the field, but more than a dozen fell hurt. Robert Zallan, 12, and Ronnie Brann, 13, died on the schoolyard. Gym teacher John Vardanian applied a tourniquet for nearly an hour to save the life of Albert Ballou—the 12-year-old's right leg was nearly severed above the knee and would have to be amputated. A doctor who ran two blocks to the scene said the heat of the explosion might have saved some lives by cauterizing wounds. Even so, 12-year-old Evan Eisner died the following day.

An engine from the DC-7 and other flaming debris fell on the field at Pacoima Junior High, killing three boys. Although 74 people on the ground were hurt, lucky breaks averted a greater tragedy.

142

Of seven crew members on the two planes, only the radarman on the F-89 survived, parachuting to a safe landing in Burbank. In all, nine people died and 74 on the ground suffered injuries ranging from burns and broken limbs to shock. The tragedy prompted so much anger about the community's lack of ambulance and medical services that Pacoima Memorial Lutheran Hospital was quickly constructed and dedicated to the three students who died.

Hometown hero

Pacoima's social isolation did not allow many heroes to emerge and make their mark, but the accomplishments of Richard Valenzuela came to matter deeply to many Chicanos. He grew up a few years behind Mary Helen Ponce, attending Haddon Avenue Elementary and Pacoima Junior High (he was absent from school the day of the midair crash, which killed one of his friends). His father died when he was 10, leaving his mother, Concepción, to raise three boys and two girls. Richard adored music from an early age. He fashioned toy guitars out of cigar boxes and broomsticks, and his heroes were Roy Rogers and Gene Autry, the singing movie cowboys who lived just a few miles away in the white Valley.

As a teenager, Valenzuela became a solid guitar picker and was invited to join the Silhouettes, a garage rock and roll band that reflected Pacoima's ethnic mix. The band had black members, a Japanese American and Chicanos like Richard,

Midair crash

As bad as it was, the toll of the midair crash over Pacoima could easily have been worse. On any other schoolday, scores of boys would have been on the playground at Pacoima Junior High in their gym clothes. Luckily, the day of the crash was just before the end of the semester, and the boys' PE activities had been canceled. Many students were in the auditorium preparing for the graduation ceremony.

Crash debris also fell on the empty playground of Terra Bella Elementary School, but the second-grade classroom, where large chunks crashed through the window, was vacant due to a field trip. Likewise, pieces of airplane ripped into nearby houses without killing or seriously harming anyone.

The planes had collided on a clear blue morning with unlimited visibility. Copilot Archie Twitchell, who perished in the DC-7, had time to radio that the big plane was going down: "Uncontrollable...uncontrollable...say good-bye to everybody."

Outrage over the accident led President Eisenhower to suspend military flight operations over the Valley.

who styled his hair in a classic low-rider waterfall. Rock and roll was becoming, in the late 1950s, the music of choice for teenagers, and the Silhouettes got gigs playing dances around the northeast end of the Valley and at parties for car clubs like the Lobos, who were Chicano, and the Lost Angels, who were white. Valenzuela's rocking guitar chords and exuberant vocals helped draw big crowds, and the 16-year-old picked up a word-of-mouth reputation as the Little Richard of the Valley.

When the Silhouettes packed the American Legion hall in Pacoima one night in May 1958, a tal-

ent scout took notice. That summer Bob Keane, the president of Del-Fi Records in Studio City, signed Valenzuela to a solo recording contract—without the Silhouettes, and with a stage name that sounded less Latino. Ritchie Valens was an immediate sensation: "Come On, Let's Go," his first single, soared on the national pop charts.

According to his biographer, Beverly Mendheim, Ritchie began composing his next hit record during a telephone call with Donna Ludwig, a girl he had met at a Panorama City party given by the Igniters, another white car club. They hung out together at San

Fernando High School, even though her parents did not want their blond daughter dating a Chicano. The love ballad "Donna" became a classic of Fifties rock, as did the flip side, "La Bamba," Ritchie's fast, electrified version of a Mexican folk song that acknowledged his Chicano heritage. At age 17, Ritchie Valens of Pacoima performed on Dick Clark's "American Bandstand" television show, stayed at the Plaza Hotel in New York and played alongside rock legends Bo Diddley and Buddy Holly and on the stage of the famed Apollo Theater. He bought his stage outfits from Nudie's, the same Lankershim Boulevard clothier-to-the-stars who dressed Elvis Presley and Roy Rogers.

For a kid who spoke almost no Spanish, his fame unloosed an immense pride in the barrios. He was not only the first rock music star of Mexican ancestry, but also the first Chicano from Pacoima, period, to achieve any status in white America. When Ritchie returned home in December 1958 he was hailed by some in the music press as the next Elvis. He played himself, alongside Jackie Wilson and Chuck Berry, in *Go Johnny Go,* a film by New York rock deejay Alan Freed. While he was home, Ritchie performed free concerts at his former schools, San Fernando High and Pacoima Junior High. Not yet 18 years old, he had forsaken his final year of high school and prepared to go back on tour.

Ritchie had feared flying since the midair crash over Pacoima Jr. High. The night before his departure he and his mother prayed at Guardian Angel church

Ritchie Valens' fame extended far beyond the Chicano neighborhoods of Pacoima. Fans made his ``Donna'' the number three song in the U.S.

for a safe trip. They also threw a farewell party at the house his success had bought for the family at 13428 Remington Street. Donna Ludwig, who had moved to Granada Hills, was forbidden by her father to attend. Ritchie called her on the phone twice, and they cooed about missing each other. "Will you wait for me?" Ritchie asked.

The Winter Dance Party tour was a miserable

experience. Bus rides through the freezing Midwest night were torturous; buses broke down and heaters malfunctioned. After performing at the Surf Ballroom in Clear Lake, Iowa, headliner Buddy Holly ditched the icy bus and chartered a small plane to the next stop in Fargo, North Dakota. One seat went to Holly's Texas buddy, J. P. (The Big Bopper) Richardson. In a coin flip, Ritchie called heads and won the final seat from Tommy Allsup, a member of Holly's band, the Crickets. The inexperienced pilot of the Beechcraft Bonanza took off in a snowstorm about 1 a.m., and within minutes the plane plunged into a cornfield and broke up. Everyone on board died, the bodies not discovered in the snow until almost midday on February 3, 1959. A letter from Ritchie's mother was found in his coat pocket: "Be good and I miss you more every day."

The news trickled out slowly, even in the Valley. This was before CNN and all-news radio, and before most newspapers began treating rock stars as celebrities. Anyway, Pacoima was another world. A brief wire notice in the afternoon *Valley Times* of February 3 reported "Rock 'N' Roll Trio Killed in Plane Crash." It was on the front page, below stories about the widening of Moorpark Street and a Reseda man who was planning a boat trip across the Atlantic. Ritchie Valens' age was given as 21—with no mention that he was a local boy. Meanwhile, radio DJs announced the news as a major tragedy. Donna Ludwig, who had transferred to James Monroe High in Sepulveda, heard about it at school from a girlfriend with a tran-

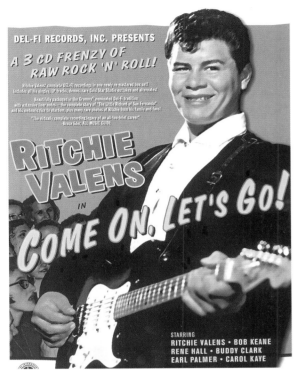

Del-Fi Records has kept Valens' memory alive, reissuing his work and pushing for his entrance to the Rock and Roll Hall of Fame.

sistor radio. "Donna"—her song—was the number three record in America, but school officials would not let the distraught senior leave campus.

While the Valenzuela family grieved, fans began appearing on Remington Street to mourn their loss. The *Valley Times* caught on the next afternoon that Ritchie was a local phenomenon, but relegated the follow-up story to page two. When the *Valley News*

and Green Sheet came out the following morning, finally there was a picture of Ritchie on the front page, and the headline became "Valley Singer, 3 Others Die." The *Los Angeles Times,* also late to the story, ran an interview that morning with Donna Ludwig. It wasn't often that a Chicano received this much attention, and anonymous callers to the Valenzuela home said they were glad he was dead.

After the body was returned home by train, a thousand mourners squeezed into St. Ferdinand's church in San Fernando for a Requiem High Mass on Saturday, February 7. As church bells pealed over the old city, nearly a hundred youths stood quietly outside "in a mist that was not quite rain," the *Times* reported. Now Richard Valenzuela again, Pacoima's first hero was buried at San Fernando Mission cemetery while "several hundred of the boys and girls who were his fans stood with bowed heads." Members of the Silhouettes served as pallbearers. "After the funeral I came home and cried like a baby for a very long time," the band's vibes player, Gil Rocha, told Valens biographer Mendheim.

On what would have been Richard Valenzuela's eighteenth birthday, his mother accepted the gold

After his burial at San Fernando Mission Cemetery, memorial dances became an annual event in the Valley. The Beatles, among others, called the young artist an influence.

Ritchie remembered

He was unknown to many at the time of his death. But today there is a Ritchie Valens postage stamp. He was elected into the Rock and Roll Hall of Fame in 2000. And he has a star on the Hollywood Walk of Fame. Del-Fi Records, his original label, has reissued his records and a boxed-set CD of his work, including the live performance before students at Pacoima Junior High on December 10, 1958, recorded on friend and classmate Gail Smith's portable tape recorder. Smith introduced him to the screaming student body as "a success story of one of last year's graduates—his first record sold over a million copies."

In Pacoima, the former Paxton Park at 10736 Laurel Canyon Boulevard became Ritchie Valens Recreation Center in 1994. An annual festival is held there in his honor, and a mural at Pacoima Junior High also pays tribute to Valens.

record for "Donna" at a poignant memorial dance in the San Fernando legion hall. The first time *Go Johnny Go* showed in the Valley, the homeboys packed the drive-ins. When Ritchie's face flashed on the big screen in the last 10 minutes of the film, car horns sounded a long and emotional salute.

Ritchie Valens had made records for all of eight months. Yet Lester Bangs, a respected rock commentator, has called him one of "that handful of folk visionaries who almost single-handedly created rock and roll in the Fifties." Of his student assembly performance at Pacoima Junior High, released as an album by Del-Fi Records after Ritchie's death, Bangs wrote, "It would be hard to find a recorded rock concert in which the performer displays more honest, humble warmth than Valens does here." John Lennon credited Ritchie's "La Bamba" with influencing the Beatles' take on "Twist and Shout." A 1987 film based on Ritchie's life, *La Bamba,* starred Lou Diamond Phillips and rekindled interest in his story. The title song, covered by the East Los Angeles group Los Lobos, went to number one in the country.

Cracks in the conspiracy

Pacoima also was the center of African American life in the Valley. Greater Community Missionary Baptist Church was founded in 1942 by the Rev. G. Pledger, and it became the mother church for other black Baptist places of worship. As more black families settled in Pacoima after the war, they formed the nucleus of a tight suburban community, albeit one segregated from the rest of the suburbs.

Any thoughts of living outside Pacoima were shut down by official and unofficial redlining, enforced by real estate brokers and builders. Typical was a restriction in the deed for a postwar subdivision on the edge of Van Nuys and Sherman Oaks, declaring that the property could never be leased, sold, used or occupied by any person "other than those whose blood is entirely that of the caucasian race…no Japanese, Chinese, Mexican, Hindu or any person of the Ethiopian, Indian, Mongolian race shall be deemed to be a caucasian." An exception was made for servants or employees. Even after such deed restrictions were ruled unconstitutional in 1948 by the Supreme Court, nothing changed.

With notable exceptions, brokers and developers policed the segregation, refusing to show houses to minorities outside Pacoima. Lenders denied loans, and landlords refused to rent apartments. The Federal Housing Administration was complicit in the redlining, routinely denying FHA mortgage insurance to blacks. When a tract of plain, boxy homes northwest of Glenoaks Boulevard and Filmore Street was sold as the Joe Louis Homes, although the enormously popular black boxer had no involvement, it seemed just another ruse to make the area attractive to blacks and keep them from trying to buy elsewhere in the Valley. The Fair Housing Council of the San Fernando Valley formed in 1960 to try to break down the walls, but progress came slowly.

Unofficial segregation was so pervasive that newspapers wrote it up when the Rice family became the first African Americans to integrate a Northridge neighborhood in 1961.

The system practiced equal opportunity racism. Sid Thompson, the future superintendent of the Los Angeles Unified School District and an African American, was blocked from moving to Mission Hills to be close to his job as a math teacher at Pacoima Junior High. He only managed to buy a house with the help of a friendly real estate agent, James Robinson, who came to the Valley in the 1950s and sold homes in Pacoima to black teachers and business people. In 1962 he became the first African American admitted to the San Fernando Valley Association of Realtors, the keeper of the property listings that brokers exchange with one another.

Another wedge was driven into the conspiracy by noted builder Joseph Eichler, a white Northern Californian who believed in open housing. Eichler made sure that his Balboa Highlands development in Granada Hills—on Jimeno and Darla avenues and Lisette and Nanette streets—was truly open to anyone with the money to buy and the desire to live in a home that didn't fit the typical Valley tract and ranch-style architecture. Eichler's homes, designed by architect A. Quincy Jones, were built on concrete slabs with atriums and radiant heat and lots of glass. Eichler went bankrupt a few years later. The policy of open housing was not to blame, said Eichler's son Ned, but he noted that "it would have been easier not to do it. The number of houses we sold to blacks and people who liked us for it was certainly offset by sales we lost and by aggravation."

While the real estate conspiracy slowly eroded, the social forces of the 1960s pushed greater change on the suburbs. The federal war on poverty pumped money into Pacoima, and the civil rights movement raised political awareness. Black power was a growing sentiment among young African Americans. God-fearing black homeowners in Pacoima viewed the angry revolutionaries—with their strident rhetoric and classes in Swahili and self-defense—with some trepidation. So those of student age turned their sights on the local institution that many blacks felt was the most racist of all: San Fernando Valley State College.

The west Valley was the most segregated and the most conservative part of Los Angeles, and the Northridge campus reflected it. While other colleges in the U.S. were being roiled by antiwar or free speech demonstrations, Valley State was quiet. Some students still wore crew cuts and ties to class, and the Fine Arts department had gained notoriety for refusing to show a sculpture by Edward Kienholz that depicted a nude pregnant mannequin.

In the fall of 1968, only about 200 of the 18,000 students were African Americans. Edward T. Peckham, who retired in 1991 as dean of students, recalled that "the only black students were on the football team or some other sports team." About the only blacks seen off campus were at Valley Skateland on Parthenia Street, and then only on Sunday nights—when whites avoided the place. "It was unheard of to find a black person in Northridge," Bill Burwell, a Pacoima activist who helped form the campus Black Students Union, recalled in the *Times* 20 years later. The campus had such a poor reputation in Pacoima that Dean Peckham struck out trying to set up a tribute after Dr. Martin Luther King was assassinated on April 4, 1968. "I called several churches. No one would come here."

Six months later, racial grievances at Valley State boiled over. The flashpoint was a football game against Cal Poly San Luis Obispo. After a black player for Valley State was roughed up during the game, another black player went to his aid but was rebuked—the black students say physically assaulted—by his own coach. After the game, fights erupted between white and black students in the Northridge locker room. The Black Student Union demanded the coach's firing. Several dozen

These women, shown at the Van Nuys courthouse, were among 27 black students arrested following the Valley State takeover. Three male student leaders were sentenced to state prison.

black students forced a meeting two weeks later with athletic director Glenn Arnett. When he insisted that only the college president could fire the coach, the boisterous group led Arnett across campus to the president's office.

Objectively, the events that followed were less violent than uprisings on many American campuses. But this was quiet suburban Northridge. People

across the Valley got mad or scared, or both, when the news flashed on November 4: Black militants had taken over the administration building at Valley State.

"All administrators and clerical staff, 37 in all, were herded into room 509, the president's conference room," according to *The Time of the Furnaces*, an account of the incident by former Black Panther Earl Anthony. One student quoted by Anthony described the emotion as "like a dog you keep on a chain. Once that dog gets free it runs wild. I guess that's the way we were on the fifth floor. We didn't want to hurt anybody, but then we were tired of taking shit from the people at Valley State. We took over the fifth floor…the young brothers were running up and down the hall just letting off steam."

The demonstrators held acting president Paul Blomgren and his staff for four hours of heated rhetoric and negotiation. No one was injured, but a knife was flashed and at least one school official was kicked. "We were not free to leave. There were weapons. There was intimidation," Dean Peckham told the *Times* in 1991.

Some 2,000 curious students, most of them white, gathered outside. Squads of Los Angeles police stood by as, upstairs, Blomgren agreed to a list of demands: the creation of a black studies department leading to a degree, recruitment of 500 new black students a year, firing of the football coach, investigation of employment practices, and immunity from prosecution for the black students. Blomgren signed the paper and went downstairs to address the crowd massed outside; the black students left through a side door.

The next day, Gov. Ronald Reagan, who advocated confronting student activists, railed that the protesters "should be dragged off by the scruff of the neck." Blomgren disavowed his acceptance of the student demands, saying it was made under duress. Police swept into Northridge and Pacoima, arresting 27 black students on charges of kidnapping, false imprisonment and conspiracy. With Reagan and local whites demanding justice, the politically ambitious district attorney assigned a top prosecutor, Vincent T. Bugliosi, to what the *Times* called "one of the most significant criminal trials in the state's history." After the students waived a jury trial rather than face a panel of angry suburbanites, the judge found 19 guilty of various charges and acquitted five. Most received county jail terms or probation, but three student leaders got prison terms of one to 14 years. Bugliosi predicted the sentences would deter student militants around the nation.

The racial upheaval in Northridge was so surprising that Life magazine announced, "People in the San Fernando Valley—suburban, conservative, largely white—are upset, confused and angered by what has happened at Valley State." The felony charges had accomplished what the Vietnam War and even the takeover could not: politicizing the apathetic commuter campus. In January 1969 a large, multiracial rally was held in support of the arrested students. After a planter was smashed through a window of the administration building, police arrested 14 students. Acting president Delmar Oviatt declared a campus emergency and banned gatherings, but it was too late. At a large rally in defiance of the ban, 286 students and faculty members were arrested. This time, most of the protestors were white. Valley State had become an activist campus. Outside groups came to support the students, while

A pastor honored

Hillery T. Broadous Elementary School is a landmark for the Valley's African American population, which has been concentrated in Pacoima since the end of World War II. The school, formerly known as Filmore Street School, was renamed to honor the late pastor of the community's Calvary Baptist Church.

Broadous founded the church in 1955 and went to work trying to break down the suburbs' pervasive racial segregation. He helped organize the Fair Housing Council of the San Fernando Valley in 1960. That year, the population of the Valley surpassed 840,000, but only 9,833 were black. Of those, 90% lived in Pacoima and many of them were poor.

When the Watts riot swept through impoverished African American neighborhoods of south Los Angeles in 1965, Broadous used his influence to defuse tensions in Pacoima and avert the spread of violence.

others urged authorities to get tougher. Bob Baker, then managing editor of the campus newspaper, the *Sundial,* and later an editor at the *Times,* wrote that in the Valley "politically, it was the equivalent of Godzilla walking over the Sepulveda Pass."

The campus—and arguably the Valley itself—was never again the white conservative bastion it had been. The college was the first in the state to create a black studies department, now the Pan-African Studies Department, staffed in part by students who had participated in the takeover. The first Chicano studies department also was founded—and most recently, the campus began to offer the first minor in Central American studies. After changing its name to California State University, Northridge, the campus became increasingly multiethnic, and by the mid-1990s no single ethnic group formed a majority. In 1992 Blenda Wilson became CSUN's first African American president.

CHAPTER 10

Coming of Age

Wednesday night was "cruise night" on Van Nuys Boulevard for more than 40 years, until police shut down the tradition by barricading the streets.

The 1960s was a tumultuous decade of adjustment to new social mores just about everywhere, but suburban enclaves such as the Valley got an extra dose. Imagine more than 100,000 teenagers reaching adolescence all at once, their hormones and rebelliousness unloosed on a place as confined and well-ordered as the Valley. Something had to give.

At the start of the 1960s, citrus groves and pastures still gave the suburbs a rural flavor, especially at the west end of the Valley. Towns held colorful local parades—Northridge had the annual equestrian Stampede, San Fernando celebrated Fiesta Days. By the end of the decade, attitudes had changed so much that the Bethlehem Star Christmas parade, a Van Nuys tradition for 21 years, was canceled for lack of interest. That same year, police arrested 70 nude dancers in raids on Valley strip clubs, and tens of thousands of young people partied at a giant outdoor rock festival in the midst of suburbia.

Rock and roll, anti-Establishment rebellion, hippies and drugs all arrived during the Sixties, and they clashed with the patriotic, crew-cut ethic that prevailed in many homes. Many fathers, if not most, earned their livelihood in some way connected to the military-industrial complex. Defense contractors like Lockheed and Litton were the biggest employers. For boys, a style statement as simple as longer hair became a divider of families and a source of trouble. High school gym coaches made it clear that hair touching the ears or collar was a lapse of moral

In the Sixties, girls wanted shorter skirts and the right to wear jeans. Boys fought for long hair.

character worthy of swats from the wood paddles they kept in their desk drawers. Northridge Military Academy made news when a 9-year-old got 20 swats for long hair, a day after taking 25 licks of the commandant's paddle for inspection demerits. "A matter of tradition," the private academy explained.

For girls, the choices became more complicated. Options in clothing, makeup and personal style were fraught with social implications. Hair was teased, straightened, curled, braided, dyed, tied into beehives or ratted into high piles, depending on the campus tribe a girl wished to affiliate with. The key battleground with authority was over short skirts and dresses, pitting girls who longed to look hipper against the fearsome authority figure known as the Girls Vice Principal. Girls deemed too immodest by the VP could be forced to kneel, and if their hem did not touch the floor a seam ripper would fix the problem.

Author Gwynn Popovac captured the humiliation of being hauled before the VP for innocently revealing too much leg in "Wet Paint," her 1986 novel about a Valley teenager coming of age at mythical Hazelton High:

Flora couldn't believe the situation she was in. She just wanted to be an anonymous tenth grader. Yet now Mrs. Baines was acting as if she knew something awful about her that she herself wasn't even aware of. It was as if Mrs. Baines had sources of secret information which, when all added up, could prove she was a bad person. It was a fearful notion...Flora went around school for the rest of the day with frayed seam-binding dangling about her calves.

Resentment that the Valley was changing too fast erupted in a 1969 brouhaha over a sexually explicit poem. "Jehovah's Child" examined in graphic language a promiscuous young woman's adventures in sex with Biblical figures, including Christ. After the poet, Deena Metzger, read the work to the English class she taught at Valley College, church leaders and conservative politicians demanded her firing. Metzger explained that the poem was intended to stimulate discussion of loosening sexual mores, as well as instill outrage "against people who use church, friends and sex for their own selfish purposes." She agreed not to read the poem again. Nonetheless, Metzger was fired—an act that was later reversed as improper by the State Supreme Court.

Under the stars

At the height of their popularity in the 1960s and 1970s, eight drive-in movie theaters operated in the Valley. Shows began each night "at dusk," the films projected onto giant outdoor screens. Countless Friday night dates were spent in automobiles parked in the back rows of the Pickwick, the Victory, the San Val and the Laurel in the east Valley, the Sepulveda and the Van Nuys in mid-Valley, and the Reseda and the Canoga in the west. Not a single drive-in screen remains.

Car culture

For teenagers of both sexes, stuck in a place as spread out as the Valley, the opening of a shopping mall qualified as a milestone. Valley Plaza in North Hollywood and Sherman Oaks Fashion Square became oases for after-school hanging out and weekend flirting on the east side of the Valley. The west side went without until Topanga Plaza in Canoga Park became the first giant mall under one roof—and an instant social center for teenagers. The Plaza, which opened in 1964, was the biggest enclosed two-level air-conditioned shopping center in the world, its promoters bragged, with a rain fountain three stories high, an ice skating rink and several department stores. For teenagers, it was a place to hitchhike or bum rides to, and to loiter away from their parents and probably see someone they knew or wanted to meet.

Without a car, weekend social life was a bleak prospect. The Valley had a nightclub for young teens, the Peppermint Stick in Sherman Oaks, and teen centers held weekend dances. There were also nearly two dozen local movie theaters, among them the California, Cornell and Magnolia in Burbank, the Centre and Crest in San Fernando, the El Portal and Guild in North Hollywood. But at age 16, the magic time when a driver's license could be acquired, the possibilities burgeoned.

Hollywood and the beaches were only a short hop away. Dates could be taken to Gravity Hill, in

Souped up cars weren't just for the boys. The Throttle Queens, shown here in 1956, took on anyone up for a race at the San Fernando Drag Strip, a popular spot for legal speeding.

Kagel Canyon, where cars set in neutral gear gave the illusion of coasting uphill. Every turnout on Mulholland Drive became a lover's lane, with views of the Valley lights. There, and at necking spots in Topanga Canyon, the north end of Zelzah Avenue and in Griffith Park, countless boys spooked their girlfriends with the urban legend of the homicidal maniac with a hook for a hand who scratches on the steamy windows of young lovers parked in the hills. In a precursor to modern rave parties, on some nights hundreds of teenagers in various stages of sobriety roamed in the dark over Tampaland, the name they gave to the ridges and gullies west of Tampa Avenue in Limekiln Canyon above Porter Ranch, which was then a new planned development.

A set of wheels also was the ticket into the oldest Valley social tradition of all—cruising Van Nuys Boulevard. The Boulevard had been the place to take Friday night dates since at least the 1930s. Robert Redford had cruised in the 1950s as a Van Nuys High senior. All of the Valley youth tribes mingled on The Boulevard: hot rodders itching for a race; customizers who drove to Tijuana for tuck-and-roll upholstery and invested in paint jobs signed by Von Dutch; lowriders who got their suspensions torched at Cohea's in San Fernando; long-haired surfers in their vans and Woodies; gnarly bikers flying the colors of the Satan's Slaves, the Valley's home-grown motorcycle gang; and carloads of shy teens who borrowed daddy's station wagon to gawk.

Wednesday night was Club Night, when car clubs from across the Los Angeles basin converged on the Boulevard to strut their souped-up Chevys and Fords. Each club had its own turf: the Los Angeles Street Racers and the Valley Hi-Los hung out in the parking lot at Van Nuys Car Wash; the Road Runners and the Associated Mopars had the Bank of America lot; the Royal GTOs, the Valley Vegas, the Vandits, the Chancellors, Associated Vans and a couple of

George Barris, seen here in 1966, was the king of the customizers and a car culture icon.

dozen others defended spots from Sherman Way south to Ventura Boulevard. On Club Night, the big attraction was to see and be seen. It could take an hour to travel a few miles in the thick traffic. "What else is there to do on Wednesday night?" a cruiser explained once to the *Times*.

The ultimate Boulevard status symbol was a Kustom Kar by George Barris, customizer for the movies and TV. At his shop in North Hollywood, he chopped, channeled, lowered, lifted, stripped chrome, removed door handles, flared wheel wells, and striped over metal flake paint jobs. Barris invented Kandy Apple Red and a line of other paint colors favored on the Boulevard, and had himself dragraced for pink slips in the 1940s. His name was local legend. He designed cars for celebrities from Sinatra to Elvis to the Beatles, and he built the Batmobile of TV fame.

Writer Tom Wolfe lionized Barris in a story for Esquire magazine, "The Kandy-Kolored Tangerine-Flake Streamline Baby." Wolfe had come to the Valley to write about hot rods and their fans. He began his research at a Teen Fair in Burbank, ogling teenyboppers dancing in slacks so body conforming "it's as if some lecherous old tailor with a gluteus-maximus fixation designed them, striation by striation." His epiphany came when he drove over to Riverside Drive to see Barris' shop. "This place is full of cars such as you have never seen before," Wolfe exulted. Barris would be better known, Wolfe wrote for his mostly Eastern audience, if he "hadn't been buried in the alien and suspect underworld of California youth." In fact, Barris remained the king of the customizers through the rest of the century.

Common ground for the Boulevard tribes was

Bob's Big Boy. The drive-in had carhops, thick malts, hamburgers and tradition. A date-night destination for decades, Bob's parking lots were places to flirt and make out, to get in fistfights over girls or hard stares, and to line up drag races. But except for Bob's and a few other food joints, business establishments were at war with the cruisers, who scared away customers. Van Nuys merchants and the police tried pleas in the newspapers, letters to parents, No Parking signs and mass arrests before finally shutting down the tradition in the mid-1980s by blocking off the entire boulevard on Wednesday nights and weekends.

It took years before the impulse to look for action on Van Nuys Boulevard finally died away. The defense of cruising was sometimes eloquent. "Who are these children of the night? Are they the muggers, burglars or vandals who inhabit our city? Are they all in need of psychological assistance? I submit that as a group they are none of these, but merely adolescents," an Encino man wrote in the *Times* in 1975. David Smith of Sepulveda praised cruising with his heart: "If it wasn't for that lighted stretch of concrete and asphalt in the San Fernando Valley, I would not be married to the lovely lady sitting next to me."

Tom Wolfe chronicled a Sixties happening of another sort in his book, *The Electric Kool-Aid Acid Test,* a journey with writer Ken Kesey and the Merry Pranksters, who traveled California in a bus painted in psychedelic colors throwing wild LSD parties. The bus stopped in February 1966 at the Sepulveda Unitarian Church on Haskell Avenue, known as The

Onion for the bulbous shape of its building. LSD was still a legal hallucinogenic drug at the time, and the Merry Pranksters were invited by the pastor to conduct the ninth in their series of mass "acid tests" in which everyone present was encouraged to turn on.

Kesey was off in Mexico, but the Pranksters contingent included Neal Cassady, the Beat Movement legend who had gone on the road with Jack Kerouac, and Hugh Romney, the poet known as Wavy Gravy. While the Grateful Dead jammed, the Pranksters rapped to the gathered hippies and curious, most everyone tripping on LSD. Wolfe wasn't there but compiled accounts, and wrote of "people dancing in the most ecstatic way and getting so far into the thing, the straight multitudes even, that even they took microphones, and suddenly there was no longer any separation between the entertainers and the entertained at all, none of that well-look-at-you-startled-squares condescension of the ordinary happening. Hundreds were swept up in an experience, which built like a

Mad Man Muntz hooked young drivers on car stereos— just as he'd sold their parents on TV sets.

Stereo from a Mad Man

His offbeat gimmicks and sales pitches to sell cars and TVs ("I want to give them away, but Mrs. Muntz won't let me. She's crazy!") made Earl "Mad Man" Muntz a fixture in postwar Los Angeles. But cruisers on Van Nuys Boulevard knew him best as the name on Muntz Stereo-Paks. The four-track tape decks put stereo sound in cars at a time when most rock radio stations were on the AM dial and dismally monaural. The decks were cheaply made and provocatively sold by "Muntz Girls," attractive young women in revealing garb who persuaded adolescent boys that they wouldn't be cool without a Muntz stereo.

dream typhoon, peace on the smooth liquid centrifugal whirling edge."

About this time, nomadic composer and author Paul Bowles stopped at Valley State College and taught existentialist literature to suburban kids, while a prominent tenured Valley State sociology professor ventured to explain the counterculture of acid trips and love-ins to mainstream America. Lewis Yablonsky's book, *The Hippie Trip,* was also his personal account of taking LSD and observing group sex at various hippie houses and communes he visited. When he began his research, Yablonsky was a 43-year-old, middle-class academic, married with two children, who had never used illegal drugs and who believed in monogamy. The year before his book was published, he was named the outstanding professor in the California State Colleges system. "Many things happened to me personally that may have shifted some of my values," he wrote of his research. At one communal house in a canyon above the Valley, he recognized a student who, he observed, spent most of the time "to use a crass 'plastic society' term, topless." The student discovered LSD that summer and, Yablonsky noted, "led a completely free sex life."

The wild summer of 1969

The summer of Woodstock began with a raucous rock and roll festival that secured a place for the Valley in 1960s lore. On the weekend of high school graduations, "Newport '69" took over the Devonshire Downs fairground in Northridge for three days and nights. The lineup of acts was the biggest of any American rock event to that time. Eric Burdon, The Byrds, The Rascals, Jethro Tull, Creedence Clearwater Revival, Steppenwolf, the Chambers Brothers and Marvin Gaye, among others, played on the field that later became the Cal State Northridge football stadium. Woodstock, held two months later, was a larger festival and came together on a rural farm in upstate New York. But the first large U.S. rock festival was held in suburbia, literally across the street from some very upset neighbors.

Everyone came to Bob's some time—especially when they were dating. These hot-rodders ordered burgers and malts in 1954.

The Pink Lady of Malibu

Lynne Seemayer was a 31-year-old Northridge artist and mother of two whose day job as a legal secretary was not her true calling. She drove Malibu Canyon regularly between the Valley and the beach, and in January, 1966 she had had enough of the graffiti, marring the rocks above the canyon's landmark tunnel. On nights when the moon was bright, she lowered herself with ropes until she hung in front of a large section of rock. Then she quietly sketched. Several months later, after a marathon 11-hour painting session, she was done.

On October 29, the sun rose on a traffic stopper: a 60-foot-high, shocking pink and joyfully naked female, grasping a handful of flowers as she cavorted on the rock above the tunnel. Seemingly appearing overnight, the black-haired, doe-eyed Pink Lady of Malibu Canyon became a sensation. "She wasn't there when I came through here two days ago," deputy sheriff William A. Sheaffer puzzled.

Crowds gathered to gawk and to ponder who could have created the apparition. Most assumed the artist was a man—or men, given

the precipitous site. County officials declared the Pink Lady a traffic hazard and tried to erase her, but this proved difficult. High-pressure water hoses only made her gleam more brightly. Paint remover didn't work. Meanwhile, the crowds grew more protective. Admirers signed petitions that called efforts to erase the Pink Lady "prudish, inartistic, inhuman and apathetic."

After several days of mystery, Seemayer came forward. She received hate mail, marriage proposals and offers to join nudist groups, and finally she lost her job. People read all kinds of meaning into the Pink Lady, but Seemayer explained, "I did it simply as an art piece, and that was all."

Fourteen gallons of drab gray paint finally obliterated the sensation, although for years afterward a faint outline of the nude form could be glimpsed in the right light over the coastal side of the tunnel.

"That rock face needed enhancing," the artist explained after coming out of hiding to accept credit. She intended to draw a bird, but didn't have room for the wings.

On Friday morning, June 20, young people from all over began crossing the Valley to Northridge—by car and van, by thumb, on foot. The music started late that afternoon, with Ike and Tina Turner, Joe Cocker and headliner Jimi Hendrix on the bill. An estimated 50,000 people made it inside the fence on Friday. Conditions were less than ideal: no provisions had been made for camping or eating, and only a few dozen portable toilets were on hand. The sound system was so inadequate that many could barely hear the music, but a party atmosphere took hold. Everyone plunked down on the grass of the old race track, and drugs were shared freely. "It was like a super big party…like a massive, massive love-in," Danny Altchuler, who played rhythm guitar for Love Exchange that night, later told the *Times'* David Wharton. Hendrix gave a lackluster performance and had trouble with his equipment, possibly due to a drink spiked with LSD. He vowed to return later in the festival to make amends.

As word spread of the gigantic party, thousands more found their way to the fairground. Many of the fans lacked the $7 daily admission charge, so they massed outside the fences on Devonshire Street and Zelzah Avenue, dancing in the traffic lanes and laying out sleeping bags on neighbors' lawns. Some stripped fruit off backyard trees for refreshment.

By Saturday, the Downs was the epicenter of a huge happening. As many as 15,000 people had simply crashed the gate the first night, and on Saturday, "we knew we had a big problem," promoter Mark

The Unitarian Church in North Hills, The Onion, became a psychedelic landmark of the Sixties when the Grateful Dead played for an "acid test" chronicled by author Tom Wolfe.

Two months before Woodstock in the summer of 1969, there was Devonshire Downs.

Robinson Jr. said. "We needed help, so we had to hire what help we could." That help came from the Los Angeles Street Racers, a car club with a tough reputation on Van Nuys Boulevard. A police inspector quipped of the Street Racers, who armed themselves with chains and boards to keep out gate-crashers, "I wouldn't want them to officiate at my wedding." Buffy Sainte-Marie, the event's unofficial earth mother, urged everybody to stay happy and enjoy the music. But outside on the streets, mobs of partyers looked for any breaks in the fence so they could join the surging crowd inside. The Street Racers got in some licks, but the wave of trespassers was too large and determined. Some who attended remember hulking Hells Angels also acting as official security, but Robinson has consistently denied that he paid any bikers.

Cory Wells, of the band Three Dog Night, described the fairgrounds as "an ocean of people out there. So many people…it was scary." With security lax, some fans were able to get on stage and backstage. Tracy Nelson, whose group Mother Earth performed on Sunday, recalled that a process server managed to hand a subpoena to one of her bandmates. Performers she knows have never stopped talking about Newport '69, she said in a recent interview with the author: "It was such a humongous show." Nelson, who went on to become a country singer in Nashville, played a part in the festival's most memorable moment, singing vocals along with Eric Burdon while a rejuvenated Jimi Hendrix jammed with Buddy Miles on drums, Cornelius Flowers and Terry Clements on saxophones, Brad Campbell on bass and Lee Oskar on harmonica. Bootleg recordings and a home movie of the hour-plus session still circulate on the Internet.

Outside the fence, tensions boiled over on Sunday after two days of no food for some of the party-goers and a long weekend of disturbance for police and residents. "Our lawn was covered with people. They weren't belligerent, but we couldn't get them off. They were drinking wine by the gallon," a woman on Romar Street complained. Police moved in force on the street scene before noon, touching off a mini-riot. Rocks and bottles were thrown and windows broken out of a police bus. One officer suffered a broken leg and another had internal injuries after being beaten. All told, 15 police officers were hurt and 387 fans were treated

West Coast country

The Valley's most celebrated music venue for decades was the Palomino Club, in a low-rent section of North Hollywood. The Palomino was the West Coast capital of country music. Country legends the likes of Buck Owens, Johnny Cash, Patsy Cline, Willie Nelson and Lefty Frizzell performed at the club at 6907 Lankershim Boulevard, which also boosted the careers of young singers such as Linda Ronstadt and Glen Campbell, both spotted at the club's weekly talent nights. After owner Tommy Thomas died in 1985, a funeral procession one and a half miles long cruised slowly past the club. The Palomino closed in 1995.

Yes, the Valley *did* rock

Devonshire Downs, scene of the Newport '69 festival and numerous smaller outdoor concerts, was razed in 2000 to make way for an industrial park, but other rock and roll landmarks remain.

On February 22, 1967, the Byrds, Buffalo Springfield and the Doors played together at the Valley Music Theatre. The Doors also performed on the football field at Birmingham High School. At Valley Skateland, now a quiet roller rink in Northridge, live acts such as Ike and Tina Turner, the Standells and Iron Butterfly played on raucous Friday nights in the 1960s. The Country Club in Reseda also has seen its share of big-name performers.

The Cinnamon Cinder, an alcohol-free nightclub for youths as young as 18, became a landmark for another reason in 1964. The club at 11345 Ventura Boulevard was run by Bob Eubanks, at the time the evening disc jockey on KRLA, a popular radio station in Los Angeles. The club's name was on a hit song by the house band, the Pastel Six, and on a TV dance show. Eubanks was also the promoter behind the Beatles' first performance

in Los Angeles, and he sneaked the band into the Cinnamon Cinder for a secret press conference. But when word leaked out that the British foursome was in the Valley, Beatlemania erupted. "More than 400 teenagers staged a mass attack" on the club, the *Valley Times* reported. A 15-year-old girl threw herself in front of the Beatles' limousine but walked away unhurt.

The Valley's less well-known rock lore includes performances by Ritchie Valens at San Fernando's Recreation Park, Bruce Springsteen trying out new material at the Sundance Saloon in Calabasas, and ex-Byrds rocker Gram Parsons holing up in a ranch house on DeSoto Avenue to write songs for the Flying Burrito Brothers. Famed drummer Sandy Nelson was seriously hurt in 1963 when his motorcycle collided on Mulholland Drive with a school bus carrying, among others, 13-year-old Bonnie Raitt.

for injuries or drug overdoses. To get the crowds off the streets, the police ordered the festival gates opened to all comers, free of charge on Sunday.

Afterward, reviewer Pete Johnson in the *Times* praised the roster of acts and said those seated near the stage "may have heard the best performance of their lives." But for most, he said, the overmatched sound system reduced the music to "one long blur of noise," and even that was drowned out by circling police helicopters. Officials estimate that 200,000 people converged on Devonshire Downs that weekend, no more than 75,000 of them paying customers. Hauled before the city police commission, promoter Robinson was asked what he would do differently next time. His answer: "I wouldn't do it." A man who lived on Zelzah Avenue quipped: "Somebody suggested they have it in Death Valley next year."

The wrong family values

The summer of 1969 concluded with unsettling revelations that caused some residents of the Valley to lose their innocence and look more closely at who lived around them. Writer Joan Didion said in her literary mosaic of the era, *The White Album:* "Many people I know in Los Angeles believed the '60s ended abruptly on August 9, 1969."

That was the day news reports carried sketchy but gruesome details of a mass murder in exclusive Benedict Canyon, in the Santa Monica Mountains. Sharon Tate, a beautiful young actress eight months

The aftermath of Newport '69 was not a pretty sight; hundreds were arrested or treated at hospitals and it took days for Northridge to recover. But these young scavengers turned litter into cash.

pregnant—the wife of Roman Polanski, director of the previous year's film sensation, *Rosemary's Baby*—was found butchered with four others in a compound protected by a high fence and electric gate. The word "PIG" was written on the front door in Tate's blood. That night, an apparent copycat killer stabbed to death grocer Leno LaBianca and his wife Rosemary in their Los Feliz area home, then scrawled "Healter Skelter" misspelling and all in blood. Gun

sales soared as alarm swept the city, especially in Hollywood circles.

On the following Sunday, the *Times* unwittingly made the connection between the Valley and the barbarous murders, but not even the police picked up on it. On the same page as stories on the Benedict Canyon murder scene and the LaBianca funerals, the missed clue was in a brief story that reported a sheriff's raid on a car theft ring at the Spahn Ranch, an old

movie location in Santa Susana Pass. Most of the 26 heavily armed suspects arrested were young women in hippie clothes.

Only months later would the connection become chillingly clear. The city's most notorious killers had roamed freely in the Valley youth culture, led by a criminal madman named Charles Manson. His "family" of young and mostly suburbia-bred women worshipped him and obeyed his commands. For about a year before the killings they had squatted at the Spahn Ranch, which became known in the Valley as a place to score drugs and hang out with free spirits who frolicked nude in the rocks. Before that, some of the girls had lived with Dennis Wilson of the Beach Boys. The band even recorded a song Manson wrote, "Never Learn Not to Love."

Manson sometimes sent the girls out of the Chatsworth rocks to do petty thefts and raid dumpsters behind supermarkets for discarded food. Other times they would dress in black, carry knives and "creepy crawl"—their name for breaking into suburban homes while the residents slept, moving the furniture, and leaving without taking anything. By the summer of 1969, Manson's mental state was unraveling. In his bestseller *Helter Skelter,* prosecutor Vincent T. Bugliosi wrote that Manson, then 35 years old, believed racial warfare would engulf the world. Manson called the coming strife "helter skelter," after a Beatles song.

On August 8, two family members were arrested in San Fernando for trying to use stolen credit cards.

Charles Manson took over the remote Spahn Ranch, plying its feeble owner with attentive girls and hiding in the old movie sets to lie low from the law.

On trial for the 1969 murders, Manson's followers included Patricia Krenwinkel, Leslie Van Houten and Susan Atkins. The three women and Manson were convicted of murder and received life sentences to prison.

Manson spotting

The list of Manson family sites in the Valley includes:

◆ Spahn Ranch in Santa Susana Pass, destroyed by fire in 1970.

◆ House at 20910 Gresham Street in Canoga Park, where the family lived between stays at Spahn Ranch.

◆ Vox recording studio at 15456 Cabrito Street in Van Nuys, where Manson cut a demo record on August 9, 1968—one year to the day before the Tate killings.

◆ 3627 Longview Valley Road in Sherman Oaks, where the gun used to shoot Jay Sebring and Voytek Frykowski was found thrown in the backyard.

◆ Gas station at Roxford Street exit from the Golden State Freeway, where the wallet of Rosemary LaBianca was found stashed in the bathroom. Manson bought milk-shakes for his followers at the Denny's coffee shop next door.

This seemed to push Manson over the edge. That night, he sent Tex Watson, Susan Atkins, Patricia Krenwinkel and a newcomer, Linda Kasabian, out to commit a crime so unforgivable that whites would blame blacks and his race war would finally explode. "Leave a sign," Manson suggested. "You girls know what to write. Something witchy." Tate's Benedict Canyon home was familiar to Manson—he had visited twice when it was occupied by record producer Terry Melcher and actress Candace Bergen. Melcher, the son of actress Doris Day, had angered Manson by rejecting his bid to record an album.

When a housekeeper discovered the carnage in the morning, blood was everywhere. The bodies of houseguests Abigail Folger and Voytek Frykowski lay splayed on the lawn, stabbed wildly as they fled. Jay Sebring, Tate's former boyfriend, was in the living room, shot and stabbed. Tate, dressed only in bra and panties, had a rope coiled around her neck and looped over a living room rafter. She had been stabbed 16 times in the chest and back; her unborn son also was dead. Steven Parent, an unlucky visitor to the compound, was found shot in his car in the driveway. Some in Hollywood speculated that the killings were some kind of sadomasochistic frenzy, due to rumors about Sebring's sexual tastes. No one blamed the black citizens of Los Angeles, as Manson had hoped.

On the night of August 9, Manson himself invaded the LaBianca home, tied up the couple and left the killings to Watson, Krenwinkel and Leslie Van Houten.

Manson's initation rite

Charles Manson's hold on the loyalties and affections of the suburban girls who became his followers and who did his killing remains a mystery. "The females in the group had as their major role the duty of gratifying the males," according to a study of the Manson family's practices conducted before the murders and reported in the Journal of Psychedelic Drugs. "Charlie set himself up as 'initiator of new females' into the commune. He would spend most of their first day making love to them, as he wanted to see if they were just on a 'sex trip' or whether they were seriously interested in joining the group."

Manson after his 1969 arrest in the desert near Death Valley, California.

The trio hitchhiked across the Valley to the ranch after they finished. Manson, meanwhile, drove to Sylmar and had Kasabian plant Rosemary LaBianca's wallet in the restroom of a gas station, hoping it would be found and incite rioting. Then he bought milkshakes for everybody at the Denny's next door.

Though Manson and the women were arrested as car theft suspects the following weekend, they were not linked to the murders and were released. The family fled to the desert near Death Valley to wait out the race war that would never come. Not until December did police announce their arrests for murder. Manson's original death sentence was converted to life in prison by the California Supreme Court in 1972. He turned 65 in prison on November 12, 1999, and is routinely rejected for parole, as are other family members.

CHAPTER 11

The Valley Myth

E.T. found the San Fernando Valley an odd yet friendly place to visit, but the cinema's favorite extraterrestrial made it clear that he wished to go home.

The San Fernando Valley is remarkably well known for a place that doesn't exist in any official sense. A mythical image of the place has permeated American culture, largely due to the proximity of Bing Crosby and later generations of showbiz folk. They have lived and played there famously. They still make their movies at studios there. And sometimes they fashion those movies—or their songs—to be about the Valley itself. Writers and authors, many of them locals too, have contributed by taking surroundings familiar to them as the settings of their stories. Outside of fiction, the Valley's image has been shaped by big news events, most notably catastrophic earthquakes and heinous crimes. The global explosion in reportage on the lives of celebrities has also given form to the myth, since so many stars of the gossip pages—among them Kevin Spacey, Jennifer Aniston and Michael Jackson—either hail from the Valley or live there now.

Just what the prevailing image is at any given moment has evolved through time. In the early 1900s the Valley was typically described as a rural haven where a hard-working family could raise peaches or white leghorns, yet still enjoy some of the perks of being close to the city. By World War II, the Valley was a famed refuge of movie stars. After the war, it became a defining American suburb, known for—and usually praised for—its comfortable, if somewhat boring, clean-cut style. But the suburbs also conjured up pictures of ugly sprawl and numbing cultural sameness, and the Valley became the occasional butt of jokes. On TV, the popular late 1960s comedy hour "Rowan and Martin's Laugh-In"—and its late-night partner on NBC, Johnny Carson's "Tonight Show"—spoofed the dubious qualities of "beautiful downtown Burbank." "The Brady Bunch" series made sugary fun of family life in a split-level, ranch-style, obviously Valley home.

Then came Valley Girls, the intelligence-challenged teenagers who shared a grating lingo and a compulsive need to shop. The stereotype of Valley Girls as bimbos in the making—and the Valley as the kind of lame place that would nurture them—swept the country in the 1980s and has never quite faded. In the end-of-century sex scandal involving President Bill Clinton, the Valley Girl label was casually applied to Oval Office plaything Monica Lewinsky, even though she was actually a product of Beverly Hills.

But gratuitous swipes at the Valley never seem out of favor. This seemed especially true in movies released in the late 1990s, a low point in the Valley's standing in American culture. In the comedy *Clueless*, Alicia Silverstone's cheerful Beverly Hills ditz Cher Horowitz is forced to spend a painful and socially humiliating night deep in the Valley. Silverstone was back again, with Brendan Fraser, in *Blast from the Past*, a romantic Cold War farce in which the Valley transforms from a Wonder Bread suburb into a "post-apocalyptic hellspace of dirt, decay and debauchery," as one reviewer put it. In *Go*, streetwise city girl Sarah Polley warns her whiny girlfriend, "Don't get 818 on me," and audiences get the area code put-down. In

His infamous beating at the hands of Los Angeles police in Lake View Terrace made Rodney King a household name.

his films *Boogie Nights* and *Magnolia,* native director Paul Thomas Anderson makes the Valley out to be a not very desirable place filled with people you probably wouldn't want to know.

The Valley even took a light ribbing in a 1999 novel satirizing New York media culture, *Turn of the Century* by Kurt Andersen. The narrator, on a West Coast business trip, drives to a television studio built on the site of a failed pornographic video company in Burbank: "Because the Valley is inherently dispiriting, the drizzle and the gray improve it in some relativistic way—the lousy weather and the Valley are in synch on a day such as this. Burbank seems less

like a failed paradise manque, and more like Cleveland."

Indeed, the Valley is rarely associated anymore with the cheery suburban optimism of "The Brady Bunch" or the blockbuster *E.T. The Extra-Terrestrial,* which never mentioned the Valley but was filmed in neighborhoods there and played on its idealized sense of place. More often now the Valley is featured as a spoiled, even menacing landscape. A good example is *187,* in which Samuel L. Jackson—who in real life is local to Encino—portrays a New York school teacher brutalized by his students. He moves west, expecting the San Fernando Valley will be a haven from urban insanity, but instead he encounters gangs that are even more murderous. This dark turn in the cinematic image probably reflects the presence of so many writers, directors and producers in and around the Valley. Living and working there, they know that the old postwar suburb has lost much of its earlier innocence. They are just showing what they know.

The Valley is no longer the pastoral outpost of 120,000 people who went the entire Labor Day weekend of 1936 without reporting a single crime. For anyone who follows the news, it is more likely to be thought of now as a crowded place with its own urban ills, ravaged by gang wars, multiple murders or some other high-profile calamity. It was on a dark street in Sun Valley where an unrepentant gun advocate, William Masters, shot a tagger in the back and bragged about it, vowing that no jury would convict him. It was in Lake View Terrace where Los Angeles

After a lengthy battle with police, this gunman's hood came off before he died on a North Hollywood street.

Children were led to safety in Granada Hills after automatic weapons fire raked their Jewish Community Center day-care facility. No one was killed in the attack.

police officers stomped Rodney King, the first in the chain of troubling events that led to the 1992 Los Angeles (and Valley) riots. In North Hollywood, live TV showed hooded bank robbers in body armor brazenly battling the cops with automatic weapons, then bleeding to death on the street. In Granada Hills, a hateful maniac opened fire on Jewish children in a day-care center, then slaughtered a postal carrier. It was even in the Valley, from a friend's hilltop home in Encino, where Orenthal James Simpson sped off in a white Ford Bronco and became—for a few sensational hours in June 1994—the nation's most famous fugitive from justice.

News coverage has helped stoke the emerging less-than-idyllic reputation, but the root of the Valley's image problem is the perception, especially strong in other sections of Los Angeles, that the Valley is simply not a very hip address. So what else is new: "When we moved to the Valley, I felt like I was being tossed into quicksand," Robert Redford, recalling his teenage days in Van Nuys in the 1950s, once told the *Times*. "There was no culture. It was very oppressive." He got out as soon as he could.

Other Angelenos, not surprisingly, can be the Valley's harshest critics. "Like, the Valley's Not a Joke Anymore!" a 1990 headline screamed in Los Angeles magazine. The article was mostly positive, yet characterized the Valley as "the strange land over the hill" and quoted a longtime resident saying "it still lacks a real personality… It's like a giant bowl of oatmeal." Even the locals are tough on themselves. When the *Times*' Valley staff invited readers to suggest witty ideas for a municipal name should the Valley secede and become a city, nominations included Minimallia, McValley, Beige-Air, Valle de Nada and Ranchos de los Ranchos. The winner by acclamation: Twenty-nine Malls.

"L.A. is surrounded by valleys, but there's only one Valley, and to everybody who lives on the other side of the hill from it, it's a standing joke," novelist Peter Israel wrote in *Hush Money*. Though not necessarily based in fact, the feeling runs deep, according to Sandra Tsing Loh, a writer, humorist and performance artist who should know. She lives in Van Nuys and wrote a monthly column on her life in the Valley for the late Buzz magazine that described the nub of the problem: "There are some L.A. addresses so unfashionable that people actually recoil in horror when you admit you live there. And of course, no basin puts people off as much as the San Fernando Valley. The feeling is absolute. The same people who'll drive from Santa Monica to Pasadena (25 miles) without blinking find lunch in Reseda (16 miles) much too far."

In her collection of essays called *Depth Takes a*

Strange doings

Space aliens in Big Tujunga Canyon? Yes, according to two young women who said they were sleeping in an isolated cabin on March 22, 1953, when lights suddenly illuminated the canyon and surrounded their house, after which time seemed to stand still. When they finally fled, one said, she saw a filmy apparition of a longhaired man.

Their account is in a 1989 book, *The Tujunga Canyon Contacts*, by Ann Druffel of the UFO investigation group SkyNet and D. Scott Rogo. Other strange phenomena reported in the canyon include soundless black helicopters, daylight flying disks and sightings of misty gray figures called "light people" by schoolchildren on camping trips.

Of more recent vintage, *UFOs Over Topanga* by Preston Dennett chronicles reported sightings in Topanga Canyon during the 1990s. On the World Wide Web, UFO watchers were especially intrigued by claims in 1996 that a huge burning ball had descended from the sky near Rocketdyne's rocket testing lab in the Santa Susana Mountains.

The Loh life

Sandra Tsing Loh's 1997 novel, *If You Lived Here, You'd Be Home By Now*, treats readers to the angst of a Gen X couple who try to earn their bohemian credentials by eschewing L.A. for a rented three-bedroom in Tujunga:

"Don't you see? Being out here is so Lancaster Desert, so Frank Zappa-esque. It's like living in Los Angeles but refusing to be a part of it. Like starting our own tribe. Denying the whole fou-fou trendy La Brea/Melrose/giving over to the style-weasels thing."

But Bronwyn, the heroine of the book, isn't buying it:

"No, 23511 Colton Place was more David Lynch than Frank Zappa. It was the sort of place where a querulous old woman with an eye patch would live with her inbred adult son, Hank, clad in a big old diaper. It was the kind of place you saw featured on 'A Current Affair.'"

Later she recoils in horror when a real estate agent sizes up her net worth and suggests that her best hope of owning a home is—"No. No. Absolutely not. Not the Valley."

Holiday, Loh put her own spin on the Valley's new face. She called it the "home of a hundred King Bear Auto Centers, a thousand Yoshinoya Beef Bowls, and ten thousand yard sales." As for the blossoming of tiny ethnic restaurants run by newly arrived immigrants, she has her favorites but wonders how some of them survive: "What inspires some folks to relocate halfway around the world to the San Fernando Valley in order to feed bad food on paper plates to their own people?"

The Valley canon

The 1.7 million souls who do live in the Valley, most of them by choice—because *they* like it—can choose from a library of books and films set in or about their hometown. The body of work runs from *Don Sagasto's Daughter*, a 1911 novel by Paul Harcourt Blades, about a proud *Californio* whose *rancho* was near Mission San Fernando, to potboiler detective mysteries.

At the top of any serious reading list should be the nonfiction works so rich with insight or direct reportage that they are quoted, by necessity, elsewhere in this book. These include *The Owensmouth Baby* and *Calabasas Girls* by Catherine Mulholland; colorful accounts of Pacoima barrio family life by Mary Helen Ponce in *Hoyt Street* and *Taking Control;* and Earl Anthony's *The Time of the Furnaces*, chronicling the 1968 black student rebellion at Valley State College. Though it is difficult to find, a true aficionado would enjoy the 1924 history of the Valley compiled by the San Fernando chapter of the Daughters of the American Revolution, whose best sources were the somewhat gilded memories of the group's own members.

The Valley received its first serious literary treatment at the hands of a local in the 1930s in James M. Cain's *The Postman Always Rings Twice*. Cain wrote in a rented two-bedroom Craftsman on Bel Aire Drive in the Burbank hills and apparently sensed an air of criminal-erotic desperation in the rural corners and roadside cafes he visited on long drives in his Ford roadster. *Postman*, regarded by some as the first modern American bestseller, was set in the general area of Agoura, in just such a gas station-cafe run by Nick Papadakis and his steamy wife Nora. She is terminally bored, both with Nick and with waiting on the motorists who pull off the highway for lunch. Into the cafe one day comes drifter Frank Chambers, who senses Nora's simmering needs and falls hard for her. The amorous couple, using an Encino rabbit breeder as their alibi, kill Nick and then fake a car accident on Malibu Lake Road in an (unsuccessful) effort to cover up the deed. In the 1946 film, starring John Garfield as Frank and Lana Turner as Nora, the Papadakis name was dropped as too ethnic—Nick and Nora became Mr. and Mrs. Smith.

Cain's second novel, *Double Indemnity*, continued on the theme of lust-begets-homicide and was set in Glendale. Adapted to the screen by Billy Wilder and Raymond Chandler, the film starred Fred MacMurray as an unassuming insurance agent who falls for Barbara Stanwyck, a scheming housewife. In Cain's story the conspirators talk themselves into killing her husband and running off with his insurance policy, confident their tracks are covered. But a dogged investigator, played by Edward G. Robinson, suspects them of foul play and makes the case. Stanwyck, who knew the Valley well from her days as a Northridge horse breeder, later played the murderous female side of a Valley married couple in *Crime of Passion*. Her character was a smart newspaper advice columnist who gives up her job to marry, then can't abide her boring existence as a homemaker. She resorts to murder to help her police officer-husband's career.

More recent crime novelists seem to like the Valley's spoiled suburbs as a locale for dastardly deeds and retrograde characters. *Fatal Convictions* by Shari P. Geller involves a serial killer exacting his own justice on Valley child molesters and is set partly at Tommy's Burgers on Roscoe Boulevard—"the only true landmark in the San Fernando Valley." Vic Daniel, the private detective in a series of books by David M. Pierce, is based in "that scurvy part of California known as the San Fernando Valley" where the smog settles in "like cheap hairspray on a home permanent." The *Ritual Bath* by Faye Kellerman involves a rape at a local yeshiva, tapping into the Valley's history of strong Jewish communities; in Barbara Seranella's *No Human Involved,* Munch Mancini is a waifish street junkie and ace car mechanic whose run from the law takes her as far as

a garage at the corner of Sepulveda and Ventura. She kicks her heroin habit at Narcotics Anonymous meetings at Reseda High School.

Some writers, especially those without strong local ties, have ascribed an apocalyptic edge to the Valley. J. G. Ballard, in *Hello America,* spun a fantasy set a century in the future with soldiers loyal to President Charles Manson digging through the ruins of the old Lockheed plant in Burbank in search of nuclear weapons to launch against Las Vegas. Ugliness reached an extreme in *The Turner Diaries,* the underground racist diatribe in which white supremacists launch their own Holocaust on Los Angeles from a secret command post in the Valley. They summarily execute Jews and anyone of mixed race, exile seven million blacks and Latinos to the desert, and hang 60,000 white "race traitors" from trees and power poles. But not all the fantasy fiction that visits the Valley is so malevolent. The futuristic Valley portrayed in *Snow Crash,* the cyber-fiction standard by Neal Stephenson, has devolved into a crazy quilt of turfs, or "burbclaves," each ruled by militias, religious cults, global corporations or the Mafia. Everything, including freeways, is privately controlled, requiring diplomacy and daredevil driving by the Deliverator, a pizza delivery boy for the Cosa Nostra. "All the people who run Cosa Nostra pizza franchises in this part of the Valley are Abkhazian immigrants," he observes. The Valley also shows up in Ed Wood's *Plan 9 From Outer Space,* called by many the worst sci-fi movie ever made. The

plot involves alien grave-robbers who take over a cemetery in the Valley.

Often, as in *Plan 9,* the Valley merely provides a convenient locale. But in some works, the Valley itself plays a key role in the story. This was certainly true in *Chinatown,* the 1974 film directed by Roman Polanski. Jack Nicholson stars as Jake Gittes, a private eye in 1920s Los Angeles who looks into the homicide of the city's water czar, Hollis Mulwray. That name is meant to evoke the memory of William Mulholland, and the story intends to echo the Valley's past as an El Dorado for water-fueled real estate speculators, but the plot details are strictly fiction. What the film lacks in historic accuracy it makes up for with twists and styling more compelling than the reality.

Gittes deciphers an elaborate conspiracy by hidden downtown powers who, at the peak of a fierce drought, dump the city's reservoir into the ocean in order to create a water shortage in the Valley. Squeezing ranchers to sell their withering orchards at distress prices is the motive; Gittes stumbles onto land deeds recorded under phony names. "Most of the Valley has been sold in the last few months," he tells Mulwray's widow, played by Faye Dunaway. The Robert Towne script oozes with intrigue. In one of the most intense scenes, Gittes is pursued through a maze of west Valley orange trees and roughed up by gun-toting country boys on horseback.

In a 1990 sequel that Nicholson directed, *The Two Jakes,* the setting flashes forward to the early postwar boom years. The orange groves are being

Walter Brennan got his Oscar before he played Amos McCoy, a comical San Fernando Valley rancher.

torn out for suburban cul-de-sacs, just as in real life. Gittes is older and mellower but allows himself to become embroiled in a murder case that turns on oil, rather than water, and on the real estate ambitions of the other Jake, the developer of "El Rancho San Fernando," played by Harvey Keitel.

The Valley's part was briefer, but explicit, in Quentin Tarantino's *Pulp Fiction,* which roamed

though many districts of Los Angeles. Gangsters Vincent Vega (John Travolta) and Jules Winnfield (Samuel L. Jackson) are driving along a main boulevard when Vega accidentally blows the head off an associate in crime riding in the backseat. They need to get off the street, since as the bad guys observe, even in the Valley cops tend to notice cars with blood-smeared windows. But where to? As Jules says, "I ain't got no partners in the 818."

Vincent: "Take it to a friendly place, that's all."

Jules: "We're in the Valley, Vincent! Marcellus ain't got no friendly places in the Valley."

Vincent: "What you doin'?"

Jules: "I'm calling my partner in Toluca Lake."

Vincent: "Where's Toluca Lake?"

Jules: "Just over the hill here, over by Burbank Studios."

Murder worked as black comedy in the offbeat *Two Days in the Valley,* in which James Spader played a sociopath-hit man and Paul Mazursky an aging film director. Director John Herzfeld called the Valley an uncredited character in the story about people who need second chances to succeed: an Olympic skier who has yet to win her medal, a detective trying to make the homicide squad, a bumbling killer working at a Domino's Pizza on Ventura Boulevard. "The movie is about a lot of people who either never achieved their goals, or screwed up their lives, or dropped the football the first time it was thrown to them," Herzfeld said in the *Times.* The funniest line comes from an older man who hears a violent fight in

the upstairs apartment and quips to his wife: "Maybe that's how they make love in Tarzana." The essential Valleyness of the film was too much for French audiences. There, the title was translated as *Two Days in Los Angeles.*

Television sitcoms set in the Valley have, not surprisingly, taken a more cheerful view. "The Adventures of the Real McCoys" was the first, about a West Virginia hillbilly family that inherits money and drives a rickety truck across country to their new farm amid the San Fernando Valley suburbs. Sponsors hated the concept, but after the show aired in 1957—as Americans by the thousands were making the same migration across Route 66—it became a hit. Viewers loved the domestic predicaments that Grandpa Amos McCoy, played by Oscar-winning actor and real-life Valley rancher Walter Brennan, found himself in each week. As an added bit of authenticity, the McCoys even had a Latino yard hand, Pepino Garcia. The show ran for seven years and spawned an imitator in "The Beverly Hillbillies."

Analyzing suburbia

Authors with something to say about suburban life have found the Valley fertile ground. Theodore Pratt's *Valley Boy* is a 1946 novel about an 11-year-old lad who finds the affection he lacks at home in a matronly next-door neighbor and a trained sea lion. The San Fernando Valley in the book is an odd place with odd inhabitants and establishments, "a fey gash in the surface of the earth that bred and molded its own brand of people and ways." There is a restaurant named Dyspeptic Bill's, a store called The House of a Good Egg, and a girl who dresses in shorts and a full-length fur coat. Pratt's Valley is an eccentric and optimistic slice of suburbia: "There was nothing else like it."

The commentary was edgier in Michael Crichton's 1996 thriller, *Airframe*. It is set in the Burbank factory of the mythical Norton Aircraft Co., a maker of wide-body airliners that mysteriously fall out of the sky. The novel's heroine, Casey Singleton, is a quality assurance vice president with a personal life not unfamiliar in the real-life Valley. She has weathered numerous layoffs in the aerospace industry and divorce from a drunk. She lives on a Glendale street where, in modern suburban fashion, she hears the pop of gunfire in her sleep and frets about sending her daughter to a school system where 50 languages are spoken. The mirage of the perfect suburban lifestyle also came in for jabs in the *The Dreyfus Affair: A Love Story,* a lighter Peter Lefcourt novel that gives the Valley an American League baseball team after the TV networks decreed, "Phoenix didn't have the demographics that the San Fernando Valley did." The Vikings play in a 125,000-seat stadium in the Sepulveda Dam basin. Their star is Randy Dreyfus, the ultimate suburban fantasy jock: the best young shortstop in the sport, "the fastest white guy in the league," and happily married to a blond Rose Queen. But Randy endures a long slump, is distracted on the field and surly at home in their gated community. He can only blame it on one thing: he is secretly in love with the Vikings' black second baseman.

Suburbia's comforts and travails were explored in perceptive detail in a pair of novels that critiqued the Valley's vaunted postwar years through the sobering eyes of teenage girls. *Wet Paint,* by Gwynn Popovac, exposed the loneliness and disillusionment that infected some family relationships in the monotonous tracts of nearly identical new houses. Her Flora Jackson attends a thinly disguised Birmingham High and is ready to burst at the strictures placed on her desires for love and adventure in the postwar Valley. Her relief comes in her fantasies about the slightly dark, slightly troubled boy from the hills south of Ventura Boulevard who shares her easel in art class. Their bohemian art teacher lets the students hang out in the studio at lunch and consummate their crushes in the supply room. The book is filled with insight into teenage pain, tracking Flora's emotional spikes as she tries to make her way socially and sexually, and portraying parents more concerned with dichondra and harsh discipline than listening and love.

My Sister from the Black Lagoon, published in 1998, covers somewhat similar ground. Author Laurie Fox bares the frigid dysfunction of a middle-class Valley family in the postwar rush, and the impact on a sensitive and aware teenager like Lorna Person. After a difficult childhood with parents who don't understand her, Lorna must change high schools when her family moves from Burbank to Tarzana. The differences between the two communities are shown as stark, and the move upsets her already lonely life. But the new school and new friends ultimately give Lorna the fresh start that she needs.

The frustrations of adolescence in the culturally deprived expanses of the Valley also inspired *Foxes,* a 1980 film directed by Adrian Lyne that follows four bored girls from the burbs who go on night-life adventures in Hollywood. Jodie Foster played the wise one who watched out for her wilder friends. The girl played by Cherie Currie, who in real life was a singer with the band the Runaways, pays dearly for her fascination with seeking out ever higher highs, while the other girls grapple with being overweight or oversexed. Another take on growing up in the Valley was presented in *La Bamba,* the 1987 film that told the Ritchie Valens story in part by fictionalizing his family relationships. In recent years, films by two young directors who have spent some of their years living in the Valley gave the most layered portrayals, depicting it as both desirable and repulsive. In *Safe,* Todd Haynes' suburbs are so smothering as to be toxic. Julianne Moore starred as a west Valley stepmother who lives behind closed gates where the new streets meet the chaparral. She seems content with a life that is attractive but numbingly empty, consumed by ordering furniture, overseeing her maid and going to aerobics classes and the hair salon. After she drives behind a smoking truck on Ventura Boulevard and breathes in fumes, she is besieged by

Julianne Moore has starred in three films where the Valley itself was the main character.

allergies and toxic reactions to the suburban environment.

Moore also starred in *Boogie Nights,* which takes place almost entirely within the dark clubs, secluded backyards and otherwise tacky milieu of the Valley's home-brewed pornography industry circa 1980. As directed by Paul Thomas Anderson, the storefronts and quiet tract neighborhoods hide secrets and disappointments. Moore serves as the mother figure to an extended family of fading porn players, wannabes and hangers-on who pine for better lives while they put on sophisticated airs at the pool and cocktail parties they hold between filming triple-XXX footage. Burt Reynolds plays the porn king of Reseda, Valley native Heather Graham is a teen porn actress who never removes her roller skates, and Mark Wahlberg is the pimply dishwasher who becomes the legendarily studly Dirk Diggler, loosely a reference to the late porn star John Holmes. Modern-day Sherman Way is the backdrop for several brutal scenes, including a robbery that turns bloody inside a doughnut shop, the stomping of a college boy by Rollergirl, and the pummeling of a destitute Diggler by gay bashers. Many in the cast, including Moore, returned to the Valley with Anderson in *Magnolia,* which portrayed a place riven with dysfunctional relationships and hit with a plague of frogs from the sky.

Any festival of Valley cinema would need to make room for at least one porn video. The Valley has been the world capital of porn production for decades, due to the ready availability of secluded backyards and post-production facilities, skilled crew members needing work and talent willing to have sex on screen. The industry also has something of a sense of local humor. One porn actress uses the screen name Tarzana, and in a film called *San Fernando Valley Girls,* rivals set up a competition to decide who deserves the title "Valley Girl." If you guessed what the competition involves, you'd be right.

Like it was a joke, OK?

Perhaps the greatest shaper of the Valley's popular image since Bing Crosby sang "San Fernando Valley" to homesick GIs was a spoof record by musician Frank Zappa and his daughter, Moon Unit. "Valley Girls" was satire, inspired by Moon's dinner table mocking of her schoolmates' syntax and incessant shopping at the Sherman Oaks Galleria. On the

Frank Zappa was a rocker of some repute in 1972, before he became the father of Valley Girls.

record she portrays Ondrya, a girl whose ultimate goal is to be popular ("otherwise people might not like you"). She whines about her mother ("like a total space cadet"), her braces ("like a total bummer") and her English teacher's homosexuality ("It's like barf me out."). The song popularized phrases like "fer shur," "gag me with a spoon" and "grody to the max."

The impact was stunning, both on the public's perception of the Valley and for the Zappas. The song zoomed to national popularity in the summer of 1982 and sold more records than any of Frank Zappa's work as a solo artist or as the leader of the avant garde 1960s band the Mothers of Invention. "I did it to amuse myself, my family and friends," Moon Zappa told Newsweek magazine. "And it was just so bizarre to have the whole world in on a joke."

Time magazine reported that from Tarzana to Tarrytown, every parent with a teenaged daughter spent that summer fretting: Is she one? The answer was yes for millions of girls who aspired to the style and sensibility of a few San Fernando Valley teenagers. Teen magazine declared that the Valley Girl style was a trendsetter in schools and shopping malls. The style was "cute:" mini-skirts, headbands, anklets and ruffles, feathered haircuts, waxed legs and manicured nails. The phenomenon had enough power that, even though the look faded long ago, the reputation of Valley Girls as airheads lives on. Not surprisingly, the put-down is not appreciated in the place where it all started.

At the height of the phenomenon, a film called

Valley Girl, directed by Martha Coolidge, sought to cash in on the buzz. In fact, the story and characters bore no resemblance to the girls in the song. Deborah Foreman played a popular high school girl who goes against her Valley friends and dates Nicolas Cage, who portrays a bad-news dude from Over the Hill. She takes him on a tour of a few local landmarks—DuPars coffee shop, Casa Vega restaurant, Encino Bowl, Mulholland Drive. The film's advertising tagline was "She's cool. He's hot. She's from the Valley. He's not." Although that film did not slight the Valley, it was followed by a torrent of film references designed to poke fun. In *Encino Man,* Brendan Fraser played an icebound caveman thawed out by nerdy Valley boys and taught how to party. A spin-off, "Encino Woman," aired on network TV. The comic high point of the genre might have been *Earth Girls Are Easy,* in which three extra-terrestrial aliens splash to Earth in the pool of a giddy Valley manicurist, played by Geena Davis. "As if things weren't bad enough," she whines, "now I've been abducted by aliens."

CHAPTER 12

Suburbia No More

In one of many clashes between the suburbs and the old Valley, Van Nuys homemakers in the 1950s went to the city to protest flies from nearby chicken farms.

In and around Los Angeles, the San Fernando Valley has a reputation for being cantankerous and self-centered, and for loudly complaining about any number of perceived grievances and slights. The image is largely deserved. Every Valley community, it seems, has a homeowner association willing to fight city hall or the homeowner group next door.

Escaping the municipal clutches of Los Angeles by seceding from the city is a big idea that comes and goes. It has, however, never ignited the popular fervor of issues like school busing or property taxes or the fears fueled by a litany of lesser horrors: low-flying jets, garbage dumps, backyard chicken coops, adult bookstores, graffiti or out-of-favor community names. Too few police, not enough ambulances. Cutting down trees, building too many apartments. Even churches have proven controversial. "Hymn singing would interfere with the peace and quiet of the neighborhood," a Wilbur Avenue man complained in the 1960s when the congregation of Northridge Missionary Church wanted to worship temporarily in a home near his.

Fevered debates over hot-button topics like oak tree preservation, the timing of traffic lights and where to install stop signs have sundered friendships and shattered neighborhood harmony. The president of the Encino Homeowners Association in the late 1980s was physically assaulted by agitated Tarzana residents at a community meeting that seethed with hostility. Los Angeles city councilman Marvin Braude, who also was jostled, complained: "I've been in public life for 25 years and this is the first time I've been pushed." The incendiary topic: Whether to extend Reseda Boulevard through the Santa Monica Mountains.

Sticking up for the Valley

Leaders have repeatedly tried to coax the communities to put aside parochial concerns and work together on behalf of the Valley. Most often, the intent was to be able to deal with Los Angeles from a position of strength.

In 1914, delegates from Burbank, Lankershim, Chatsworth Park, Zelzah, Monte Vista, the Little Landers colony in Tujunga and the new towns of Van Nuys and Owensmouth met in San Fernando. They named a chairman, John T. Wilson, who was a respected pioneer resident and foreman of George K. Porter's ranches and subdivision enterprises. They organized themselves as the San Fernando Valley Federated Commercial Bodies and agreed to cooperate for the good of the region.

But town rivalries soon undermined the effort. Lankershim and Owensmouth, for instance, stayed behind in 1915 while most of the Valley joined the City of Los Angeles. Later, property owners along San Fernando Road—the only north-south highway across the Valley—objected when Van Nuys merchants cooked up a scheme to steal motor traffic off the road. The Van Nuys upstarts had posted an electric sign that directed Los Angeles-bound motorists down a narrow blacktop through orange groves and dairy farms and into Van Nuys, a detour that added several miles to the trip. Under pressure the Van Nuys group finally altered the sign—to snare motorists bound for UCLA, which had just opened in Westwood.

After World War II, when Van Nuys Army Airfield was offered to the city for one dollar as war surplus, new divisions opened. Neighbors and chambers of commerce could not agree whether a civilian airport in the middle of suburban development would be a good idea; many residents just wanted the city to reopen Saticoy Street, which had been closed when the wartime runway was lengthened. The offer was ultimately accepted, but the proposed name—San Fernando Valley Airport—caused a dispute. The city of San Fernando had its own airport and objected that the name could be confusing. Everyone finally settled on Van Nuys Airport.

Some of the fiercest fights broke out in defense of the Valley's new rural-suburban lifestyle. The first heated land-use battle of the postwar era was over plans by Forest Lawn, which ran a famous memorial park in Glendale, to open a second cemetery on a slope of the Santa Monica Mountains, adjacent to Griffith Park. The site was a landmark in Valley history, the locale where D.W. Griffith filmed *The Birth of a Nation* and part of the Lasky movie ranch. But the fight was over rezoning and preserving the land as open space. Anti-Forest Lawn rhetoric included

She said no—for as long as she could—but there was no stopping the Golden State Freeway from gobbling up this property owner's home in 1958. Battles over eminent domain condemnations were common.

Tales of
Forest Lawn

◆ The original Forest Lawn Memorial Park in Glendale inspired the British novelist Evelyn Waugh to write *The Loved One,* his satirical take on California's funerary culture.

◆ Hours after the Los Angeles city council in 1948 gave conditional approval to open the new Forest Lawn in Hollywood Hills, the operators moved swiftly to bury six bodies obtained from the downtown General Hospital. The maneuver, under state law, automatically dedicated the land as a permanent cemetery—cutting off any chance the council might have to change its mind.

assertions that contamination from the corpses would seep down to the water supply, with the Los Angeles River just below the hilly acreage. "Study This and Shudder!" newspaper ads screamed. Rezoning was granted, however.

Bulldozers clearing routes for freeways incited many skirmishes over neighborhood preservation and condemnation of private property. But the defin-

ing quality-of-life controversy in the 1950s and 1960s was over how much land to set aside for growth—in particular, for industry. The Valley's growth boosters wanted to encourage factories and plants so that residents could work near home and not have to drive every morning into Hollywood or Los Angeles. Horse ranches with white-planked fences and expansive citrus groves still covered the west end of the Valley, but many developers and businessmen gleefully foresaw a future population of one or two million.

A new power, the Industrial Association of the San Fernando Valley, formed in 1949 to push for industrial zoning. Its leadership came from banks and savings and loans, real estate interests, newspapers and the city Department of Water and Power—interests that all stood to gain if manufacturing plants replaced pastures and orchards. The association took on the mission of persuading the city to designate West Valley land for industry before new neighborhoods invaded the prime open space along the Southern Pacific railroad tracks, which would service the plants.

Opposition came mostly from the West Valley Homeowners Protection Association, which held rallies, testified before city committees and filed lawsuits—tactics that would become common tools of slow-growth homeowner groups in the Valley. Many homeowners liked the orange and walnut groves encircling their tracts and treasured the space to ride horses and raise a few peacocks—

Sprawl happens

A city planning consultant warned in 1956 that the suburban character of the Valley was already endangered: "The valley is neither as livable nor as efficient as it might have been." Not enough land had been set aside for parks and public spaces to help form cohesive communities, and the practice of lining boulevards with strip shopping was "not only inefficient in that it strangles traffic movement, but is violently ugly and blighting to the residential areas fringing it."

More serious, the consultant concluded, suburbia had been allowed to "sprawl uniformly over mile after mile, with little variation in density or dwelling type, making for monotony not only of view but of inhabitants."

while still living within driving distance of jobs in the city. But in the mid-1950s a swath exceeding 7,000 acres was zoned industrial, mostly along the tracks in Canoga Park, Northridge and Chatsworth. From then on, ranching was all but finished as a big-time occupation.

As the Valley filled with people, its political clout grew stronger. A major coup was the state's decision

Sam Yorty of Studio City became the first beneficiary of Valley political power.

to place a coveted four-year college in the area. Proposed sites were adjacent to the Sepulveda veteran's hospital, at the former Birmingham Army Hospital—not yet a high school—or near Hansen Dam. Ultimately, 165 acres of squash fields and orange groves were selected in Northridge. The bill to create San Fernando Valley State College was carried by local assemblyman Julian Beck, a former teacher at San Fernando High School, and the deal may have been sealed when Valley lobbyists picked up the check at a secret dinner for 23 lawmakers at the Brown Derby restaurant in Los Angeles. In 1961, the Valley flexed its muscle again to elect the mayor

of Los Angeles. Residents annoyed by a city ordinance requiring them to separate cans and bottles from other home trash made Sam Yorty of Studio City the first and so far only Valley inhabitant to occupy the mayor's office.

In the Cold War, defense contracts became the lifeblood of the Valley. A congressman elected from Van Nuys in 1960, James Corman, rose to become a power broker in the Democratic majority that funneled money to the plants—Lockheed, Litton, Bendix, Rocketdyne—that employed so many Valley fathers. While Corman wielded influence in Washington, another Democrat from Van Nuys, Robert Moretti, in 1971 became the speaker of the state Assembly, a post then considered second in statehouse power only to the governor. (The speakership would be claimed by a Democrat from the Valley again in 2000, when Bob Hertzberg of Sherman Oaks gained the post.)

By the mid-1970s, homeowners of all political stripes had become anxious over a new issue. As Valley homes rose in value, property tax bills soared. Many worried they might be forced to move, since the tax levy did not respect whether a person's income was rising or falling—the tax was keyed solely to the appraised value of the home. This was especially hard on people who planned to retire in their suburban castles—they may have bought for $29,995 after the war and since paid off the mortgage, but now they had to scrape together money to pay taxes on a theoretical market price of $100,000

or more.

An army of stirred-up suburbanites—some truly fearful of having to sell out to survive—was primed to act. Howard Jarvis, a pugnacious activist who had been on the periphery of local Republican circles for decades, came to the Valley to mobilize support for an initiative to roll back property taxes. Jarvis had tried and failed to place earlier tax-cutting measures on the ballot. But this time he partnered with a Sacramento-area activist, Paul Gann. The Jarvis-Gann

Homeowners packed the North Hollywood High auditorium in 1954 to protest rising property taxes.

initiative, Proposition 13, appeared on the June 1978 ballot and passed overwhelmingly, dramatically lowering taxes and altering how they are calculated. The Valley had been the hotbed of property tax anger and its reputation as a political force swelled. A Republican assemblyman from Woodland Hills, Paul Priolo, emerged as his party's leader in Sacramento.

At about the same time, an even more homegrown movement erupted among parents of school children. Under legal pressure to desegregate its classrooms, the Los Angeles board of education had come up with a plan to bus thousands of students across the city. Many parents in the Valley moved their children to private schools or left for smaller suburban enclaves with their independent systems. Others became politically active for the first time in their lives. Parents at Lanai Road Elementary, a secluded campus in the Encino hills, were among the first to organize. From their ranks emerged Bobbi Fiedler, a tireless mother who roused parents across the Valley to pack raucous meetings, carry protest signs and circulate petitions at shopping centers. Fiedler and another parent, Roberta Weintraub, were elected to the school board as anti-busing reformers.

A court ordered the buses to roll in 1978, but the whole idea ran counter to a basic value of the suburbs. Geographic isolation was no accident; rather, it was strongly preferred by most in the Valley, and only in part due to racial fears. Many dreaded the prospect of sending their children on buses over the hill, or across the Valley to areas they viewed as less safe—or even to receive inner-city students on their campuses. Some Valley inhabitants had come to resent the city, unwilling to go anywhere near downtown except, perhaps, to Dodger Stadium or the Coliseum. The anti-busing cause ultimately prevailed, defeating busing in 1981, and it morphed into a local political machine with Fiedler at the helm.

As Ronald Reagan was winning the White House in 1980, she took on Jim Corman, the Valley's most influential voice in Congress, and beat him by 752 votes out of 153,770 cast. Fiedler served six years before leaving to pursue unsuccessfully the Republican nomination for U.S. Senate. Roberta Weintraub went on to spend 14 years on the school board, serving as president several times before leaving public life.

Secession fever

The notion that the Valley should divorce itself from the City of Los Angeles has a long history. Northridge ranchers—seeking more home rule—pushed a secession bill in the Legislature in 1941, but it stalled. The west Valley's city councilman, Pat McGee, in 1960 advocated a borough system much like New York's, but it died for lack of interest. Same for a three-and-a-half year push to promote secession in the early 1960s by an organization called the

After spending years on the political fringe, Howard Jarvis led his tax cutting revolt to victory in 1978.

Bobbi Fiedler rode the busing issue all the way to Congress but lost her bid for the Senate in 1986.

Valleywide Better Government Committee, although the group's main agitator, Reseda mortician Don Lorenzen, was elected to the City Council.

In the mid-1970s, with city hall occupied by a mayor, Tom Bradley, whose focus was over the hill, some in the Valley's conservative-dominated chambers of commerce actively encouraged secession. They had connections in Sacramento and made the idea sound feasible enough that Los Angeles lobbied hard in the state capital and won veto power over any breakaway. That change in the rules, and a lack of public passion over the issue, killed the effort for the moment—although once again a prime mover, Northridge retailer Hal Bernson, was rewarded with a powerful platform by being elected to the City Council.

Talk of secession never fully dies—and may be the logical extension of the Valley's ingrained separateness. At the core of such sentiment is a widely held belief that the Valley is a superior place to live, but that it suffers the disrespect of Los Angeles. Hardcore secessionists also feel in their guts that, despite the plethora of new schools, streets, parks and libraries built in the suburban era, the city has never given the Valley its rightful share of government largesse. This belief may be "merely felt and sensed," in the words of USC political scientist H. Eric Schockman, but it is strongly embraced by many who have no need to see proof in black and white.

Serious discussion of quitting Los Angeles re-emerged in the 1990s—and this time began attracting wider interest. In the United States, only the cities of New York, Chicago, Houston, Philadelphia and the remainder of Los Angeles would have more people than an independent city of the San Fernando Valley. The London news weekly The Economist, calling the Valley "its own world, the quintessential suburban enclave," noted that secession movements are usually prompted by oppression. But, the magazine observed, in the Valley it was the bourgeois trying to escape from what they saw as a withering city. Secession even got laughs on late-night television. Jay Leno, host of NBC's "Tonight Show," did a bit about possible new names for a liberated Valley, and proffered a tongue-in-cheek list that stung some local sensibilities: Off-Ramp Acres...Asphalt-By-The-Sea...Smogadena ...Pornadelphia...Newer Jersey...Unknown Actorville ...Little Appalachia. Bobbi Fiedler, who by then had become a vocal secession advocate, retorted in the Times that "Jay Leno could have his chin in Los Angeles and his (backside) in Chatsworth and not know the difference."

The Valley's most influential industry figures and politicians have tended to view secession warily, since it promises a convulsive disruption without a clear upside—and without clear popular backing. But in the 1990s the cause was joined by some grass-roots voices previously silent. Homeowner groups, for example, play key roles in the organization responsible for a petition that collected the signatures of 130,000 voters to force a formal study of secession's feasibility. The group, Valley Voters

Since 1962, when this sign went up, communities in the Valley have enjoyed quasi-official status at city hall.

Organized Toward Empowerment (Valley VOTE), proposed a detailed municipal divorce in which the city's huge and profitable Department of Water and Power would be jointly operated by the two cities and most other civic assets would generally be divided by geography.

Valley VOTE claims more members than any earlier secession drive, but it has had limited financial backing. Only under pressure did the group's

The annual Chatsworth holiday parade and others like it promote community pride. Reflecting the area's rural roots, equestrians are prominent in most of the Valley's local parades.

most generous angel reveal itself in 1998: the Woodland Hills-based *Daily News* ran a small story disclosing that the newspaper had secretly contributed $60,000, a third of the organization's income at the time. The newspaper, successor to the old *Valley News and Green Sheet* and now owned by the Denver-based newspaper mogul Dean Singleton, has made greater Valley autonomy a front-page crusade. In editorials, it has urged residents to sign secession petitions, and likened secessionists to the American colonists who went to war to break free of England: "What did those 13 puny colonies want? A little respect. A little recognition. A lot of services for their money." The editorial page of the *Los Angeles Times,* which competes with the *Daily News* in the Valley market, has strongly opposed secession as a bad idea for the Valley and for Los Angeles.

Both papers have published gobs of stories on moves to secede from the city and to break from the Los Angeles Unified School District, even though the public at large has seemed mostly apathetic. Polls routinely find moderate support for the idea of secession, but there has been no rising drumbeat out of the neighborhoods to make it happen. To the contrary, at the first public hearing on the official secession study—the furthest any secession petition had ever gotten—only a few leaders of the cause and no member of the general public showed up. They blamed the embarrassment on inconvenient timing—9 a.m. on a weekday—but that seemed a lame excuse. The Valley has proven itself plenty ready to turn out when its passions are stoked, and it also is a community of early risers—hundreds of residents lined up their cars before dawn throughout that summer to buy Krispy Kreme doughnuts when an outlet opened in Van Nuys.

In fact, the Valley—formerly a hotbed of suburban rage—seems to have lost much of its zest for matters political. When an opportunity arose to send a message of protest over the hill—the most sweeping reform of city government in decades, on the 1999 ballot—voter turnout was abysmal. It was no aberration. Two years earlier, so few voters felt it important enough to secure a stronger local voice on the City Council that a Valley candidate lost to a Westsider in a district that straddles both areas.

A more fundamental obstacle for backers of secession is that, every year, the Valley becomes a little bit more like Los Angeles. People in the Valley are more likely now to shop at the same stores and be fans of the same celebrity chefs as trendsetters in the city—only those chefs have now opened sister restaurants along Ventura Boulevard. Brand names that once connoted the Valley—local favorites like Bob's Big Boy, DuPar's coffee shops, Baskin-Robbins, Gelson's markets, KGIL radio—either stopped emphasizing their roots or faded away entirely, unable to keep up with the chains.

But it goes much deeper than that. Secession also suffers from its image as an issue mainly of interest to older white homeowners and business people, at a time when the Valley has turned into one of the nation's most diverse areas. Valley VOTE has some minority board members, but the group's motives have remained suspect among minority leaders. One explanation may be that the voices that have complained loudest about the Valley not getting its "fair share" have never seemed especially bothered by Pacoima getting less than Northridge or Sherman Oaks.

A bigger factor is the changing nature of the Valley itself. A city of the San Fernando Valley would be a paradox—the whitest big city in America because it would lack an urban core of African Americans, but also a stewpot of tongues and sensibilities and aspirations. On an old suburban thoroughfare like Reseda Boulevard, there are store signs today in Farsi, Arabic, Armenian, Spanish and Korean. In Panorama City, the first planned suburb of the postwar boom, the old-line stores are gone and shopping crowds flock now to La Curacao, a Mayan and Aztec-themed department store where the clerks speak Spanish and purchases may be picked up—at the shopper's option—by family members back home at one of the retailer's outlets in Latin America.

After English and Spanish, the most commonly spoken languages in Valley public schools are, in order, Armenian, Korean, Tagalog, Vietnamese, Farsi, Russian, Thai, Punjabi, Arabic and Khmer. Of all campuses in the huge Los Angeles school system, the one with the most languages spoken in a 1998 survey was Granada Hills High School. A generation earlier, when Granada met San Fernando High for the city football championship in 1970, the game was widely anticipated as a symbolic showdown between the old and the newly emerging Valley: Granada's student body was almost all white, San Fernando was led by black and Latino players. In front of 16,000 charged-up fans at Birmingham High School, Granada won 38-28 and a melee in the stands ended the contest early. Granada Hills High now is a symbol of the Valley's diversity. Its students speak 28 native languages other than English: Spanish, Korean and Cantonese the most frequent, but also Punjabi, Tagalog, Greek, Hebrew, Croatian and Gujarati. Of the 20 campuses in the school system with the most resident languages, 13 are in the Valley. The least diverse sections of the Valley now are the traditional minority enclaves. Pacoima elementary schools such as Haddon Street and Telfair Avenue feature just one non-English language: Spanish.

The trend is unmistakable. In 1980 the U.S. Census found that a quarter of the Valley's population was foreign born. That share had grown to a third in the 1990 count, and will likely be higher again when the 2000 census is fully reported. The Valley has become a prime settling area for middle-class immigrants drawn from around the world to Southern California. Miles and miles of economically built and rapidly aging—and thus more affordable—tract homes and apartments provide places for new arrivals to live in a semblance of the fabled American suburbia.

Signs of the Valley's globalization are everywhere: More than 3,000 Armenian-American athletes competed in the 24th annual Navasartian Games at Birmingham High. A cricket match in Sepulveda Basin in 1999 was broadcast to England, Singapore, Australia and Pakistan. During that year's warfare in the Kosovo province of Yugoslavia, more than a dozen ethnic Albanian refugees made their way to the Valley to wait out the terror with countrymen here. Enclaves of immigrants exist in nearly every Valley community, with ethnic tensions sometimes at play. At Grant High School in Valley Village, ill will between Armenian and Latino students has been brewing since the 1980s, and in October 1999 spilled over into a melee that brought the LAPD to campus and sparked some anti-Armenian graffiti the principal called "nasty, terrible stuff."

Evidence of the new, more complicated demographic face is readily visible in Valley institutions. At

Cal State Northridge, a survey of student enrollment in the late 1990s showed 38% white, 22% Latino, 14% Asian, 8% black and the remaining 18% "other," including some few American Indians. A few blocks from campus, the Lutheran church built by Norwegian settlers in the farming outpost of Zelzah in 1917, still nicely preserved, now houses the Korean Los Angeles Antioch Church. And how's this for symbolism: the Budweiser brewery on Roscoe Boulevard, hailed when it opened in the 1950s as a paragon of all-American industry, since 1994 has turned the vats over once a week to a Japanese brewmaster who turns gallons of Owens Valley water into bottles of Kirin beer.

The Valley seems sometimes to seethe with barely concealed anger at the changes. After the First Presbyterian Church of Van Nuys, a fixture on Friar Street for 85 years, closed because the English-speaking membership had dwindled away, the longtime church secretary admitted to the *Times*: "It's been very hard to take, a lot of people do resent it." Sandy Banks, a *Times* columnist who is African American, has written about apartment vacancies vanishing when she knocks on the door, about a landlord who welcomed her and then confided, "We don't rent to the Mexicans," and about her own struggles to accept a Korean family in her close-knit Porter Ranch cul-de-sac.

It's not surprising, then, that the last issue to stir real passion in the Valley was not secession but Proposition 187, an initiative on the California ballot

The Venkateswara Temple was built for local Hindus on Mulholland Drive in Malibu Canyon.

Immigrant churches flourish across the Valley, often in makeshift surroundings. These services for a Serbian Orthodox congregation in Sylmar were held in 1993.

intended to bar illegal immigrants from schools and other public services. The 1994 measure served in many minds as a referendum on the demographic changes that have transformed the Valley.

On one side, there were big turnouts by supporters at voter forums. On the other, protesting students walked out of high schools and marched through Van Nuys, Chatsworth and other communities. Some Valley organizations found their members badly divided. The United Chambers of Commerce, normally a conservative body, split into camps and finally voted 15-10 to endorse the measure. "People are saying, 'I don't like this Third World takeover.' It is literally an invasion and very upsetting," said Guy Weddington McCreary, a Valley VOTE donor whose family helped settle North Hollywood. But a member of the Mid-Valley Chamber, which opposed Proposition 187, said it would hurt people in the Valley. "We didn't feel that requiring medical and educational personnel to be INS cops was appropriate," James Stewart said. The debates were wrenching. "I've been a member here for 30 years and I've never seen us so badly split," said lawyer David Fleming of the rhetoric at the Valley Industry and Commerce Association, successor to the organization that formed in 1949 to push for industrial growth.

The Valley's reputation as suburbia incarnate endures, even if the reality no longer fits the image so cleanly. For instance, Time magazine's New York editors thought it enough of a cultural milestone to report on the closure in 1999 of the Sherman Oaks Galleria, the Ventura Boulevard shopping mall-cum-teenage hangout that helped inspire the Valley Girl phenomenon. But the Valley now has its own satellite suburbs—places beyond the mountains like Simi Valley, Stevenson Ranch and Westlake Village—where baby boomers who grew up in the Valley relocated in search of the less-urban existence they remember and want for their own children. Exiles in these small truly suburban cities, among them Agoura Hills and Santa Clarita, are now almost as likely as diehard Angelenos to avoid visiting the floor of the Valley.

Even many natives are less likely to sing the praises of their home turf. When the *Los Angeles Times* Poll asked inhabitants of the Valley what they thought of their community for a 1999 series on the suburbs, the responses were disheartening. One in four respondents said they regard the Valley as more urban than suburban, 35% said they no longer considered the Valley a good place to raise children, and most damning of all, 39% said they were thinking seriously of moving away within two years. In contrast, in newer suburban refuges in Ventura and Orange counties, upwards of 90% said they were happy with their lives.

Within the Valley, the existence of gated com-

Monteria Estates, near Chatsworth, is one of the gated communities where residents with wealth are taking refuge.

munities is on the rise—many of them enclaves of million-dollar homes and estates. Also, more neighborhoods are adapting to the changes by fashioning their own mini-secession—redrawing the quasi-official boundaries between communities to get away from names tainted with a bad reputation, or inventing new names entirely. North Hills, known as Sepulveda for 60 years, abandoned the name because it was thought to be soiled by association with gangs, crime and soft property values. Parts of Canoga Park became West Hills and niches of North Hollywood won approval to call themselves Valley Village and West Toluca Lake. La Tuna Canyon broke from Sun Valley, and Arleta has battled with the U.S. Postal Service to separate its zip code from Pacoima.

Van Nuys, once the quintessential Valley address, is now the name that seems the most shunned. One corner broke off and declared itself to be Valley Glen, other sections have fought to be recognized as part of the more posh Sherman Oaks, and some residents near Sepulveda Dam basin have hopes of coining a new neighborhood name: Lake Balboa. "We're embarrassed to say we live here—we say we live across the street from Encino," one Van Nuys resident said in the *Times*. Homeowners in Van Nuys say all this disrespect is a bum rap: "Soon all we are left with will be the bad parts," a Van Nuys man moaned

Hidden Hills is an incorporated city located entirely behind guarded gates. The roughly 2,000 residents treasure their seclusion.

Citizens of the newly christened district of West Hills celebrated their secession from Canoga Park in 1987.

when Valley Glen won its separate status in 1998.

In the end, the question of secession from Los Angeles may never be put before the populace. The Los Angeles City Council no longer has veto power, thanks to a law pushed by Paula Boland, a former Valley member of the state Assembly. But state law still requires a detailed study to show that the separation can be accomplished without harming or unduly benefiting—in a financial sense—either the citizens of Los Angeles or those in the Valley. If splitting up cannot be done in a neutral way, the process is dead. Even if secession survives the study, a majority of all voters in Los Angeles must vote yes for the split to occur. As yet, no one from the Valley has gone over the hill to seriously try to sell the benefits of secession to the inner city. It's also anybody's bet whether most residents of the Valley would even want secession once the details are calculated, especially if it means higher taxes or curtailed services or both.

Practicalities aside, there are some tantalizing arguments for secession. Think what could happen to all the apathy, all the cynicism, if a place as diverse as the Valley actually came together to invent a new type of city—America's first 21st century metropolis. Secession presents an enticing opportunity to engage new ideas and to start over. And what befits the Valley's past more? The newlyweds who came after World War II—and all the explorers and immigrants before them—were just looking for a new start in the San Fernando Valley.

A new municipality in the Valley, with more than 1.5 million residents, would be the sixth most populous city in the U.S.—not exactly the profile of a suburban refuge. It would face most of the problems of a large concentrated urban area: aging neighborhoods and business districts in decline, gnawing pockets of poverty and gangs, a spreading sense that the environment and quality of life are declining. But a new city also would begin its life with impressive strengths and assets, and perhaps most important with a shared history and lore that define the Valley as a place unlike anywhere else.

"I grew up in a place
that has vanished,
in a world that can
be recalled by only
a very few."

—Catherine Mulholland,
granddaughter of
water engineer
William Mulholland,
in the *Los Angeles
Times* Magazine.

Everyone who lives in the Valley occupies a piece of ground with some connection to the stories told in this book. People digging in their yards have found grave markers, old cannonballs from the 1845 artillery battle between Gov. Micheltorena and *Californio* rebels, and Indian artifacts. History here is what you make of it, what you allow your eyes to see.

My family's half-acre in the Sherwood Forest section of Northridge had once been dry forage for longhorn cattle bearing the brand of Mission San Fernando Rey. It lay five miles southwest across the plain from the mission compound, past a shallow arroyo that somehow came to be called Bull Creek. Our little parcel then became part of Andres Pico's rancho and, later, a remote corner of George K. Porter's middle ranch. After William Mulholland's aqueduct brought irrigation water, our rectangle of land belonged to a walnut grove that sprawled southward from Parthenia Street—a narrow country lane connecting the settlements of Zelzah and Mission Acres—down to the Southern Pacific's Coast Line tracks.

We moved in late in 1956, among the first of the new suburban arrivals on Parthenia. Through the long summers we enjoyed the voluptuous shade cast by two giant, thick-limbed walnut trees. They served as second base in innumerable ballgames and kept us, and the squirrels, stocked in nuts. I realize now that every vacant lot down the block had a mature walnut tree at its center, and that they lined up in perfect rows. They were the survivors of the old way, and as the street filled in the houses were simply erected between the trees.

Such pleasing vestiges of the Valley's past can still be found by anyone with a curious eye. I drive the marathon boulevards and side streets looking for anything out of the ordinary in the suburban sprawl—a clump of tall eucalyptus trees, or an oversize corner lot where the lack of curbs and sidewalks signals the existence of a surviving ranchette. I enjoy finding hidden farmhouses tucked between fenced subdivisions, secret creeks with swimming tadpoles and dirt roads that seem out of place in modern Los Angeles. On one foray, I peeked over a brick wall on Lemarsh Street, in a tract built where I remember the pasture of the Northridge Farms thoroughbred ranch, and discovered the abandoned fruit orchard that actor Jack Oakie had planted six decades earlier, on the ranch he acquired from Barbara Stanwyck.

Orange groves dating from the heyday of citrus remain on the south edge of the Cal State University Northridge campus, at Orcutt Ranch Park in West Hills, and at the working Bothwell Ranch in Woodland Hills. Remnant olive groves may be spotted on Roxford Street and other old thoroughfares in Sylmar, the former olive capital. A splendid rank of olive trees lining Lassen Street in Chatsworth has been around so long they hold cultural monument status, as do the wooly deodar cedars shading White Oak Avenue in Granada Hills, planted by the foreman of the Sunshine Ranch before suburbia arrived.

This scene of sheep grazing on the hills along Ventura Boulevard in Woodland Hills was captured in 1956, but it could have been a century earlier.

Right on busy Vanowen Street, in Shadow Ranch Park, are the last physical remains of the Lankershim wheat ranching empire, which harvested nearly the entire southern half of the Valley from 1869 to 1909 and exported grain to Europe. The house was the headquarters of Lankershim's Workman Ranch, an outpost in a sea of wheat. Nearby, two gargantuan gum trees planted by foreman Al Workman as windbreaks more than 120 years ago are the last of his eucalyptus to have survived gales, freezes and the bulldozers.

In the Weeks Colony section of Winnetka and the Fuller Farm section of Northridge, I enjoy spotting what's left of the one-acre chicken ranches that lured so many to the Valley in the years after World War I. In Woodland Hills are still a few last examples of the speculative cottages built by land schemer Victor Girard, now shaded by mature trees he planted in the 1920s; from the same era, several dozen homes built of boulders can still be found in the Stonehurst subdivision, near horse corrals and unpaved streets in Sun Valley and Shadow Hills; and in central Van Nuys and Burbank and Northridge and Canoga Park are still homes and a few business structures left from each town's early years.

In some cases, we are fortunate to still have these evidences of the past. After the buried foundations of an old adobe were discovered across Lankershim Boulevard from Universal Studios, local historians said the building was probably the Rancho Cahuenga house where Andreas Pico and Col. John Fremont completed the surrender of California to American rule in 1847. Thanks to pressure from citizens who appreciate Valley history, the foundations will now be exposed to public view as part of the Campo Cahuenga monument that commemorates the surrender. Volunteers have saved the Andres Pico adobe in Mission Hills, perhaps the oldest remaining private house in the Valley, and which now contains a small museum and the holdings of the San Fernando Valley Historical Society. Nearby, the San Fernando adobe of the Lopez family that ran Lopez Station has also been restored. The Bolton Hall community meeting house in Tujunga was saved by the Little Landers Historical Society, which also operates a museum. The Hill-Palmer homestead house has been lovingly restored and maintained by the Chatsworth Historical Society. The last home of Miguel and Espiritu Leonis is open to the public in Calabasas, sheltered beneath a truly gargantuan oak. Other museums are dedicated to the history of Burbank and of Canoga Park-Owensmouth.

I have come to treasure all of these locales where the days that came before can be examined and quietly remembered. Some of them exude a palpable sense of history. The mouth of Bell Canyon in the Simi Hills is one of those unexpected spots for me. The creek that has flowed from the canyon for centuries is now fenced and channeled in concrete, but the rocky ridge looming overhead still looks just as it did when Spaniards gave it the name *El Escorpión*. It is not so hard to picture how the canyon must have looked when the Indian border settlement of *Huwam* stood beside the creek.

The grounds of Mission San Fernando Rey are another place where the air is thick with history. Visitors can absorb the grandeur of the *sala*, the great room, with its heavy doors beyond which the entire Valley once unfolded in a panorama of grass and foxtails. Or they may pause in the small graveyard out behind the church to ponder the 2,000 Indians whose remains were buried there. Earthquakes, vandals and time tore down the original adobe bricks, but restorations have created an historical oasis. In recent years, Pope John Paul II and, somewhat ironically, the King of Spain have walked the same corridors where Spanish padres once led prayers.

My favorite locale for observing the ghosts of the past is in an unlikely spot—on busy Ventura Boulevard, just east of Balboa Boulevard in Encino. I ignore the speeding traffic and the smoke belching from a Mexican restaurant, and instead picture a path worn in the dirt by boots and hooves and stagecoach wheels. In continuous use for more than 200 years, the path has gone by several names—*El Camino Real, Camino de las Virgenes*, Ventura Road, and now to many just The Boulevard. The sidewalk in front of Los Encinos State Historic Park is about the closest a Valley history chauvinist can get to hallowed ground: it just may be the location of *Siutcanga*, the village where the 1769 Portola expedition enjoyed Tongva hospitality. Inside the park, a warm water spring could well be the same abundant water source that

The Valley's oldest remaining wood-frame house and eucalyptus trees—the last vestiges of the Lankershim ranching empire—are located in Shadow Ranch Park in West Hills.

Portola's diarist, Fray Juan Crespi, and later correspondents wrote about.

This much is known: against the hillside on the far side of the boulevard, in the excavation for an office building, archaeologists in the 1980s found the richest trove of Tongva remains and artifacts ever unearthed. They and the media took to calling it the Lost Village of Encino. Nearby, they also found the detritus of a roadhouse and tavern run by Frenchman Jacque LaSalle that served Basque sheepherders on the Encino ranch. In the tavern's old dumping pit were found late-19th-century bottles, china and table implements, enough to reconstruct what food and liquors were served to travelers on the dusty highway. Both of those sites are now buried beneath an office building and parking garage.

But within Los Encinos park, other treasures remain on view. The acreage was saved by sharp-eyed residents who saw a developer's subdivision sign go up in the building frenzy after World War II. Their efforts preserved the last remaining piece of historic *Rancho Encino,* granted by Pio Pico to mission Indians and snatched from them by Vicente de la Osa, a local land schemer. In the park today, two buildings that look starkly out of place in the modern San Fernando Valley stand at angles to each other, guarded by California pepper trees and thorny tangles of *nopalera* cactus. The long, low adobe house was built facing the *camino* in 1851 by de la Osa, who used it as his home and as a roadhouse for travelers. The larger, two-story farmhouse was erected of limestone

The Leonis Adobe near Calabasas is a museum to the memory of Miguel and Espiritu.

The de Osa adobe in Encino was a real estate office in 1948, until neighbors acted to preserve it within a historic park.

quarried locally by the ranch's next owner, the French sheep breeder Eugene Garnier. The house bears a stunning resemblance to farmhouses found in Basque country in the French Pyrenees. It was Garnier who captured the waters of the famous spring in a pool shaped like a guitar. His initial and the date, 1872, appear on a metal gateworks on the pool.

Both old homes suffered severe damage in the 1994 earthquake. At least they are still standing— even though many longtime residents of the Valley whom I spoke with have no idea that the park and its treasures are there. The relics of the lost village gather dust in a warehouse, which seems a waste. Think how much richer the Valley's claim to have a distinct heritage would be if the village had been resurrected as an educational park—perhaps even as a spiritual home for the offspring of San Fernando Valley Indians, who struggle to hold onto some kind of identity.

Like the lost village, many of the landmarks and noteworthy places mentioned in this book have vanished. There is nothing left to remind us, for instance, of the crowds that jammed the Jeffries Barn boxing arena on Victory Boulevard, or the Valley Garden Arena on Vineland Avenue, or the Garden of the Moon dance pavilion in Tujunga. Likewise, all traces have disappeared of the once-popular Pop's Willow Lake resort on Big Tujunga Wash, of the RKO studio ranch where Jimmy Stewart stumbled through the winter snow of Bedford Falls on a hot summer Encino day, of Richard Neutra's modernist von

Sternberg home or of the original control tower at Van Nuys Airport seen in *Casablanca*. Among the missing are landmarks of more suburban vintage such as the drive-in movie theaters, the Bob's Big Boy burger joints where Wednesday night cruisers gathered on Van Nuys Boulevard, the General Motors factory that made Panorama City possible and the Sherman Oaks Galleria made notorious as the 1980s hangout of obnoxious Valley Girls. The only vestige left of the old Busch Gardens theme park—at one time a haven of lakes and free beer at the Anheuser-Busch brewery—are the feral parrots and parakeets that squawk across the Valley sky and feast on backyard sunflowers.

In the months that I had the pleasure of working on this book, the old Valley has continued to disappear. Bulldozers took a large bite out of the arboreal knoll south of Ventura Boulevard where Gen. Harrison Gray Otis built his hacienda and planted exotic trees, and where Edgar Rice Burroughs coined the name Tarzana. An industrial park and a golf course went up beside the cascades in Sylmar where Mulholland's aqueduct makes its splashy arrival. Subdividers also began to carve up a piece of Plummer Hill where, for many decades, stands of eucalyptus and pepper trees have stood watch over a hidden creek. Graders were scouring out new homesites in the mountains above Porter Ranch, and big plans were underway for the former Ahmanson Ranch west even of West Hills, which used to be the end of the Los Angeles sprawl. Developers had their eyes on the

abandoned Chatsworth Reservoir and on the Warner Ridge at Pierce College, both among the few places where one can catch a glimpse of what the Valley floor must have looked like when it was covered in grass. With each new subdivision and mini-mall, another irreplaceable piece of our past is lost.

In my old hometown of Northridge, I have watched the landmarks inexorably disappear. The reliable well that watered the laborers who laid the Southern Pacific tracks across the blazing Valley at the start of the 20th century—and that inspired the community's original name, Zelzah, a Biblical oasis—was buried beneath an auto parts store. The pre-suburbia, two-story grammar school in the center of town was removed for a bank. Most recently, to make

The Northridge train depot was razed five years after this 1956 picture showing station master E. J. Hillings. The station had served the original settlers of Zelzah.

Thoroughbred yearlings in training for racing careers romped at Northridge Farms in 1957. The land is now a subdivision.

way for another industrial park, bulldozers razed the last evidence of Devonshire Downs, home turf of the equestrian lifestyle that not so long before defined the west end of the Valley.

When my family first moved to Northridge, the community still seemed a bit like a country town and possessed much of its rustic charm. Horses grazed in inviting pastures behind white-plank fences on Reseda Boulevard. Neighbors of ours kept backyard stables, bred cottontails, and exercised their pigeon flocks every evening. We had encounters with garter snakes, alligator lizards and possums. But the transformation into suburbia was already moving at a gallop. The orange and walnut growers were moving away to less crowded places. Soon the thoroughbred ranches were gone, along with the board sidewalk in front of Brown's feed store and the wood-framed SP passenger depot at Reseda and Parthenia. In their spots rose apartment houses, a Zody's department store and a modern underpass to speed traffic beneath the train tracks.

Zody's is long gone, and some of those apartments stood for barely a generation before collapsing in the 1994 earthquake. The center of Northridge itself has shifted west a mile or two, to the clusters of shopping centers built over top of the old citrus and walnut groves, including the orchard of Catherine Mulholland's father, Perry Mulholland. Perhaps this is what people mean when they say that history doesn't count for anything in the suburbs. But that is a sentiment I can no longer accept as valid and accurate. For more than two centuries the San Fernando Valley has been filling up with people who left somewhere else to find a better life here, and they have made a past worth remembering.

This book is blessed with the kindness and talents of many people whom I have never met as well as more than a few friends and former colleagues. The first group includes the literally hundreds of people who have, fortunately for me, committed their feelings or observations about the San Fernando Valley to writing in the 200-some years before I began to research the topic. There is no possible way to give them sufficient credit. But I would have no story to tell without the writings of eyewitnesses like Fray Crespi and Benjamin Truman, or the biographical examinations of important figures like William Mulholland (by Catherine Mulholland, Margaret Leslie Davis and others) and Ritchie Valens (by Beverly Mendheim). The published memoirs of such former inhabitants as Lucille Ball, Jane Russell, Major Horace Bell and others also provided valuable anecdotes and insights.

Among past writings on the Valley, certain works stand out for their depth or scholarship. Msgr. Francis J. Weber of the Catholic Archdiocese of Los Angeles wrote the book—several of them actually—on the history of Mission San Fernando Rey. Frank Keffer, W. W. Robinson, Robert Durrenberger, Leonard Pitt, Jackson Mayers and Lawrence C. Jorgensen compiled essential facts about the San Fernando Valley in works that stand up to the test of time. Historians Remi Nadeau, Abraham Hoffman, Kevin Starr and Mike Davis enlightened with their analyses of events that shaped the Valley as we know it.

In my research I enjoyed the good fortune of open access to the choice trove of material on the Valley that resides in the editorial library of the *Los Angeles Times*, which has been reporting on the Valley since the 1880s. The work of scores of *Times* writers and editors appears here, without specific credit, and I'm grateful for that. Library director Dorothy Ingebretsen and her staff were superlative and Mike Lange arranged important access to the rare holdings of the *Times*' history center. Of course, the paper's former owners, Gen. Harrison Gray Otis and the Chandlers, had a few things to say about the course of history in the Valley and the *Times* remains an important community force. But to the paper's credit, no one sought to influence the conclusions or content of this book.

I also took advantage of the many archival treasures maintained by the San Fernando Valley Historical Society; my thanks to Harold Rockwell for opening the door. Thanks also to the robustly informed staff of the Los Angeles Central Library, particularly the specialists in the history and genealogy department. They toil in a room deep below the ground but never tire of answering strange questions. The library at California State University at Northridge, the Valley College historical museum and the volunteer docents of the Little Landers, Chatsworth and Canoga Park-Owensmouth historical societies also were helpful. Just as valuable were the insights shared by Valley progeny past and present, especially those of Jeffrey Styler and Lisa Landworth. Marc Wanamaker provided rare background on the studios in the Valley. From Nashville, Tracy Nelson looked back 30 years to share her memories of being on stage at the Newport '69 rock festival. To my surprise, the Internet proved to be an essential resource, connecting me with a wealth of lore, people and photographs that might otherwise have gone unnoticed.

Special thanks are due the photographers whose work graces these pages, among them more than two dozen *Times* photographers. Great pictures don't just happen. Nor do they just reappear when you want to put them in a book. Gay Raszkiewicz of the *Times'* photo library found and edited many hundreds of images, never tiring of the hunt. At the Los Angeles Central Library, senior librarian Carolyn Kozo Cole graciously assisted my search of the remarkable photography archives she maintains. Dace Taube, curator at the Regional History Center of the University of Southern California Library Department of Special Collections, helped greatly. Morgan P. Yates, corporate archivist for the Automobile Club of Southern California, the staff of the Seaver Center for Western History Research and the Margaret Herrick Library of the Academy of Motion Picture Arts and Sciences all made valuable contributions. Bryan Thomas of Del-Fi Records gave me material on Ritchie Valens. Stacey R. Strickler provided good visual sense and Rikki Sax ensured the images look as great in the book as in their original form.

Now that the project is complete, my heartfelt thanks go to Carla Lazzareschi, the director of the *Los Angeles Times* book division, who heard out my unformed idea and said, "I think this could be a book." Her spirit refused to flag and her good advice kept flowing as the months ran into years. The learned editing eye of Noel Greenwood raised the level of the final product immeasurably, as did the suggestions of a thoughtful historian offered by Professor Gloria Ricci Lothrop. The overall look of the book is a credit to the talents of Patrik Olson and Gillian Gough at G&O Design in Pasadena, California, with valuable input from Tom Trapnell. The maps were created by Roger Kuo. As good copy editors should, Pat Connell and Steven Hawkins made the manuscript better and taught me things.

Inevitably, writing the book became a family affair. My parents, Julie and Rod Roderick, opened their memories to me. My siblings—Chris, Steve and Peter—endured my countless stories and gave freely of their own. The support and patience that counted most came from Judy Graeme, my wife, and our daughter Sean Roderick. They put up with my absences and writing funks and assured me it was OK, asking only a few times, "When is it going to be done?" Well now it is, and I couldn't have done it without their love.

About the author

Kevin Roderick came to the subject of the San Fernando Valley both as a curious journalist and as a product himself of the suburbs. He grew up in Northridge, roaming the tracts of newly minted neighborhoods that came into being in the 1950s and 1960s. After attending James Monroe High School and studying the craft of journalism at California State University, Northridge, he went to work for the *Los Angeles Times* as a cub reporter covering the Valley. His career path steered him into other reporting endeavors and the newspaper's senior editor ranks, but the untold stories of the Valley always beckoned.

Roderick is currently the Los Angeles bureau chief for The Industry Standard magazine and lives in Santa Monica, Calif.

BIBLIOGRAPHY

Newspapers

Extensive use was made of the news archives of the *Los Angeles Times*, which began publishing in 1881. Material also came from these newspapers, some of them no longer in existence: *Lankershim Laconic, Los Angeles Examiner, Los Angeles Herald-Examiner, L.A. Weekly, New Times Los Angeles, San Fernando Sun, Valley Times, Van Nuys News and Call* (later the *Van Nuys News, Valley News and Green Sheet* and *Daily News of Los Angeles*.)

Books

Alleman, Richard. *The Movie Lover's Guide to Hollywood.* New York: Harper Colophon Books, 1985.

Andersen, Kurt. *Turn of the Century.* New York: Random House, 1999.

Anthony, Earl. *The Time of the Furnaces: A Case Study of Black Student Revolt.* New York: The Dial Press, 1971.

Atkinson, Janet I. *Los Angeles County Historical Directory.* Jefferson, NC: McFarland & Company, 1988.

Ball, Lucille with Betty Hannah Hoffman. *Love, Lucy.* New York: G.P. Putnam, 1996.

Bancroft, Hubert Howe. *The Works of Hubert Howe Bancroft, History of California.* Santa Barbara: Wallace Hebberd, 1969, from 1886 edition.

Bartlett, Donald L. and James B. Steele. *Empire: The Life, Legend, and Madness of Howard Hughes.* New York: W.W. Norton & Company, 1979.

Basinger, Jeanine. *The It's a Wonderful Life Book.* New York: Alfred A. Knopf, 1986.

Bell, Maj. Horace. *Reminiscences of a Ranger or Early Times in Southern California.* Published originally in 1881. Santa Barbara: Wallace Hebberd, 1927.

————, edited by Lanier Bartlett. *On the Old West Coast, Being Further Reminiscences of a Ranger.* New York: William Morrow, 1930.

Blades, Paul Harcourt. *Don Sagasto's Daughter: A Romance of Southern California.* Boston: The Gorham Press, 1911.

Bowman, Lynn. *Los Angeles: Epic of a City.* Berkeley: Howell-North, 1974.

Bravin, Jess. *Squeaky: The Life and Times of Lynette Alice Fromme.* New York: Buzz Books, 1997.

Breeden, Marshall. *The Romantic Southland of California.* Los Angeles: Kenmore, 1928.

Brewer, William H.; Francis P. Farquhar, ed. *Up and Down California in 1860-1864: Journal of William H. Brewer.* New Haven: Yale University Press, 1930.

Brodsly, David. *L.A. Freeway: An Appreciative Essay.* Berkeley: University of California Press, 1981.

Brown, Karl. *Adventures With D.W. Griffith.* New York: Farrar, Straus and Giroux, 1973.

Brown, Peter Harry and Pat H. Broeske. *Howard Hughes: The Untold Story.* New York: Dutton, 1996.

Bugliosi, Vincent with Curt Gentry. *Helter Skelter:*

The True Story of the Manson Murders. New York: Bantam Books, 1974.

Cacioppo, Richard K. *The History of Woodland Hills and Girard.* Panorama City: White Stone, 1982.

Cain, James M. *Cain x 3: Three Novels by James M. Cain.* New York: Alfred A. Knopf, 1969.

Carey, Harry Jr. *Company of Heroes: My Life as an Actor in the John Ford Stock Company.* Metuchen, NJ: The Scarecrow Press, 1994.

Cary, Diana Serra. *Whatever Happened to Baby Peggy: The Autobiography of Hollywood's Pioneer Child Star.* New York: Thomas Dunne Books, 1996.

——-. *The Hollywood Posse.* Norman, OK: University of Oklahoma Press, 1975.

Caughey, John and Laree Caughey. *Los Angeles: Biography of a City.* Berkeley: University of California Press, 1976.

Chase, Jo Smeaton. *California Coast Trails: A Horseback Ride from Mexico to Oregon.* Boston: Houghton Mifflin, 1913.

Clary, William W. *History of the Law Firm of O'Melveny & Myers 1885-1965.* Los Angeles: Privately printed, 1966.

Cleland, Robert Glass. *The Cattle on a Thousand Hills.* San Marino: The Huntington Library, 1951.

Cohen, Chester G. *El Escorpión: From Indian Village to Los Angeles Park.* Woodland Hills: Periday, 1989.

Crichton, Michael. *Airframe.* New York: Alfred A. Knopf, 1996.

Crosby, Bing as told to Pete Martin. *Call Me Lucky.* New York: Simon and Schuster, 1953.

Daughters of the American Revolution. *The Valley of San Fernando.* Published by DAR, California State Society, San Fernando Valley chapter, 1924.

Davis, Margaret Leslie. *Rivers in the Desert: William Mulholland and the Inventing of Los Angeles.* New York: Harper Collins, 1993.

Davis, Mike. *City of Quartz.* London: Verso, 1990.

——-. *Ecology of Fear: Los Angeles & the Imagination of Disaster.* New York: Metropolitan, 1998.

Didion, Joan. *The White Album.* New York: Washington Square Press, 1979.

Ditto, Jerry. *Eichler Homes: Design for Living.* San Francisco: Chronicle Books, 1995.

Drinkwater, John. *The Life and Adventures of Carl Laemmle.* New York: Arno Press, 1978.

Druffel, Ann and D. Scott Rogo. *The Tujunga Canyon Contacts.* New York: New American Library, 1989.

Durrenberger, Robert, Leonard Pitt and Richard Preston. *The San Fernando Valley: A Bibliography and Research.* Northridge: San Fernando Valley State College Center for Urban Studies & Bureau of Business, 1967.

Dwiggins, Don. *Hollywood Pilot: The Biography of Paul Mantz.* Garden City: Doubleday & Company, 1967.

Eberts, Mike. *Griffith Park: A Centennial History.* Los Angeles: Historical Society of Southern California, 1996.

Eliot, Marc. *Walt Disney, Hollywood's Dark Prince.* Secaucus: Birch Lane Press, 1993.

Fein, Art. *The L.A. Musical History Tour: A Guide to the Rock and Roll Landscapes of Los Angeles.* Boston: Faber, 1990.

——-. *The L.A. Musical History Tour, 2nd edition.* Los Angeles: 2.13.61 Publications, 1998.

Fenton, Robert W. *The Big Swingers.* Englewood Cliffs: Prentice-Hall, 1967.

Fogelson, Robert M. *The Fragmented Metropolis: Los Angeles 1850-1930.* Cambridge: Harvard University Press, 1967.

Fong-Torres, Ben. *Hickory Wind: The Life & Times of Gram Parsons.* New York: Pocket Books, 1991.

Ford, Dan. *Pappy: The Life of John Ford.* Englewood Cliffs: Prentice-Hall, 1979.

Foster, Mark S. *Henry J. Kaiser: Builder in the Modern American West.* Austin: University of Texas Press, 1989.

Fox, Laurie. *My Sister From the Black Lagoon: A Novel of My Life.* New York: Simon and Schuster, 1998.

Fradkin, Philip L. *The Seven States of California: A Natural and Human History.* New York: Henry Holt and Company, 1995.

Friedrich, Otto. *City of Nets: A Portrait of Hollywood in the 1940s.* Berkeley: UC Press, 1986.

Gable, Kathleen. *Clark Gable: A Personal Portrait.* Englewood Cliffs: Prentice-Hall, 1961.

Garceau, Jean with Inez Cocke. *"Dear Mr. G—":*

The Biography of Clark Gable. Boston: Little, Brown, 1961.

Gaye, Laura B. *Last of the Old West: A Book of Sketches About the Calabasas Area.* Laura B. Gaye, 1965.

——. *Land of the West Valley.* Laura B. Gaye, 1975.

Gebhard, David. *Schindler.* New York: Viking, 1971.

Gebhard, David and Robert Winter. *Architecture in Los Angeles, a Compleat Guide.* Salt Lake City: Peregrine Smith Books, 1985.

——. *A Guide to Architecture in Southern California.* Los Angeles: The Los Angeles County Museum of Art, 1965.

Geller, Shari P. *Fatal Convictions.* New York: Regan Books, 1996.

Gish, Lillian with Ann Pinchot. *Lillian Gish: The Movies, Mr. Griffith and Me.* Englewood Cliffs: Prentice-Hall, 1969.

Gottlieb, Robert and Irene Wolt. *Thinking Big: The Story of the Los Angeles Times, Its Publishers and Their Influence on Southern California.* New York: G.P. Putnam, 1977.

Gray, Mike. *Angle of Attack: Harrison Storms and the Race to the Moon.* New York: W.W. Norton, 1992.

Grenier, Judson A., ed. *Guide to Historic Places in Los Angeles County.* Dubuque: Kendall/Hunt Publishing, 1978.

Griffin, Nancy and Kim Masters. *Hit and Run: How Jon Peters and Peter Guber Took Sony for a Ride in Hollywood.* New York: Simon and Schuster, 1996.

Guinn, J. M. *Historical and Biographical Record of Los Angeles and Vicinity.* Chicago: Chapman Publishing, 1901.

Gumprecht, Blake. *The Los Angeles River: Its Life, Death and Possible Rebirth.* Baltimore: Johns Hopkins University Press, 1999.

Harmetz, Aljean. *Round Up the Usual Suspects: The Making of Casablanca.* New York: Hyperion, 1992.

Harrison, Benjamin S. *Fortune Favors the Brave— The Life and Times of Horace Bell, Pioneer Californian.* Los Angeles: Ward Ritchie Press, 1953.

Hart, Lincoln. *Our Town.* Los Angeles: Boulevard Press, 1942.

Hayne, Donald, ed. *The Autobiography of Cecil B. DeMille.* Englewood Cliffs: Prentice-Hall, 1959.

Henderson, David. *'Scuse Me While I Kiss the Sky: The Life of Jimi Hendrix.* New York: Bantam Books, 1996.

Henderson, Robert M. *D. W. Griffith: His Life and Work.* New York: Oxford University Press, 1972.

Higham, Charles. *Cecil B. DeMille.* New York: Charles Scribner's, 1973.

——. *Warner Brothers.* New York: Charles Scribner's, 1975.

Hise, Greg. *Magnetic Los Angeles: Planning the Twentieth-Century Metropolis.* Baltimore: The Johns Hopkins University Press, 1997.

Hoffman, Abraham. *Vision or Villainy: Origins of the Owens Valley-Los Angeles Water Controversy.* College Station: Texas A&M University Press, 1981.

Jewell, Richard B. with Vernon Harbin. *The RKO Story.* New York: Arlington House, 1982.

Johnson, Clarence L. with Maggie Smith Kelly. *More Than My Share of It All.* Washington: Smithsonian Institution Press, 1985.

Jorgensen, Lawrence C., ed. *The San Fernando Valley, Past & Present.* Los Angeles: Pacific Rim Research, 1982.

Kahrl, William L. *Water and Power: The Conflict Over Los Angeles' Water Supply in the Owens Valley.* Berkeley: University of California Press, 1982.

Keffer, Frank. *History of San Fernando Valley.* Glendale: Stillman, 1934.

Khrushchev in America: Full text of the speeches made Sept. 15-27, 1959. Translated from book published in USSR entitled Live in Peace and Friendship. New York: Crosscurrents Press, 1960.

Lasky, Betty. *RKO: The Biggest Little Major of Them All.* Englewood Cliffs: Prentice-Hall, 1984.

Layne, J. Gregg. *Annals of Los Angeles From the Arrival of the First White Men to the Civil War.* San Francisco: California Historical Society, 1935.

Leader, Leonard. *Los Angeles and the Great Depression.* New York: Garland Publishing, 1991.

Lefcourt, Peter. *The Dreyfus Affair: a Love Story.* New York: Random House, 1992.

Lillard, Richard G. *Eden in Jeopardy: Man's Prodigal Meddling With His Environment, the Southern California Experience.* New York: Alfred A. Knopf, 1966.

Loh, Sandra Tsing. *Depth Takes a Holiday: Essays from Lesser Los Angeles.* New York: Riverhead Books, 1996.

——-. *If You Lived Here, You'd Be Home By Now.* New York: Riverhead Books, 1997.

Lombard, Sarah R. *Rancho Tujunga: A History of Sunland-Tujunga, Calif.* Sunland: Sunland Woman's Club, 1990.

Los Angeles Aeronautics 1920-1929. Northrop Institute of Technology, 1973.

Louvish, Simon. *Man on the Flying Trapeze: The Life & Times of W. C. Fields.* New York: W.W. Norton, 1997.

Lovell, Mary S. *The Sound of Wings: The Life of Amelia Earhart.* New York: St. Martins Press, 1989.

Madsen, Axel. *Stanwyck.* New York: HarperCollins, 1994.

Marion, Frances. *Westward the Dream.* Garden City: Doubleday, 1948.

Marx, Arthur. *The Secret Life of Bob Hope.* New York: Barricade Books, 1993.

Mason, William M. and Dr. John A. McKinstry. *The Japanese of Los Angeles.* Los Angeles: Los Angeles County Museum of Natural History, 1969.

Massman, Patti and Susan Rosser. *Just Desserts.* New York: Crown Publishers, 1991.

Mayers, Jackson. *The San Fernando Valley.* Walnut: John D. McIntyre, 1976.

Mayo, Morrow. *Los Angeles.* New York: Alfred A. Knopf, 1932.

McKee, Lavonne and Ted Schwarz. *Get Ready to Say Goodbye.* Far Hills: New Horizon, 1994.

McPhee, John. *The Control of Nature.* New York: The Noonday Press, 1989.

Mendheim, Beverly. *Ritchie Valens: The First Latino Rocker.* Tempe: Bilingual Press, 1987.

Moore, Charles, Peter Becker and Regula Campbell. *The City Observed: Los Angeles.* New York: Random House, 1984.

Mulholland, Catherine. *Calabasas Girls: An Intimate History 1885-1912.* Berkeley: Elmwood, 1976.

——-. *The Owensmouth Baby: The Making of a San Fernando Valley Town.* Northridge: Santa Susana Press, 1987.

——-. Chapter in *California Childhood: Recollections and Stories of the Golden State.* Gary Soto, ed. Berkeley: Creative Arts, 1988.

——-. *William Mulholland and the Rise of Los Angeles.* Berkeley: UC Press, 2000

Nadeau, Remi A. *City-Makers: The Men Who Transformed Los Angeles from Village to Metropolis During the First Great Boom, 1868-76.* Garden City: Doubleday & Co., 1948.

——-. *The Water Seekers.* Bishop: Chalfant Press, 1950.

——-. *Los Angeles: From Mission to Modern City.* New York: Longmans, Green, 1960.

Newmark, Maurice H. and Marco R. Newmark, eds. *Sixty Years in Southern California, 1853-1913: Containing the Reminiscences of Harris Newmark.* New York: The Knickerbocker Press, 1926.

Nunis, Doyce B. Jr., ed. *Mission San Fernando, Rey de España, 1797-1997: A Bicentennial Tribute.* Los Angeles: Historical Society of Southern California, 1997.

Oakie, Jack. *Jack Oakie's Double Takes.* San Francisco: Strawberry Hill Press, 1990.

Oakie, Victoria Horne, ed. *Dear Jack: Hollywood Birthday Reminiscences to Jack Oakie.* Portland: Strawberry Hill Press, 1994.

——-. *Jack Oakie's Oakridge: A Cultural Heritage Monument in Northridge.* San Francisco: Strawberry Hill Press, 1990.

Outland, Charles F. *Stagecoaching on El Camino Real: Los Angeles to San Francisco 1861-1901.* Glendale: Arthur H. Clark, 1973.

Ovnick, Merry. *Los Angeles: The End of the Rainbow.* Los Angeles: Balcony Press, 1994.

Palmer, Edwin O. *History of Hollywood, Vol. 1.* Hollywood: Arthur H. Cawston, 1937.

Parrish, Robert. *Growing Up in Hollywood.* Boston: Little, Brown, 1976.

Pierce, David M. *Down in the Valley.* London: Penguin Books, 1989.

——-. *Angels in Heaven.* New York: The Mysterious Press, 1992.

Ponce, Mary Helen. *Hoyt Street: An Autobiography.* Albuquerque: University of New Mexico Press, 1993.

———. *Taking Control.* Houston: Arte Público Press, 1987.

Popovac, Gwynn. *Wet Paint.* Boston: Houghton Mifflin, 1986.

Porges, Irwin. *Edgar Rice Burroughs: The Man Who Created Tarzan.* Provo: Brigham Young University Press, 1975.

Pratt, Theodore. *Valley Boy.* New York: Duell, Sloan and Pearce, 1946.

Rasmussen, Cecilia. *Curbside L.A.: An Offbeat Guide to the City of Angels From the Pages of the Los Angeles Times.* Los Angeles: Los Angeles Times, 1996.

———. *Los Angeles Unconventional: The Men and Women Who Did Los Angeles Their Way.* Los Angeles: Los Angeles Times, 1998.

Reynolds, Debbie with David Patrick Columbia. *Debbie, My Life.* New York: William Morrow, 1988.

Rich, Ben R. and Leo Janos. *Skunk Works: A Personal Memoir of My Years at Lockheed.* Boston: Little, Brown, 1994.

Richard Neutra Buildings and Projects. Zurich: Editions Girsberger, 1951.

Rieff, David. *Los Angeles: Capital of the Third World.* New York: Simon & Schuster, 1991.

Ring, Frances Kroll. *Against the Current: As I Remember F. Scott Fitzgerald.* San Francisco:

Donald S. Ellis, 1985.

Robinson, W. W. *The Story of the San Fernando Valley.* Los Angeles: Title Insurance and Trust, 1961.

———. *The Spanish and Mexican Ranchos of the San Fernando Valley.* Highland Park: Southwest Museum, 1966.

Roderick, Kevin, ed. *In Pursuit of Justice: The People vs. Orenthal James Simpson.* Los Angeles: Los Angeles Times, 1995.

Rogers, Roy and Dale Evans, with Jane and Michael Stern. *Happy Trails, Our Life Story.* New York: Simon & Schuster, 1994.

Russell, Jane. *Jane Russell: My Path and My Detours.* New York: Franklin Watts, 1985.

Ryan, Carolyn L. *Winnetka's Heritage: A Man With a Dream.* Crown Gibraltar Graphic Center, 1977.

Samit, Michele. *No Sanctuary: The True Story of a Rabbi's Deadly Affair.* New York: Birch Lane Press, 1993.

San Fernando Valley and Vicinity: A.B.C. Directory, 1949-1951. A.B.C. Directories.

San Fernando Valley Directory, 1921. Los Angeles: Los Angeles Directory Co., 1921.

Schickel, Richard. *The Disney Version: The Life, Times, Art and Commerce of Walt Disney.* Chicago: Elephant Paperbacks, 1997.

Schrag, Peter. *Paradise Lost: California's Experience, America's Future.* New York: The New Press, 1998.

Scott, Allen J. and Soja, Edward W., eds. *The City: Los Angeles and Urban Theory at the End of the*

Twentieth Century. Berkeley: University of California Press, 1996.

Seranella, Barbara. *No Human Involved.* New York: Harper Paperbacks, 1997.

Sherman, Robert G. *Quiet on the Set!: Motion Picture History at the Iverson Movie Ranch.* Chatsworth: Sherway Publishing, 1984.

Sieh, Kerry and Simon LeVay. *The Earth in Turmoil: Earthquakes, Volcanoes and Their Impact on Humankind.* New York: W.H. Freeman, 1998.

Silva, Fred, ed. *Focus on The Birth of a Nation.* Englewood Cliffs: Prentice-Hall, 1971.

Starr, Kevin: *Endangered Dreams: The Great Depression in California.* New York: Oxford University Press, 1996.

———. *The Dream Endures: California Enters the 1940s.* New York: Oxford University Press, 1997.

Stephenson, Neal. *Snow Crash.* New York: Bantam Books, 1992.

Stewart, Maria Helena. *Los Encinos' Past and Present.* Maria Helena Stewart, 1965.

Stockdale, Tom. *They Died Too Young: Jimi Hendrix.* Philadelphia: Chelsea House Publishers, 1998.

Summers, Anthony. *Goddess: The Secret Lives of Marilyn Monroe.* New York: Macmillan, 1985.

Tarakanoff, Vassili Petrovitch. *Statement of My Captivity Among the Californians,* translated from Russian by Ivan Petroff. Los Angeles: Glen Dawson, 1953.

Truman, Maj. Ben C. *Semi-Tropical California.*

San Francisco: A.L. Bancroft & Company, 1874.

Underwood, John. *Madcaps, Millionaires and "Mose."* Glendale: Heritage Press, 1984.

Verge, Arthur C. *Paradise Transformed: Los Angeles During the Second World War.* Dubuque: Kendall/Hunt, 1993.

Waldinger, Roger and Mehdi Bozorgmehr, eds. *Ethnic Los Angeles.* New York: Russell Sage Foundation, 1996.

Wallis, Hal and Charles Higham. *Starmaker: The Autobiography of Hal Wallis.* New York: Macmillan, 1980.

Walsh, Raoul. *Each Man in His Time: The Life Story of a Director.* New York: Farrar, Straus and Giroux, 1974.

Ward, Elizabeth and Alain Silver. *Raymond Chandler's Los Angeles.* Woodstock: Overlook, 1997.

Warner, J. L. *My First Hundred Years in Hollywood.* New York: Random House, 1964.

Watson, Virginia. *Chatsworth History.* Chatsworth Historical Society, 1991.

Wayne, Aissa with Steve Delsohn. *John Wayne, My Father.* New York: Random House, 1991.

Wayne, Jane Ellen. *Stanwyck.* New York: Arbor House, 1985.

Weaver, John D. *Carnation, The First 75 Years 1899-1974.* Carnation Company, 1974.

Weber, Rev. Francis J. *Mission San Fernando.* Los Angeles: Westernlore Press, 1968.

——, ed. *The Mission in the Valley: A Documentary History of San Fernando, Rey de España.* Santa Barbara: Kimberly Press, 1995.

——. *Memories of an Old Mission.* Mission Hills: Saint Francis Historical Society, 1997.

Wilson, Jane. *Gibson, Dunn & Crutcher, Lawyers: An Early History.* Los Angeles: Gibson, Dunn & Crutcher, 1990.

Wolfe, Tom: *The Kandy-Kolored Tangerine Flake Streamline Baby.* New York: Farrar, Straus and Giroux, 1965.

——. *The Electric Kool-Aid Acid Test.* New York: Farrar, Straus and Giroux, 1968.

Woolsey, Ronald C. *Migrants West Toward the Southern California Frontier.* Claremont: Grizzly Bear Publishing Co., 1996.

Wynne, H. Hugh. *The Motion Picture Stunt Pilots and Hollywood's Classic Aviation Movies.* Missoula: Pictorial Histories Publishing, 1987.

Yablonsky, Lewis. *The Hippie Trip.* New York: Pegasus, 1968.

Zavattero, Janette. *The Sylmar Tunnel Disaster.* New York: Everest House, 1978.

Published articles

Barrows, Henry D. "Pio Pico: A Biographical & Character Sketch of the Last Mexican Governor of Alta California." *Annual Publication of the Historical Society of Southern California,* 1894.

Bennett, Charles and Milton Breivogel. "Planning for the San Fernando Valley." *Western City,* April 1945.

Busch, Noel. "The San Fernando Valley." *Holiday,* Dec. 1951.

Carr, Susan, et al. "The Public Health Response to Los Angeles' 1994 Earthquake." *American Journal of Public Health,* April 1996.

Chanslor, Roy. "San Fernando Valley." *Holiday,* Oct. 1957.

Davis, Mike. "How Eden Lost Its Garden: A Political History of the Los Angeles Landscape." In *The City: Los Angeles and Urban Theory at the End of the Twentieth Century,* Allen J. Scott, ed. Berkeley: UC Press, 1996.

Dionne, Roger. "Tarzan's Valley." *Westways,* Aug. 1977.

Dixon, Elizabeth I., ed. "Early San Fernando: Memoirs of Mrs. Catherine Dace." *Southern California Quarterly,* Sept. 1962.

Dolkas, James B. "Men With a Mission: The Porters of San Fernando." *California Historian,* Spring 1997.

Duncan, Gerald. "The San Fernando: Valley of Surprises." *Coronet,* March 1951.

Greengard, Samuel. "Like, The Valley's Not a Joke Anymore." *Los Angeles,* Feb., 1990.

Hamilton, Andrew. "Small Cities Can Lick Crime, Too!" *Coronet,* May 1956.

Harris, Sheldon. "Meanwhile, Back in the Valley." *Commonweal,* May 23, 1969.

"Hell's Angels Completed." *American*

Cinematographer. Jan. 1930.

"In Pursuit of Vanished Days." *Annual Publication of the Historical Society of Southern California,* 1928.

Jackson, Wesley. "How Pleasant Was Our Valley." *Frontier,* April 1956.

Johnson, John R. "The Indians of Mission San Fernando" in *Mission San Fernando, Rey de España, 1797-1997,* Doyce B. Nunis Jr., ed.

Kahn, Gordon. "As the Escrow Flies." *Atlantic Monthly,* Feb. 1945.

La Barbera, Joseph. "Joe Fawkes and the Aerial Swallow." *Westways,* Feb. 1964.

Lauria, Steve. "Laughs in Beautiful Downtown Burbank." *USA Today Baseball Weekly,* Jan. 29-Feb. 11, 1992.

Lothrop, Gloria Ricci. "A Pictorial History of Mission San Fernando" in *Mission San Fernando, Rey de España, 1791-1997,* Doyce B. Nunis Jr., ed.

McBroom, Patricia. "The Ducal Life in Northridge." *Los Angeles Magazine,* Sept. 1963.

Mulholland, Catherine. "Something Lost, Something Gained." *Los Angeles Times Magazine,* Jan. 10, 1999.

Nadeau, Remi. "Wheat Ruled the Valley." *Westways,* April 1963.

———. "The Men Who Opened the Valley." *Westways,* May 1963.

Neuerberg, Norman. "Biography of a Building" in *Mission San Fernando, Rey de España, 1797-1997,* Doyce B. Nunis Jr., ed.

Nevin, David. "Uneasy Peace at Valley State." *Life,* March 14, 1969.

Newmark, Marco R. "Historical Profiles: Isaac N. Van Nuys." *Quarterly of the Historical Society of Southern California,* Vol. 38.

Packard, Francis H. "The Politics of Smog." *Frontier,* April 1956.

Polley, Frank J. "Americans at the Battle of Cahuenga." *Annual Publication of the Historical Society of Southern California,* 1894.

Preston, Richard E. "The Changing Landscape of the San Fernando Valley Between 1930-64." *California Geographer,* Vol. VI.

Rial, J.A. "The anomalous seismic response of the ground at the Tarzana hill site during the Northridge 1994 Southern California earthquake." *Bulletin of the Seismological Society of America,* Dec. 1996.

Ripley, Vernette Snyder. "The San Fernando Pass and the Traffic That Went Over It." *The Quarterly of the Historical Society of Southern California,* Vol. 29.

Robinson, W. W. "Rancho Story of San Fernando Valley." *The Quarterly of the Historical Society of Southern California ,* Vol. 38.

Rogers, Bogart. "Four Million Dollars and Four Men's Lives." *Photoplay,* April 1930.

Scott, Allen J. "High-Technology Development in the San Fernando Valley and Ventura County." In *The City: Los Angeles and Urban Theory at the End of the Twentieth Century,* Allen J. Scott, ed. Berkeley: UC Press, 1996.

Stocker, Joseph. "Citizens Learn to Eavesdrop." *Nation's Business,* June 1951.

Stowe, Noel J., ed. "An Interview with David Otto Brant." *California Historical Society Quarterly,* Vol. 47.

Straw, J.E. "The Fertile San Fernando Valley." *The Rural Californian,* June 1893.

Talese, Gay. "Charlie Manson's Home on the Range." *Esquire,* March 1970.

"The St. Francis Dam Disaster Revisited." *Southern California Quarterly,* Spring/Summer 1995.

Thompson, Donald J. "On the Citrus Front." *California Citrograph,* July 1942.

Van Nuys, J. Benton. "My Memories of San Fernando Valley." *The Quarterly of the Historical Society of Southern California,* Vol. 38.

Von Blon, John. "The Olive's Royal Swartness." *Westways,* March 1934.

Warren, Viola Lockhart. "The Eucalyptus Crusade." *Southern California Quarterly,* 44.

Williams, Michael Wayne. "From Orange Groves to High-Tech in the San Fernando Valley: Boosterism, Rezoning and the Emergence of an R&D Regional Economy." *Southern California Quarterly,* 1998.

Woehlke, Walter V. "The Rejuvenation of San Fernando." *Sunset,* Feb. 1914.

Papers, reports and miscellaneous documents

Abbiss, Kenneth Tector. "A History of the Warner Ranch for class in California History, 7-10 Tuesdays." 1964. Typewritten manuscript on file at Los Angeles Central Library.

"Amusement Map of Los Angeles County," 1929. On file at Los Angeles Central Library.

Baur, John E. *William Paul Whitsett: A Biographical Sketch.* Sponsored by the W. P. Whitsett Endowment; filed in Department of History, California State University, Northridge, 1987.

Bell, Maj. Horace. "Horace Bell manuscripts, typewritten notes from 'The Spiritual Conquest of California, from the Manuscript of Don Guillermo Embustero y Mentiro re: Serra in San Fernando Valley and Chief Cahuenga.' " Los Angeles Central Library rare collection.

"Birmingham General Hospital," brochure given to patients. At San Fernando Valley Historical Society.

Brandt, Gladys Lillian. "The San Fernando Valley: A Study in Changing Adjustment Between Its Economic Life and Its Natural Environment." Master's dissertation. University of Chicago, Department of Geography, 1928.

Bunton, George W. "Van Nuys (Within Los Angeles) California: The Hub of San Fernando Valley." Brochure printed by Van Nuys Publishing Co., 1922. Los Angeles Central Library rare collection.

"California Earthquake History 1769-Present." U.S. Geological Survey Web site.

Carpenter, Bruce R. "Rancho Encino: Its Historical Geography." UCLA master's thesis. 1948

Christin, Mrs. Charles A. Typewritten interview with John T. Wilson, on file at Los Angeles Central Library.

Cruikshank, Kenneth M., et al. "Winnetka Deformation Zone: Surface expression of coactive slip on a blind fault during the Northridge earthquake sequence." Portland State University, Geology Department, 1996.

"Destination '90: Policies for Planning." Citizens Advisory Committee report. 1968.

Dixon, Kathy, et al. "Beyond Suburbia: The Changing Face of the San Fernando Valley." UCLA master's thesis in Urban Planning, June 1993.

Ewing, Paul A. "The Agricultural Situation in San Fernando Valley." U.S. Dept. of Agriculture, 1939.

"Growth and Economic Stature of the San Fernando Valley." Security First National Bank Research Department, 1960.

Heath, George Joseph. "Geographical Influences on the History of the San Fernando Valley." USC master's thesis in history. 1966.

Hodgkinson, Kathleen M., et al. "Damage and Restoration of Geodetic Infrastructure Caused by the 1994 Northridge, California, Earthquake." U.S. Geological Survey, 1996.

Izzard, Alex Edwin Jr. "Factors Influencing the Agglomeration of the Electronics Industry in San Fernando Valley." UCLA master's thesis in geography. 1961.

Jenkins, Gordon. *San Fernando Valley* lyrics. New York: Edwin H. Morris & Company, 1943.

Killian, Chris. "Aircraft Wrecks in Southern California." Web site.

Knight, Albert. "Stonehurst—A 1920s Stone House Neighborhood." March 24, 2000.

Leask, Samuel Jr. "CAO Report to the Board of City Planning Commissioners on the Los Angeles City Planning Department." Nov. 1956.

Lothrop, Gloria Ricci. "Pro Fidem: Franciscan Missionary Efforts in Alta California." 1999.

Lyon, Laura Lucile. "Investigation of the Program for the Adjustment of Mexican Girls to the High Schools of the San Fernando Valley." USC School of Education master's thesis. 1933.

"Map of San Fernando Valley, California." Security Trust and Savings Bank, 1924.

Mayers, Jackson. *The San Fernando Valley Story.* Pamphlet.

"Mid San Fernando Valley." Pamphlet. Valley College Historical Museum Association, 1998.

"Memories of Early California on Sepulveda Trail, Programme and Historical Notes." Brochure. Sept. 27, 1930.

"1955 Master Plan Restudy of San Fernando Valley." Los Angeles City Planning Department, 1955.

"Official Map of Greater San Fernando Valley."

The American Surveys, 1926.

Olmsted, Frederick Law, et al. "A Major Traffic Street Plan for Los Angeles." May 1924.

Petit, Stanley N. "Valley Agriculture." *Valley History,* 1999 pamphlet.

Porter, Florence Collins, ed. "The Story of the McKinley Home for Boys." Woman's Auxiliary of the McKinley Home for Boys, 1921. In Los Angeles Central Library rare collection.

"Report and Recommendations of a Comprehensive Rapid Transit Plan for the City and County of Los Angeles." Kelker, De Leuw & Co., Chicago. 1925.

"San Fernando Valley Calendar of Events." Title Insurance, 1951.

Scientific Resource Surveys Inc., "Archaeological/ Historical Reports on the Encino Towers and Casa Balboa Property." First Financial Group, 1978.

"35th Anniversary of San Fernando High School, 1896-1931." Brochure, 1931. At San Fernando Valley Historical Society.

"Valley History." Pamphlet. Valley College Historical Museum Association, 1999.

"USGS Response to an Urban Earthquake— Northridge 1994." Prepared by the U.S. Geological Survey for the Federal Emergency Management Agency, 1996.

Shaffer, Ralph E. "Letters From the People: The Los Angeles Times Letters Column, 1881-1889."

Tiernan, Mary Lee. "The Roscoe Robbers and the Sensational Train Wrecking of 1894."

Wood, Charles L. "Would the San Fernando Valley Be Fed or Drained by Rapid Transit Connection with the Metropolitan Center?" Board of City Planning Commissioners, Los Angeles, 1930.

Zappa, Frank and Moon Zappa. *Valley Girls.* (recording) Barking Pumpkin Records, 1982.

Films

Birth of a Nation, The. Dir. D.W. Griffith. David D. Griffith Corp., 1915.

Boogie Nights. Dir. Paul Thomas Anderson. New Line Cinema, 1997.

Chinatown. Dir. Roman Polanski. Paramount Pictures, 1974.

Earth Girls are Easy. Dir. Julien Temple. Vestron Pictures, 1989.

Encino Man Dir. Les Mayfield. Warner Brothers, 1992.

Foxes. Dir. Adrian Lyne. United Artists, 1980.

Go. Dir. Doug Liman. Columbia Pictures, 1999.

Hell's Angels. Dir. Howard Hughes. United Artists, 1930.

La Bamba. Dir. Luis Valdez. Columbia Pictures, 1987.

Magnolia Dir. Paul Thomas Anderson. New Line Cinema, 1999.

Postman Always Rings Twice, The. Dir. Tay Garnett. Metro-Goldwyn-Mayer, 1946.

Pulp Fiction. Dir. Quentin Tarantino. Miramax, 1994.

Safe Dir. Todd Haynes. Sony Pictures Classics, 1995.

San Fernando Valley. Dir. Yakima Canutt and John English. Republic Pictures, 1944.

San Fernando Valley Girls. Excalibur Films.

2 Days in the Valley. Dir. John Herzfeld. MGM-UA, 1996.

Two Jakes, The. Dir. Jack Nicholson. Paramount Pictures, 1990.

Valley Girl. Dir. Martha Coolidge. Atlantic Pictures, 1983.

This book includes photographs made available by the *Los Angeles Times* and from other archives. The photographers whose images appear courtesy of the *Times* include Lacy Atkins, Tony Barnard, Larry Bessell, Frank Q. Brown, Bob Carey, Harry Chase, Carolyn Cole, Gil Cooper, Bruce Cox, Don Cormier, Anne Cusack, Alan Duignan, Michael Edwards, Steve Fontanini, George Fry, Dave Gatley, Gordon Grant, Pete Grant, Ray Knudsen, Joel Lugavere, Irfan Khan, John Malmin, Al Markado, Howard Maxwell, Rick Meyer, Cal Montney, Mary Nogueras, Maxine Reams, Art Rogers, Joe Vitti and George Wilhelm. Others whose names do not appear in the *Times* archives deserve equal credit.

Photographs not from the *Times* appear on the following pages, courtesy of and with thanks to the sources:

i Regional History Center, USC
ii Seaver Center for Western History Research
iii Los Angeles Public Library
iv Los Angeles Public Library
3 Seaver Center for Western History Research
5 Los Angeles Public Library
6 Los Angeles Public Library
9 Seaver Center for Western History Research
10 Regional History Center, USC
18 Regional History Center, USC
21 Regional History Center, USC
23 Regional History Center, USC
27 San Fernando Valley Historical Society

29 Regional History Center, USC
30 Regional History Center, USC
31 Seaver Center for Western History Research
36 Regional History Center, USC
37 Los Angeles Public Library
38 San Fernando Valley Historical Society
39 Regional History Center, USC
40 Los Angeles Public Library
42 Los Angeles Public Library
46 San Fernando Valley Historical Society
47 Seaver Center for Western History Research
58 Los Angeles Public Library
59 Los Angeles Public Library (top)
60 Automobile Club of Southern California
61 Regional History Center, USC
63 Huntington Library
70 Seaver Center for Western History Research
71 Los Angeles Public Library
73 Regional History Center, USC (Michigan Avenue)
   Los Angeles Public Library (Bolton Hall)
75 Los Angeles Public Library
76 Automobile Club of Southern California
77 Los Angeles Public Library (Red Car)
   Regional History Center, USC (Pacoima)
78 Los Angeles Public Library
80 Associated Press
84 Academy of Motion Pictures Arts and Sciences, Margaret Herrick Library
85 San Fernando Valley Historical Society
87 Bison Archives
89 Los Angeles Public Library
90 Los Angeles Public Library
91 Academy of Motion Pictures Arts and Sciences, Margaret Herrick Library

92 San Fernando Valley Historical Society
93 Los Angeles Public Library
97 Associated Press
105 Automobile Club of Southern California
106 Los Angeles Public Library
108 Regional History Center, USC
111 T. Christian Miller (photocopy)
114 Regional History Center, USC
120 Los Angeles Public Library
121 Los Angeles Public Library
126 Seaver Center for Western History Research
125 Seaver Center for Western History Research
130 Los Angeles Public Library
131 Los Angeles Public Library
138 Los Angeles Public Library
140 Los Angeles Public Library (children)
   Los Angeles Public Library (farmer)
144 Del-Fi Records
145 Del-Fi Records
147 Los Angeles Public Library
153 San Fernando Valley Historical Society
155 Los Angeles Public Library
158 Los Angeles Public Library
164 Associated Press (Spahn Ranch)
168 Copyright 2001 by Universal City Studios, Inc. Courtesy of Universal Studios Publishing
170 Associated Press
180 Regional History Center, USC
184 Los Angeles Public Library

Page numbers in italics indicate photographs and maps.